Big

Wayward

Girl

HERBERT L. PHILLIPS

Big

Wayward

Girl

AN INFORMAL POLITICAL HISTORY OF CALIFORNIA

DOUBLEDAY & COMPANY, INC.
GARDEN CITY, NEW YORK
1968

For Frances

"Now, here, you see, it takes all the running you can do to keep in the same place. If you want to get somewhere else, you must run at least twice as fast as that!"

The Queen in Lewis Carroll's
Through the Looking-Glass

ACKNOWLEDGMENTS

In the preparation of this book, the author has drawn heavily not only on the standard politico-historical works of an earlier California and the personal recollections and impressions of his own time but, frequently and with much profit, on the political and governmental reports of the San Francisco *Chronicle*, the Sacramento *Bee*, the San Francisco *Examiner* and the Los Angeles *Times*. In addition, these books of memoirs, comment, biography and discussion of special subjects are among the many which have been sources of valuable reference: *Earl Warren*, by Irving Stone; *Six Crises*, by Richard M. Nixon; *California in Our Time*, by Robert Glass Cleland; *The California Progressives*, by George E. Mowry; *California: The Great Exception*, by Carey McWilliams; *Incredible Land*, by Basil Woon; *The Lobbyists*, by Karl Schriftgiesser; *I, Candidate for Governor*, by Upton Sinclair; *The Legislature of California*, by C. C. Young; *Party Politics in the Golden State*, by Dean R. Cresap; *The Story of California*, by Henry K. Norton; *Glory Roads*, by Luther Whiteman and Samuel L. Lewis; *Crime in America*, by Estes Kefauver; *Olson's New Deal for California*, by Robert E. Burke; *Legislative Investigative Report*, by H. R. Philbrick; *Our California State Taxes*, by H. Dewey Anderson; *The Western Public, 1952 and Beyond*, by Alfred de Grazia; *The Year of Decision: 1846*, by Bernard De Voto; *The Politics of California*, by David Farrelly and Ivan Hinderaker; *Professional Public Relations and Political Power*, by Stanley Kelley, Jr. The author is also particularly grateful to the McClatchy Newspapers of California for permission to reproduce many of the pictures with which the book is illustrated.

H.L.P.
Sacramento, California

CONTENTS

Foreword

STATE OF UNPREDICTABILITY

California is a big girl now, with magnificent measurements and all the self-assurance of a repeated beauty contest winner, but she still has a persistent, nationwide reputation for waywardness. This is so in many respects, especially in the field of politics, with which this book will concern itself. The complaint of professional politicians around the country is that the stunning object of their growing attention is altogether too fickle and not in the least disposed to settle down to a maidenly decorum that can be depended upon. By fits and turns over the years, California has exhibited all the eccentricities, ambition, charm and unpredictability of an old-time Hollywood movie queen.

The abrupt rise of Ronald Reagan from film and television sound-stages to the governor's chair is merely the latest example of a capricious California temperament which other regions find difficult to understand. The state's dazzling switches of devotion at election time were in evidence long before Reagan came along. Its government has undergone two complete upheavals in eight years and numerous others in the last several decades. Republican and Democratic leaders in turn have been abandoned without notice. Ideological attachments have shifted at a dizzying pace from conservatism to progressivism and then suddenly back again. Attempts to account for the often whimsical political behavior of the place have been pursued with increasing eagerness of late as a consequence of the national population leadership attained by California in the early 1960s, with a corresponding gain in prestige and possible national campaign influence. Political parties, from the time of Theodore Roosevelt to the election retention of Lyndon B. Johnson, have needed the electoral votes of either New York or California, sometimes both, for Presidential year success. It is plain enough why Ronald Reagan's Republican California, so recently Democratic—and still heavily Democratic in voter registrations—is eyed with such misgivings and profound yearning by partisan fortune hunters.

The purpose here is an informal survey of this enticing and extraordinary state's political history and some of the personalities and lessons it has produced. It will range from the time of Gaspar de Portolá, who took office as California's first Spanish governor seven years to the very month before the Declaration of Independence, to the tumultuous opening months of Governor Reagan's incumbency. California has lived under half a dozen flags in something over four centuries. If its political antics have been a little on the peculiar side at times, if its sudden changes of mind defy prediction in advance, the almost unbelievable phenomenon of westward mass migration must rank high among the basic reasons. Newcomers have been pouring into California in successive waves since the Franciscan fathers began colonization in the eighteenth century and in infinitely greater numbers since the Gold Rush, the Mexican and Civil Wars and the turn of the present century. All too often they find themselves politically rootless in a strange land, in many instances ripe to be led, or misled, by the first persuasive charmer who comes along. This rich, expansive domain of 158,693 square miles is more bountifully blessed by nature than most but without the uniformity of population background or readily foreseeable conduct patterns of many of its sister states with a somewhat less chaotic mode of development. An original Spanish civilization was replaced long ago by the widely divergent attitudes, prejudices, aspirations and political credos of forty-nine other American states and almost as many foreign lands. California's occasionally quixotic digressions in odd and unexpected directions largely reflect this mishmash of idiosyncrasies.

Any account of California's ballot-box vagaries must deal, too, with the state's existence during most of the first half of the twentieth century under a most unusual set of election laws which permitted candidates to "cross-file" for multiple party nominations and allowed voters, even at party primaries, to register one way and vote another. Since the nomination seekers were not required for many years to reveal their party affiliations on the printed ballot, the confusion of an already flustered electorate was tremendously multiplied. Until this system was discontinued in 1959, it was periodically characterized by less adventurous parts of the country as a kind of West Coast silliness and cited regularly to support the theory that political campaigns in California were a form of vaguely organized pandemonium.

Even in the late 1960s, a nonpartisan independence of spirit was still strikingly evident in the state's surging, restless population. It must be admitted at the outset that fascinating, unconventional California, over nearly two centuries of political history, has frequently deserved her notoriety as an outrageous flirt, capable of breaking political hearts and engagements with madcap impulsiveness. With her Spanish antecedents and rough mining-camp upbringing, the headstrong *señorita* remains lighthearted and fancy-free, altogether an extremely perverse, complex and alluring personality which nobody in his right senses had better take for granted.

1

THE FIRST GOVERNOR

There is, up in the Sierra Nevada, a town called Portola, without the Spanish accent. Around California a scattering of streets, lanes, plazas and perhaps a few schools and other public places bear the same name. Not much else remains to remind today's Californians of Gaspar de Portolá, the first governor of the Californias, Upper and Lower. The latter was what now is Mexico's Baja California, which may have accounted for the early European belief that all of California was one great peninsula.

Portolá is overshadowed in the history books by the famous Father Junípero Serra. Whereas many of the original white settlers along the Atlantic came to the New World after breaks with Catholicism and, in some instances, following discontent with European Protestant establishments, the real colonizers of California were the Franciscan padres. With a handful of soldiers and fellow priests, Serra arrived in the southern end of Alta California in the summer of 1769, intent on bringing the Christian faith to the natives. Although Juan Rodríguez Cabrillo, back in 1542, had stumbled into what is presently San Diego Bay and vaguely explored the south-central coast, staking out Spain's claim to territorial title, the Indian inhabitants had had the place to themselves, without the blessings of organization, reli-

1

gion, European ethics, enforced civil tranquillity or even European interference, for well over two centuries. So California's governmental and political history did not actually begin until 227 years after Cabrillo* and 190 years after Sir Francis Drake's explorations. It was about the time the British were busy suspending East Coast colonial assemblies and Virginia was petitioning the king of England for redress of grievances.

Generously described in afterthought as the "New World Francis of Assisi," Father Serra was middle-aged, visionary, dedicated and, by some reports of the day, pretty stubborn. With him was Gaspar de Portolá, representing Spain's military and civil might, such as it was in this backwater of empire. The two quarreled almost immediately.

Gubernatorial power in the name of the Spanish throne was assumed by Portolá on July 1, 1769. On July 16, Father Serra founded Mission San Diego de Alealá on the shore of San Diego Bay, near the spot where Cabrillo had landed in the sixteenth century. While there was a theoretical division of authority between the church and the military, the determined father-president of the mission system eventually gained the upper hand and, incidentally, most of the glory for the joint operation. From the very beginning, Portolá found California less than salubrious. He was disenchanted with the whole mission and colonization project and wanted to give it up and go back to Mexico. What Portolá overlooked was the fact that he was dealing with a founding father—a kind of Catholic, West Coast William Bradford or Roger Williams. Digging in his sandaled heels, Father Serra resisted sturdily. Portolá insisted, even issued a flat order. Serra disobeyed it. And the idea of giving California back to the Indians a second time was abandoned. This little power struggle was somehow typical of what lay ahead. Californians have been intermit-

* Sent on a Pacific exploratory voyage by Hernán Cortés, conqueror and governor of Mexico, Cabrillo discovered what is now California on September 28, 1542. He died on one of the Santa Barbara Islands off the southern coast the following January 3.

tently in passionate controversy over numerous and frequently less significant issues ever since.

Portolá took a second and happier view of things after his more or less accidental discovery of San Francisco Bay. He had been trying to locate Monterey Bay which the Cabrillo expedition had reported long before. Evidently pleased with what he did find, the doughty captain decided to stay around and search awhile longer. In 1770, after Monterey Bay finally had been rediscovered, the Governor participated with Father Serra in a mission-founding ceremony close beside it and solemnly claimed the whole domain as the property of His Catholic Majesty Charles III, king of Spain.

California, by the way, has endured the good and bad offices of sixty-six titular rulers under various banners, not counting the governor of the Russian settlement at Fort Ross, various bickering pretenders to authority during Mexico's control or the president of the Bear Flag Republic. It has been exceeded in number of governors only by some of the original Eastern colonies. Since 1769, there have been ten Spanish royal governors of California, sixteen Mexican provincial rulers, seven holders of gubernatorial authority under the United States military regime of the late 1840s and, since statehood in 1850, thirty-three American civil governors, as of 1967.

There was actually very little for Portolá to rule in California's infancy: the stark, empty grandeur of a thousand-mile coastline, largely unmapped; the rugged, unexplored Sierra Nevada; a vast, Indian-occupied central valley, stretching off for leagues like a Midwestern plain. It was quite different from the old Marco Polo tales of a fabulous land off the coast of Asia, a region ruled by Amazons with gold as its only metal. Unearthing the gold was still nearly eighty years in the future, and females of extraordinary proportions and tyrannical arrogance were seldom recognized as a staple California commodity until the invention of Hollywood. The days of guitar-strumming and lovable Latins performing the picturesque hat dance were also yet to come. Portolá appears to have faced a Western equivalent of Captain John Smith's Virginia hardships—without Pocahontas.

Slowly, however, the chain of missions and presidios moved up the coast. San Juan Capistrano and those persistent swallows appeared in 1776. The time-spread between the construction of the first mission at San Diego and the twenty-first and final one, San Francisco Solano, was more than half a century. Credit for this first conquest of California rests with the Church, with the Franciscans rather than with their protective military allies, especially since the awed and perplexed native inhabitants offered little or no organized opposition. It is surprising, on the whole, that so few scalps were taken in early California. But West Coast Indians were a fairly docile lot compared with the proud and warlike tribesmen farther east. At one time, thousands of them lived and worked hard around the coastal missions, while other thousands, evidently preferring relative idleness and freedom to sweat and salvation, stayed far away.

So the paleface invasion prospered. The missions flourished, some of them ultimately acquiring what in that primitive region was enormous wealth. And California finally was launched on her very long and outlandish history. After considerable indecision, this immense, anomalous land, at long last, had been formally added to the white man's burden. The white man picked up this burden with less alacrity and much less dedicated and puritanical zeal than marked the behavior of East Coast colonists, whether in New England, New Amsterdam or the South. By no stretch of the imagination was Spanish California a go-getter land. California's reputation in that respect came quite a bit later. It may be just as well that Serra and Portolá were not around to see it.

2

CASTANETS AND SIESTAS

For many years after Father Serra and Governor Portolá, for that matter even after the Mexican Revolution, Spanish California was the Western Hemisphere's gayest colony north of the Rio Grande. There were twenty-six Spanish and Mexican governors over a period of seventy-seven years. Their rule was oftentimes rather perfunctory, however, and the colonists, scattered over an area as extensive as that from New England to the Carolinas, did pretty much as they pleased. Portolá's immediate successor, Felipe de Barri, for example, lived at Loreto in Baja California, which was proclaimed the capital of both provinces, and never even visited Alta California. The Franciscans were around, of course, but there was much more to the place than simply somber padres, mission bells and the energetic conversion of the Indians.

California provincials of the late eighteenth century and early nineteenth approached life with an agreeable lightheartedness. They behaved at times as though they were doing a lively musical comedy, complete with rhythmic Latin tunes and all the rest. The script, as with later Hollywood imitations, was hazy and unpredictable, but they managed to get a lot of sparkle into it. For one thing, Spanish Californians, or at least most of them, worked sparingly and, when

5

they had the *dinero,* dressed resplendently, sang and danced a lot, dined well, gambled a little, drank a good bit and occasionally stole a few horses. There were more swirling skirts and flashing castanets than New England's Puritans ever would have tolerated. Moreover, New Spain's holiday feasts generally outdid even the Pilgrims' much publicized first Thanksgiving in lavish menu and festive conviviality. The wine alone was enough to make the difference. So was the popular mode of dress—*señoritas* in silks, velvets and laces, men and boys in elaborately embroidered jackets and slashed trousers, with bright red sashes and multicolored serapes. The wealthy among them seemed perpetually making ready for a costume ball.

Between acts in all this pageantry, Alta California found time somehow for the longest colonial nap on record. It basked lazily in the sun from 1769 until the American conquest in 1846. It was a place vastly different from twentieth-century California which was to pass New York in number of inhabitants to the accompaniment of pronounced national attention and much hurried examination of the West Coast's bustling, many-sided economy; its crowded, multilane freeways; its booming industries and electronics enterprises; its motion-picture and television production factories; its grotesque real-estate developments; its sunshine and smog, its politics, folkways, beatniks, hippies and "urban sprawl." Whether some lurking carry-over from California's novel beginning, so different from the average American colony, may have influenced its habits later on, particularly its fitful reluctance to embrace conformity, is an arresting though perhaps unanswerable question.

There was precious little bustle in the Spanish days, and no cities worthy of the name. San Diego, Monterey, Santa Barbara and San Francisco, originally Yerba Buena, were just starting out. Then there was a little southern village which the Indians used to call "Yang-na." The padres renamed it Nuestra Señora de los Angeles.

All this while, the church followed its traditional course in a dominion untouched by the European Reformation. Although the people were reasonably happy, carefree and inclined to a gentle somnolence

6

—to put as nice a phrase to it as possible—the pueblos and ranchos came into being and gradually began to thrive along with the missions and presidios. Cattle ranged over spacious land-grant acreages where the owner was virtually a king. Hospitality, extravagant living and courtly good manners were the hallmark of these little "monarchies." The conquistador's helmet and armor quickly gave way to the sombrero and the gold- and silver-embellished garb of the vaquero, the ranchero and the landed don. The latter frequently spent more on the equipment of his favorite horse than the average colonist on the other side of the continent could afford for personal wardrobe. It was the custom in well-to-do homes to leave a pile of coins in every guest room. The temporarily embarrassed visitor was expected to take what he needed. In such homes, the head of the family was treated with a respect he certainly would whistle for in vain nowadays. His hand was ceremoniously kissed by all his sons and daughters before they trotted off to bed. Juvenile delinquency was no problem in the well-ordered hacienda. Even a middle-aged man, so the story goes, thought twice before smoking or wearing his sombrero indoors in his father's presence.

The ten Spanish royal governors left no particularly lasting impression on the largely unsettled area they ruled. Although some of them may have been reluctant to admit it, there is every indication that the mission system predominated in influence and that the titular representatives of the crown, aside from pomp and ceremony, played second fiddle a good part of the time in California's earliest days. After all, seven out of the ten served before the War of 1812, during a period when the young, struggling American Republic offered no more than an imaginary threat to Spain's pretensions on the Pacific. Old Portolá is remembered nowadays chiefly as the discoverer of San Francisco Bay; his successors are recalled, if at all, probably because of the resounding names some of them left in the history books. The ruler in 1814, for instance, was José Joaquín de Arrillaga. The last of the Spanish gubernatorial line, in 1822, was Pablo Vicente de Solá. As for the Mexican governors, next on the scene, Figueroa,

Castro, Pico, Argüello, Chico and Alvarado still persist as place names, mostly in the southern end of the state, though modern Californians suspecting their significance are few and far between. By and large, the even tenor of Spanish-Mexican life was undisturbed in the late 1700s and early 1800s, except for trifling local rivalries now and then and occasional rumors of English, French or American "invasion." Foreign encroachment was generally limited, though, to a few trading ships or smuggling craft.

Then, in 1812, the Russians came. Already in Alaska as early as 1798, they founded a California fur-trading post and settlement north of San Francisco Bay and erected a stout redwood stockade. They bought the site from the Indians for a handful of trinkets and three blankets. In this, at least, northern California resembles Manhattan. The somewhat alarmed Latins called this stronghold of the intruders "the Fort of the Russians." Years later, American settlers shortened it to "Fort Russ." And that may be the genesis of Fort Ross, the present name of the old ruins. At any rate, the Russians stayed only until 1841. They sold out to Captain John A. Sutter, a Swiss soldier of fortune who had become the founder of New Helvetia, a spreading Mexican land-grant empire in the valley of the Sacramento River. His 1839 Sutter's Fort eventually expanded into Sacramento, California's present capital.

In the spreading rancho system, meanwhile, Spanish Californians pursued their languid, unworried way of life. Even politics and factional warfare campaigns were conducted lackadaisically. Leo Carrillo, the stage and screen actor, a colorful fellow of impeccable Spanish-Californian descent, used to tell of a great, long-ago battle, waged at a mountain pass in southern California, between the forces of one of his distinguished ancestors and an equally eminent rival "general."

"They fought for two days and two nights," said Carrillo, "and then, on the third day, they got together for a barbecue and fiesta."

It was not all rodeos, feast days and rounds of unblemished merriment, of course; not for the early mission system's Indian converts

8

anyhow. Some of these reportedly were worked to the point of virtual slavery. But for Californians of Spanish heritage, the years between Mission San Diego de Alcalá and the Gold Rush provided a colorful, drowsy, idyllic existence in which the siesta was favored over such institutions, say, as the New England town meeting, and the fandango was more prevalent than the witch hunt. There were disputes over whether the Spanish seat of government should be Loreto in Baja California or Monterey in Alta California, the latter winning out by royal decree after 1775. The alcaldes, ordinarily thought of as mayors or local judges, appear to have doubled often in the early mission period as overseers of native laborers. After Mexico became a republic, California was entitled to a representative, or *diputado,* in the Mexican congress. But he was without a vote in that parliamentary body and might, with some justification, be classed as California's first legislative lobbyist, the forerunner of a horde of spokesmen for public and private interests in the lawmaking affairs of the California that lay ahead. In the beginning, however, the *diputado* was more especially concerned with such regional questions as whether the capital of the California Mexican territory ought to be Los Angeles or Monterey. At the same time, colonial officialdom had to cope with a growing California dissatisfaction with the central government, a local feeling, evidently widespread, that Mexico was neglecting the interests of her thinly settled northernmost province.

Nonetheless, the oddly charming *manâna* quality of this extensive royal and then republican domain was not appreciably altered by the Mexican War of Independence which, in the early 1820s, changed California from Spanish to Mexican control; nor by the Bear Flag Revolution of the 1840s; nor even, at first, by the War between the United States and Mexico which, in 1846, made California an American possession. Yet "Sutter's gold," only two years later, generated a convulsive upheaval of all that had gone before. The old political establishment toppled abruptly, making way for a new and brisker manner of government, a new conglomeration of races, a new set of rulers. More than that, a whole concept of living was changed. It was

9

the first of California's many transformations. Had Portolá and his long chain of Latin gubernatorial successors been around half a decade after it started, they would have been hard pressed to recognize the old place.

"It seems to me," said Mariano Guadalupe Vallejo, who had established the most northern of Mexican garrisons and colonies in the Sonoma Valley, "that there never was a more peaceful and happy people on the face of the earth than the Spanish, Mexican and Indian population of Alta California before the American conquest."

Sonoma had been the scene of the Bear Flag uprising. A town on an arm of the San Francisco Bay still bears Vallejo's name. The accepted California pronunciation of the Spanish word nowadays is "val-lay'-ho." Eastern newcomers have been calling it "Valley-Joe" for generations.

For Spanish California, the gold years of 1848 and 1849 had a shorter word, much easier to pronounce, much more final and uncompromising: *Adios.*

3

MANIFEST DESTINY'S HELPER

America has produced a good many distinguished men named Marshall, but probably none at once so influential and so unknown to the general population as James Wilson Marshall. Even California's incalculable mineral deposits which he inadvertently discovered became known in time as "Sutter's gold." As it happened, neither Sutter nor Marshall got very much of it. And Marshall wound up as a casual footnote in many a history book. True enough, he found the gold by accident and was as surprised, no doubt, as Cabrillo had been when he came upon San Diego Bay. As a matter of fact, though, Marshall, indirectly at least, had as much to do with what has been called "the winning of the West" as anybody around during the roaring 1840s.

The spirit of expansionism had been growing in America all that decade—and for a variety of economic and political reasons. The doctrine of "manifest destiny," under President James K. Polk, was persuasive.

This was an enticing slogan of the 1840s, epitomizing the American urge to westward expansion, the concept that the institutions, ways of life and governmental credos of this relatively new nation were foreordained to spread over the vast expanse of empty lands beyond the continental divide and ultimately to the Pacific. There was a growing desire to acquire such far-off and alien-claimed territories as Oregon, New Mexico and California by Yankee infiltration, annexation or even conquest if need be. It is not difficult, in retrospect, to see the prevailing trends of those days, with their economic and romantic motivations, or the expansionist goals envisioned by Polk, who has sometimes been called the only "strong" President between Jackson and Lincoln. Some enthusiasts, indeed, apparently looked upon a transcontinental sweep of American empire as the grand design of Providence.

The addition of a profit motive, a glittering one at that, had more than a little to do with the outcome. The lure of something for practically nothing impelled the adventurous to pull up stakes and risk the hazards of a transcontinental trek not only willingly but eagerly. A newspaper editor coined the phrase "manifest destiny" in 1845. Marshall put the frosting on the cake in 1848. On January 24 of that year, he became the unwitting cause of California's first great population influx—an explosive termination of the easygoing Spanish-Mexican pueblo and rancho system and the brand of politics and agrarian economics which marked it. When this New Jersey wheel-wright, a hired hand in John A. Sutter's "New Helvetia" Mexican land-grant operation, found flakes of gold at a Coloma sawmill site, the history of California and Western America was changed in a twinkling.

It would be a vast oversimplification, of course, to underrate other factors. The Bear Flag Revolt and the American conquest had come two years earlier. Polk had had his eye on California for a long time. So had France and England, not to mention Russia's brief, experimental interest. Then too, Mexican rule in the 1840s had been weak and plagued by petty controversies. It must be remembered that, at the start of 1846, the map of "California" included the present states of California, Nevada, Utah, Arizona, New Mexico and portions of Colorado and Wyoming. And "Oregon" was mapped to take in not only that future state but likewise Washington, Idaho, parts of Montana and another segment of Wyoming, plus areas ranging northward to Canada. Thomas O. Larkin, American consul at the Monterey provincial capital, had been instructed to do what he could to bring about the defection of California from Mexico. Other figures also were on stage, including the striking, restless and ambitious John Charles Frémont whose Western explorations centered importantly on California where he did considerable marching and countermarching just prior to the Bear Flag incident.

At daybreak on June 14, 1846, some thirty-odd American ranchers surrounded Vallejo's house at Sonoma and launched the Bear Flag Revolt. History tells us that not a few of them got fairly high on Vallejo's wine before accepting the General's "surrender." Sober heads prevailed, however. One of the soberest men, William B. Ide, took charge of Vallejo and things generally. He told his fellow "revolutionists" they could go down in history as a gang of brigands or as the "saviors" of California. They settled for the latter and a new flag. Something of a dreamer, Ide then penned a wordy proclamation, declaring the existence of the "California Republic." He cast himself in the temporary role of "President." His evident goal was independence to be followed by American annexation.

But first came the Bear Flag. This was fashioned from a piece of white cotton, with a broad red stripe across the bottom and a red star in the upper left-hand corner. To distinguish it from the emblem of Texas, already in the republic business, a grizzly bear was painted in black at the center. Some complained that the original drawing more nearly resembled a plump pig. This minority was quickly silenced. On the whole, the somewhat tattered revolutionary council, mostly clad in fringed leather hunting costumes à la Kit Carson, had pride enough in its handiwork, and the homemade banner was enthusiastically hoisted in brief triumph. It still flies, by the way, over California public buildings. The bear nowadays is plainly recognizable.

It goes almost without saying that the Bear Flag Revolt had more than its share of comic opera overtones. It was something of a West

Coast Boston Tea Party, undertaken with complete seriousness and later hallowed in patriotic tradition. "President" Ide had scarcely begun his incumbency when Frémont moved in and smoothly placed himself at the head of the movement. Ide bitterly denounced Lieutenant-Colonel Frémont's intrusion. As it turned out, the Colonel's reign over the new governmental setup was also amazingly short. With the Mexican War under way, the American flag was raised at Monterey and Sonoma before the summer was over and the "republic" folded up as unceremoniously as it had started.

Two years later, in a California still sketchily governed by the military, Marshall found his precious flakes of gold on the American River, a tributary of the Sacramento. His discovery, verified behind the carefully locked doors of a Sutter's Fort office not much bigger than a modern bathroom, was the worst-kept secret in the annals of California or any other state. The fast-spreading word attracted the serious attention of the Anglo-Saxon world to California for the first time, even though Drake had visited the place and recounted some of its virtues and shortcomings 269 years earlier. In a practical sense, Marshall's discovery outshone Drake's. It set the Gold Rush in turbulent motion—the westward stampede of thousands by wagon train across the plains, by pack train over the Isthmus of Panama and by ship around the Horn. For better or worse, it furnished California with a new and stormy cast of characters, a new set of values, an immensely revised and more strenuous manner of existence. The late Bernard De Voto called 1846 "the year of decision" in the conquest of the "Great American Desert," the largely unmapped lands west of the Louisiana Purchase. Where California is concerned at least, 1848 and 1849 might be described as the years of activation—with James Marshall the unexpected little helper of manifest destiny.

The first marketed gold dust from the Coloma discovery site was spent in the Sutter's Fort settlement for a jug of brandy. The seemingly inexhaustible flow of the Mother Lode's yellow metal led, directly and indirectly, to other results infinitely more intoxicating: statehood came to California in two years. Tiny villages became sprawling young cities. Population jumped from an estimated 6000 (aside from native Indians) in 1840 to 92,000 in 1850, to 380,000 by 1860 and to 560,000 by 1870. Stagecoaches and the colorful Pony Express were followed by the first transcontinental railroad. The gold seekers were followed by migrations of artisans, farmers, merchants and homeseekers. Only eight years after gold discovery, California mounted its first ambitious attempt to elect a President.

John Charles Frémont, the native Georgian who had helped California win independence from Mexico, was sworn in as a United States Senator of his adopted state the day after it was admitted to the Union. He was a Free-Soil Democrat and his opposition to slavery cost him re-election. In 1856, he became the state's first candidate for the White House, the first nominee of the newly-formed Republican party. As was the case with General Dwight D. Eisenhower nearly one hundred years later, Frémont, ultimately a general too, was touted not only by the Republicans but by certain Democratic party elements for the Presidential nomination. Like Ike, he chose the GOP. And he ran up a respectable 114 electoral votes for his two-year-old party against 174 for Democrat James Buchanan.

California gave an early demonstration of its capricious political tendencies. Though seemingly elated and not a little prideful over Frémont's nomination, it backed away from its erstwhile revolutionary hero on election day and went Democratic.

4

"PACIFIC REPUBLIC" PLOT

In the growing, varied and shifting population of modern California, perhaps relatively few know much about the abortive scheme, a little more than a century ago, to turn this first Far Western state into an independent "Pacific Republic." It was cooked up some thirteen years after the Bear Flag Revolution and nine years after California had been admitted to the Union. The Bear Flag figured only as the emblem which this short-lived but serious movement proposed to raise as its national banner.

At about the same time, in another but related political enterprise, the six counties of southern California voted to withdraw from the state and form a new commonwealth of their own. The proposal to divide California into two separate states was to be advanced intermittently in later years, even in the twentieth century, usually by hotheads upset over regional political differences. On this first occasion, the southern counties came within an ace of making the plan a reality.

California's first decade of statehood was a wild one. The problem of law and order alone was almost impossible to master. Many had come to the West in quest of gold without the trouble of digging for it. Murders and robberies were commonplace, not only in the haphazardly expanding young cities but in the smaller settlements and mining camps. Life was cheap. There were few jails in this frontier society, so the punishment of convicted lawbreakers, at least as miners' tribunals meted it out, was usually swift and often harsh. But official findings of guilt were seemingly infrequent. The vigilantes, citizens' law-enforcement committees, had to be organized in San Francisco, then the largest community, to put down violence and deal with the criminal element. One old chronicle reports that, between 1849 and 1854, over 4000 murders were committed in California, 1200 of them in San Francisco, with only one legal conviction. California office seekers, even nowadays, are forever crying out against intolerable "crime conditions," but these almost unbelievable early-day statistics really gave the authorities something to worry about, particularly when one remembers that, in 1850, the state's inhabitants totaled only 92,579, with 34,000 of them huddled together in San Francisco and a mere 1610 in Los Angeles.

Starting with Peter H. Burnett, the new state had six governors in its first ten years, all Democrats save for one representative of the American party. John McDougall and John Bigler were Burnett's immediate successors in the early 1850s, when the gubernatorial term was only two years. Then came the American party's John Neely Johnson, followed by Democrats John B. Weller and Milton S. Latham. The second decade produced still another Democrat, John G. Downey. It was not until the threatening cataclysm of the Civil War that California, like the nation, turned to the Republicans, with the governorship election of Leland Stanford. All this while, the state operated under the constitution of 1849, which prevailed until a new one was adopted in 1879. The slavery question lurked in the back of a lot of minds at that first constitutional convention. Among the delegates, including Sutter and Vallejo, former Northerners outnumbered those originally from slave states, however, and California rejected slave owning. It had reputedly been the hope of Southerners to bring into the Union the whole enormous western area which had been called California before statehood, and then ultimately divide its

17

southern half into one or more slave states. Despite their sharp set-back, the issue, in slightly different form, was to bob up again within a few years. Meantime, California undertook the trying task of or-ganizing its government, the State Legislature variously meeting in San Jose, Vallejo and Benicia before Sacramento finally was settled upon as a permanent capital.

In the closing half of the 1850s, the "wild West" became more preoccupied than ever with the slavery question, along with the rest of the country. While the new state was loyal to the Federal Union in theory, it had gone against the Republicans in the national election of 1856. And, actually, there were large pockets of Southern sym-pathizers, particularly in southern California. The State Legislature of 1859 contained strong proslavery factions, as a matter of fact. Among these, and some of their non-legislative backers, there devel-oped a proposal to transform all of California into a separate nation and invite the countries of the world to recognize it as such, an in-dependent republican realm. It was the eve of the Civil War. The idea, in that troubled era of emphasis on the sovereignty of each in-dividual state, was to save California from the fate of a Union feared to be on the verge of collapse. That was the excuse anyhow, if not the basic motivation. In the northern and central sections of the state, however, public sentiment was strongly in favor of the national gov-ernment in the impending clash. Union demonstrations were held in many communities. It became evident that a majority of Californians, aside from areas where there had been substantial migrations from Dixie, wanted no part of unilateral independence. So the bizarre plot for a "Pacific Republic," so boldly entered into even in advance of the formation of the Confederacy, ended in frustration almost as soon as its real purposes became generally known.

An alternate proposal was trotted out promptly. The proslavery interests among the lawmakers had real strength at that stage and were not to be underestimated. They gained authorization for an election in the six southernmost counties on the proposition that these should separate from the rest of the state. Here again, the formation of a new slave state appeared to be the controlling object. Writers on that agitated period classify Governor Milton S. Latham, who held office briefly in 1860, as sympathetic to the projected breakaway and incipient slave state plan, calculated, among other things, to restore a United States Senate power balance. He was a Lecompton Democrat who resigned shortly to go to the Senate as a replacement for Senator David C. Broderick, killed in a duel by State Supreme Court Justice David S. Terry after a political quarrel in the fall of 1859. Formal dueling was frowned upon, as were impromptu gun fights, even in that far-off day, but nonetheless such happenings played a part in the sporadic violence of the times. The Broderick-Terry duel, due to the prominence of the participants, is still remembered and argued about, at least by historical researchers. Eventually, balloting was held on the plan for six counties to withdraw from the state, and the undertaking received a majority. The Civil War came before this withdrawal could be accomplished. Otherwise, California, like the Carolinas, the Dakotas and Virginia, would have been divided.

California's first great political showdown of this period came in the Presidential election of 1860. There was a fierce campaign in the new state, as elsewhere. But, finally, the pro-Union, antislavery forces prevailed. California's electoral votes, at that time only four, went to the second Presidential candidate of the Republican party, Abraham Lincoln. The firing on Fort Sumter in the spring of 1861 had its repercussions in California. Thereafter, the intended secession of southern California counties was abandoned. In the circumstances, further promotion of it would have amounted to an act of treason. There was no longer much room for compromise, even in a region so remote from the fields of battle. Yet, in some localities, a remarkable amount of friendly feeling for the South persisted. As in the turbulent population of modern California, political concepts were clung to tenaciously in that complicated pioneer society and often seemed to depend, as at present, on what part of the country the newly arrived Californians had come from. In any case, another determined state political fight came later that year. It ended in the reorganization of the Legislature along pro-Union lines and in the election of Leland Stanford, a member of California's "Big Four" in the transcontinental railroad enterprise and later the founder of Stanford University, as the state's first Republican governor.

The old story goes that when Stanford went to the mansion which was to serve as his executive residence, the then-uncontrolled Sacramento River was at flood stage and he had to make his approach by rowboat, entering the house through a second-story window. True or false, the incident is typical of a water problem with which California was confronted for generations, a condition of periodic flood danger in many northern districts and a seasonal shortage of water in the southern counties.

Returning to the war crisis of 1861–1862, California's new Legislature adopted resolutions of Union loyalty almost immediately, along with promises of aid to the nation's security and the Government's preservation. So far as the Legislature was concerned, this represented a marked majority change of face in two years. The new promises were kept. The military ranks of the Confederacy received their share of Californians, many from areas where much sentiment continued to lie in that direction because of pre-California background. The state as a whole provided approximately sixteen thousand men —infantry, cavalry and mountaineers—in response to the Union's call for troops. It has been California's claim, upon occasion, that General William Tecumseh Sherman was one of its contributions to the Union cause. Sherman, though born in Ohio, was a banker in San Francisco, among other varied civilian pursuits in several states, after his graduation from West Point and his participation in the Mexican War.

Safely in the Loyalist column as the Civil War dragged on, California gave a majority to President Lincoln for his second term. Its home record during the great conflict, in addition to disposing of the "Pacific Republic" idea and blocking the state's dismemberment, included managing domestic affairs with sufficient skill and alertness to prevent agents or adherents of the Confederacy from gaining any meaningful Far Western foothold. In the last analysis, though, California's gold counted most. Both North and South's economy faltered more than once in the long struggle. Historians have agreed frequently that California's contributions to the national economy played a major, perhaps a decisive, role in the successful prosecution of the war.

5

RAILROAD EMPIRE

The domination of post-Civil War California politics by the railroad interests may have been reprehensible, morally squalid and all the other censorious things history has said about it, but, looking back at the roistering young state of one hundred years or so ago, the economic and political pressures that came about were perhaps fairly inevitable. Transportation was among the most demanding requirements of California, cut off from the rest of the country by largely unpeopled expanses of wilderness and prairies. Those who opened up the way for ready transport of settlers, goods and, most important, the shipment of California products, played a role of tremendous consequence in the state's early development and were hailed as public benefactors who, in the beginning at least, could do no wrong. Great wealth and power flowed from their enterprise, and with these rewards came the temptation to mold the destiny of a land where no corporate organizations of comparable influence then existed.

With a mere handful of inhabitants, in terms of the migration floods which came later, the California of the closing third of the nineteenth century offered an economic and political vacuum which the railroad pioneers and their successors, operating in financial self-interest and from a monopolistic position of towering strength, hastened to fill. It was an infant state, just learning to walk. Get-rich-quick inclinations were prevalent; politics was infused with an earthy pragmatism; a compelling sense of probity in public affairs appears, in many localities, to have been developed only sketchily. Of this loosely-knitted domain, gay, attractive San Francisco, the "Paris of the West," was the financial capital. The Central Pacific Railroad, and the Southern Pacific which succeeded it, presently assumed control over the politico-economic aspects of California as though it were a private empire. Many closely-reasoned volumes have described those days, accounting for every turn and twist of the strange and often sordid doings of that period in meticulous detail. It is the generous thesis of some of these that neither the "Big Four" of the Central Pacific (the crusty old tycoon Collis P. Huntington, and his associates, Crocker, Hopkins and Stanford) nor those who followed them in influence set out deliberately to throw California affairs into disorder, but rather that political corruption was inherent in the easy morality of the times. With the passage of many years, in fact, the railroad giants have become legendary, possibly, as is the way with legends, a shade more heroic than even they would have imagined possible. The wheeling and dealing of a bygone era are comfortably forgotten in such immense achievements as the first transcontinental railroad and such picturesque ceremonies as the driving of the Golden Spike.

For that matter, the California of the late nineteenth century and early twentieth certainly did have its full quota of little political manipulators as well as big ones. Nonetheless, by 1900, the Southern Pacific and its hired minions carried vast, almost unexampled weight in California's political kingmaking, party conventions, election campaigns, patronage appointments, legislative sessions and, not infrequently, in local politics. William F. Herrin, chief counsel for the railroad until 1910, was the head of what came to be known as the "Southern Pacific Political Bureau." The great central valleys had begun shifting from the production of wheat and cattle to fruits

23

and vegetables. With the advent of irrigation, still expensive at that time, California's agriculture was undergoing a revolution of its own. Still in railroad control were millions of acres of land from the public domain which had been granted by the federal Government in original rail project charters. An important part of the state's population gravitated to the cities, where political bossism flourished along with crime and skulduggery. It was a rough, tough milieu by any standards, but not too difficult to handle on essential political matters where overriding corporate interests were at stake. Years later, in his book *The California Progressives,* George E. Mowry summarized the situation like this: "California, like so many of her sister commonwealths at the turn of the century, had only the shadow of representative government, while the real substance of power resided largely in the Southern Pacific Railroad Company. To a degree perhaps unparalleled in the nation, the Southern Pacific and a web of associated economic interests ruled the state." He went on to quote Herrin as having once told Lincoln Steffens (Steffens' *Autobiography*) that the Southern Pacific, in order to keep California "safe," was forced to allow all the little grafters and vice rings in the state to obtain their share of the public loot.

Against the arrogant machinations of what was commonly termed "the Machine," California reform groups became active, and eventually triumphant, in this century's first decade. A termination of the almost naked power of the railroad interests and their complex of associates did not come, however, until the Hiram Johnson political "revolution" of 1910. It would be a great mistake, of course, to assume, as sometimes has been done in the hero worship of later years, that Johnson broke the sway of the Southern Pacific singlehanded. In time, as governor, he was an important political instrument in a remarkable change of California affairs, but he had substantial help, both before and after he reached executive status. At the outset, indeed, he was a comparatively minor voice, though one of considerable eloquence, in the better-government movement which culminated in various political reform committees at both ends of the state and finally in the formation of the League of Lincoln-Roosevelt Republican Clubs. In agreement with the long-term aims of these undertakings, at various times in the prolonged struggle against political bossism, were such men, to name a few, as Dr. John R. Haynes and Rudolph Spreckels; such reform-minded figures as Meyer Lissner, Marshall Stimson, William Kent and James D. Phelan, later a Democratic United States Senator; such lawyers as Johnson and Francis J. Heney; such editors as Fremont Older of the San Francisco *Bulletin,* Chester Rowell of the Fresno *Republican,* C. K. McClatchy of the Sacramento *Bee,* Irving Martin of the Stockton *Record* and Edward A. Dickson of the Los Angeles *Express.* There were numerous others committed to progressivism and political rebellion. Once California's political style had changed, the Johnsonian government encountered no shortage of manpower from which to recruit the advisers and makers of a new order. Power is never surrendered willingly, though, and the stormy preliminaries dragged out over ten years or more. As far back as 1899, for instance, the State Legislature, apparently concerned over the anti-railroad cartoons of Homer Davenport, not to mention the tender sensibilities of the railroad operators, actually passed a law which sought to prohibit the publication of certain types of journalistic lampoons. It was an off-beat demonstration of the extent to which lawmaking influence, under given conditions, sometimes can be carried. This, of course, was before the monopolistic status of the railroad "machine" had been somewhat dented by the advent of the Santa Fe and Western Pacific lines. In its day, so Dr. Haynes was to declare at one point, the Southern Pacific setup, together with Herrin and his aides, had the political potency to dominate the selection of public officials "from the village constable to the Governor of the state."

Curiously enough, the Progressive movement, as it developed in California anyhow, did not appear to be essentially anti-corporation in nature, though bent on diminishing the S.P.'s political power; nor did it, on the whole, seem predominantly prolabor in a state where labor union organization had been rapid. The typical Progressive of that time has been pictured as middle-class, or even upper middle-class; better educated than many; often a professional man of determined personal independence; basically committed to reform of public institutions, better regulation of private utility companies and improvement of political practices, rather than to any attempt to tinker with the established economic structure. Despite their temporary involvement in a "movement," the Progressives were largely unfettered individualists, some of them politically ambitious, almost all of them intent on remedial action as distinguished from anything which nowadays might be called radicalism. Most of them, though not all, were of Republican background, not surprising in a state where the GOP had prevailed in every gubernatorial election since the turn of the century.

There is an interesting story that when Chester Rowell conferred with Mrs. Hiram Johnson on the question of Johnson running for governor in 1910, she observed that she would "rather die" than have him seek the governorship, was sure that he would lose, objected to living in Sacramento, disliked the demands of public life and would much prefer that her husband, if he ran at all, try for the United States Senate. In the long run, Johnson sought and captured both jobs.

6

A STRANGE LITTLE GIANT

In a little more than four and a half decades between the administration of Leland Stanford and the election of Hiram Johnson in 1910, California had fourteen governors—eight Republicans, five Democrats and one member of the Union party. The interesting thing is that, in spite of California's far-flung reputation for quick, unheralded shifts of attachment, the Republicans took over the governorship in the closing years of the 1890s and appeared to have a permanent lease on the executive mansion for an unbelievable time thereafter. The electorate bounced back and forth between liberal and reactionary preferences during that period, but did so within the framework of the Republican party. When Democratic Governor James H. Budd ended his term in the Spanish-American War year 1898, the Democrats found themselves unable to promote another gubernatorial winner for forty years.

It was quite different in the decades between the Civil War and the Spanish-American, with much more fluctuation of party strength. After Stanford's governorship concluded in 1863, Union party Governor Frederick F. Low took over. Serving in the 1870s were Democrat Henry H. Haight, Republicans Newton Booth and Romualdo Pacheco and Democrat William Irwin, in that order. The 1880s produced another mixed bag: first Republican George C. Perkins, then Democrats George Stoneman and Washington Bartlett, followed by Republican Robert W. Waterman, the lieutenant governor when Bartlett died after brief incumbency. The state's two top officials in 1887 had represented opposite parties, emphasizing the somewhat patternless political habits of that era, at least in the matter of partisan regularity at the polls. The nineteenth century's windup years later brought on Republican Governor Henry H. Markham and, finally, Democrat Budd.

Turn-of-the-century chroniclers noted the power of the railroad interests in almost every important party convention of the early 1900s, influencing the elections of Republican Governors Henry T. Gage (1899–1902, under the revised four-year-term system), George C. Pardee (1903–1906) and James N. Gillett (1907–1910). Although Pardee was eager for renomination in 1906, the Southern Pacific support went to Congressman Gillett. One possible factor, talked about at the time anyhow, was Pardee's encouragement of the new Western Pacific. At all events, after the S.P.'s switch away from him, former Governor Pardee supported the Lincoln-Roosevelt League and the candidacy of Hiram Johnson in 1910. The Gillett administration was the last before railroad might was curbed in California and the long Johnson regime began.

It has always seemed to this writer that 1910 is a fine dividing point, psychologically at least, between the old California of the Gold Rush, the vigilantes and the Hispano-Mexican days and the more recent California of, say, Hollywood and Vine, Earl Warren, Edmund G. (Pat) Brown, atom smashers, Warner Brothers and, eventually, Ronald Reagan. Approximately sixty post-Gold Rush years by then had already wrought many sweeping changes, but the spirit of the nineteenth century, and even a few vestiges of the eighteenth, carried on through the first decade of the twentieth. At the end of that decade, the most striking and debatable California political figure of his time, the remarkable Hiram Warren Johnson, made his controversial debut. More than fifty years later, the influ-

28

ences of his appearance on the scene were still clearly discernible. In 1910, the unsure commonwealth, destined to attract a population of some 19 million within a couple of generations, boasted fewer than 2.4 million. These were predominantly the children of the gold-questing pioneers and *their* children. The twentieth century's westward migration was under way but not on anything like the scale it later was to attain. Los Angeles, a tough little Spanish-American town until around 1880, was smaller than San Francisco. The interior of the state was dotted with small, dozing hamlets—often in winter flood danger, hot and dusty in summer—their unpaved principal thoroughfares, with narrow sidewalks under wooden arcades, not very different from "Main Street" nowadays in a television western.

Californians born before the turn of the century well may have memories of San Francisco, on her magnificent hills, painfully recovering from the earthquake and fire of 1906; of Los Angeles, a latent urban Gargantua just beginning to stir south of the Tehachapi; of Sacramento, the capital city, which by then had spread around Sutter's Fort into a slowly growing market town of 44,000; of Victorian mansions, occasionally still lighted by gas or kerosene lamps, and of other large, square pioneer homes, sometimes built of bricks shipped around the Horn. Those reared in smaller communities—on the banks of the Sacramento, say, or the San Joaquin —may yet recall the smells and sounds of the rivers on which stern-wheelers towed barges stacked high with bags of grain, at that time still classed as one of the chief money products of the potentially rich but undercultivated interior valleys. Many of these villages were secluded, almost self-contained economic units, largely undisturbed by the world beyond the river bottom lands and the surrounding hills.

Into every cranny of this often misruled urban and unorganized semirural setting the word came, in 1910, that Republican Hiram Johnson was bent on becoming California's fifty-sixth or twenty-third governor, depending on how one reckoned it. Most of the time Johnson brought the message personally, riding in an early-model automobile, generally attended by a fife and drum corps and invariably concentrating his oratorical attacks on the Southern Pacific Railroad and how it must be taught to "keep its dirty hands out of politics." This performance signaled the advent, at least on any significant, successful statewide basis, of the Western Progressive movement in California. The Republican nomination at that particular stage of events, and for many subsequent years, was tantamount to gubernatorial election. The main question was what brand of Republicanism should prevail. In the light of later developments, it is possible to pass lightly over the doings of some of Johnson's immediate predecessors, but highly difficult to dismiss Johnson himself or the tremendous public metamorphosis his emergence brought about—a revolutionary upheaval in California government, not to mention the Republican party.

Encountering this energetic, aggressive and oddly frustrated little political magician, whether in those formative days or later on in the 1920s, the 1930s and the early 1940s, when he was a United States Senator, it was hard to escape the feeling that somehow one was in the presence of a living legend, however self-consciously contrived. Johnson's gubernatorial career, at marked variance with parts of his senatorial record, stood by itself and still does, a singular example of the impact of a forceful personality on the course of politics and on a hitherto essentially regressive and even self-complacent "old frontier" style of life. It is a commonplace to say of Johnson that he "threw the Southern Pacific out of California politics." More to the point, he and the set of public officials who joined him, by election or appointment, headed the state in new political directions which, after periodic, perhaps inevitable backsliding, ultimately affected its social, economic and governmental development to a much greater degree than was originally suspected.

Bossism and corruption had reigned in California's politics, particularly in its State Legislature, for a considerable time prior to 1910. Easy virtue ruled in a lot of local governments, too. Graft, bribery and extortion were freely talked about in writings of the day, and many specialized accounts since then have dealt extensively with situations apparently intolerable. It is perhaps well to remember that, aside from actual records in the main stream of political history, the colorful side incidents, so treasured by researchers, often gain currency from the recollections of older participants in past events and may be touched up, more than a little, by the parts they played and the prejudices they had. It is plain enough, though, that organized private interests, the railroad interests in particular, were in ruthless control of many phases of state politics in the period just before and after the turn of the century, and that in San Francisco, then the state's metropolis with a population ranging from 350,000 to a little over 400,000, the machinations of the Schmitz-Ruef regime were notorious. Eugene E. Schmitz was the San Francisco mayor and Abraham Ruef, until his indictment on extortion charges, was widely known as the "Curly Boss" of the city's politics. Hoodlumism and shady political dealings were reported generally after the great earthquake and fire of 1906. The San Francisco *Call,* on September 11 of that year, printed a story to the effect that Ruef had been paid twenty thousand dollars by Herrin interests for delivering San Francisco support to the Southern Pacific-favored candidate for governor at the Republican nominating convention. This was revealed, according to the *Call,* by one of Ruef's political underlings, said to have been disgruntled because the money had not been divided. Extensively published after the convention was a victory banquet photograph which included GOP nominee Gillett with his arm on Ruef's shoulder. That picture evidently caused as big a furor in the California of that day as the one, four decades later, of Arthur H. Samish, the liquor lobbyist, holding a Charlie McCarthy-like dummy on his knee and saying, according to a *Collier's* Magazine caption, "That's my Legislature." The San Francisco graft trials started in 1906 and, in some aspects, dragged on for several years. The bitter flavor of the times is illustrated by the fact that, when criminal indictments eventually reached a court of law, Francis J. Heney, the chief special prosecutor, was shot down in the courtroom. After the near-fatal gunning compelled Heney to withdraw from the case, Hiram Johnson was one of those who agreed to carry on the prosecution. Ruef was convicted and, after prolonged appeals to higher courts, finally went to San Quentin Prison.

The Lincoln-Roosevelt Republican League, committed to reform, obtained nominal but ineffective control of the Legislature in 1909. The real turning point came with Johnson's election as governor in 1910. In some sense, give or take a few years, it paralleled the movement into power of the Western Progressives elsewhere, the elder La Follette in Wisconsin, Norris in Nebraska, Borah in Idaho and the rest. Most of them provided a rallying place for the advocates of liberal reform at a time when Republican forces were badly split on this question and the Democratic party, in many regions, was weak, cautious or dormant. The accomplishments of Johnson's first Legislature in 1911 and the record of his first term continue to be regarded with some astonishment. It may be that Johnson was a little astonished himself before he died.

Hiram Johnson was a vigorous, two-fisted, bespectacled attorney of stocky build and average height who parted his hair in the middle and wore a high, stiff collar almost closed in the front, somewhat in the style later favored by Herbert Hoover. At the outset of his life in politics, he was ambitious, progressive, implacable in his assaults on his opponents and, at the same time, seemingly given to a moody sense of pessimism and insecurity. Senator William E. Borah was once quoted as saying that Johnson actively hated any man who opposed him. Always a man who "ran scared" in a campaign, Johnson feared defeat at the hands of "the machine" until nearly election time in 1910. Faced finally with the prospect of victory, he viewed the problem of what to do afterward with some trepidation. As Franklin Roosevelt was to do nationally twenty-two years later—to say nothing of Ronald Reagan fifty-six years later in California—Hiram called in his friends and advisers and improvised at almost the eleventh hour.

It was little short of a miracle that so far-reaching a program came out of these improvisations at so early a date, especially with reactionary hostility to the new governor so formidable. The Johnson forces, reform Republicans and a few friendly Democrats, accomplished, among other things, the authorization of the initiative, the referendum and the recall; the approval of woman's suffrage; the reorganization of private utility regulation, with rate-fixing by the state; the enactment of a wages and hours law for women; the revitalization and revision of the direct primary law, and the inauguration of workmen's compensation insurance. Johnson's six years in the executive mansion provided a model for numerous other jurisdictions and set the California legislative mood for a long time to come. Compulsory compensation coverage for industrial accident victims, bitterly assailed in Johnson's day as an invitation to "malingering," helped initiate the broad system of social insurance which now exists generally throughout the country and is taken pretty much for granted. State control of public service corporation rates became a permanent and accepted thing. The innovation of direct legislation gave the voters an early and lasting, though sometimes misused, weapon against the inaction of recalcitrant or lobby-controlled legislative bodies.

The Johnson administration had a long-lasting effect upon the careers and fortunes of succeeding governors. It became the fashion for many of them, even after the passage of half a century, to compare their own records as favorably as possible with Johnson's and, when caught uncomfortably in a political jam, to cite Johnsonian precedents as though quoting Holy Writ.

7

CROSS-FILING AND FRUSTRATION

In accounting for the fantastic ups and downs of California politics, the unique institution of primary election "cross-filing" is not to be overlooked. From the standpoint of election campaigns, it was by far the most important heritage of the Hiram Johnson era. It exercised an immeasurable pressure on California state affairs from that long-ago period until its abolition in 1959. The rest of the country ridiculed it for years as another instance of California eccentricity and regarded it with professed horror.

This singular method of operation, spelled out in California's election laws, permitted a primary candidate for partisan state office to file for and receive the nominations of as many political parties as he wished. He was limited in this only by his electioneering ability and by a proviso that he simultaneously win his own party's endorsement. But he was not required, in the beginning and for a long time thereafter, to list his party affiliation on any of the printed primary ballots. The utter confusion of the votors, in a state of rapidly changing population, was incalculable.

The California program bypassed, or rather abandoned, the theory generally accepted elsewhere that a primary election is strictly a party affair and that the selection of public office nominees ought to be made exclusively by the members of each party. Advanced as a countertheory was the contention that all voters, regardless of party, should be allowed an unlimited hand in all primary nominations as well as in general election decisions. This undertaking, with its authorization of multiple nominations, was a sweeping departure from average voting procedures around the nation. Little wonder, perhaps, that the politicians of other states dubbed it ludicrous. These unusual regulations, it must be recalled, however, grew out of an intensive power battle between the progressive and reactionary forces within the California Republican party, comparable, although on different issues, to the left-right disagreements which were to divide that same party some fifty years later. The state's reformers had managed to outlaw the old system of choosing nominees by party conventions, an arrangement under which professional party chieftains had flourished, often in league with the interests of the Southern Pacific and other business and industrial groups with an appetite for kingmaking. The cross-filing plan, added to a re-vamped and expanded direct primary, was hailed by its sponsors as a further insurance against the hand-picking of candidates by party bosses, in this case by the conservative bosses who had controlled political machinery prior to Johnson's election. It was pictured, in fact, as the death knell of political bossism against which Governor Johnson declaimed bitterly.

The cross-filing system, intended to encourage voting "for the man, not the party," worked, in actual practice, to the distinct advantage of incumbents. Usually much better known than their challengers, officeholders often were able to gain double and even triple nominations at the summer primaries and thus avoid serious November runoff contests. The California primary automatically became as important as it is in some of the one-party Southern states. At the outset, the Republicans profited most by cross-filing, since they already held a top-heavy majority of the state offices when the program started. It helped them to continue in substantial control of affairs, particularly in the Legislature, for decades, even for

35

a while after California voter registrations had switched, as they did in the mid-1930s, in favor of the Democrats. The Democrats succeeded in carrying California at times in national elections. Yet, for more than fifty years, the Republicans captured the governorship and usually the Legislature with monotonous regularity. During that time, only two Democrats reached the state's executive mansion, both of them after the late 1930s.

As it turned out, the Johnson aggregation fostered a primary pattern which had the effect of California state election domination by Republicans who were frequently much more conservative than the old reformers of the 1910–1916 period had ever intended. In later years, Johnson himself, as a United States Senator, won re-election more than once through the aid of multiple nominations. As late as 1950, as an example of the system, 92 candidates for 134 statewide constitutional, congressional and legislative offices won both major party nominations at the primary. There were 57 Republican double winners and 35 Democrats. The point is that only 42 out of the 134 offices remained to be filled at the November general election. It was not until the early 1950s that the practice was modified to require the party identification of each partisan primary candidate on every voter's ballot. Thereafter, through appeals to party loyalty, the Democrats improved their lot. They had, by then, been leading in number of registered California voters since 1934.

California retained cross-filing until 1959 when Governor Edmund G. (Pat) Brown and his fellow Democrats, finally in legislative majority, abolished it. There was political irony in this action. The Democrats, long committed doctrinarily to the elimination of cross-filing, repealed it at a time when they themselves had come to California power and were in position to benefit by the odd practice much as the GOP had done for so many years. What is significant is the fact that cross-filing proved to be the only major program of the Johnson days which California abandoned in fifty years. Johnson as governor, like F.D.R. as President later on, was much hated by many adversaries, but few had the political courage or muscle to undo what he had accomplished.

Haunted by restless ambition, and no doubt by some of the ideas for which he had campaigned in 1910, Governor Johnson teamed up with Theodore Roosevelt as Vice-Presidential candidate in T.R.'s Progressive party bid for the White House in 1912. In the Republican split which simplified Democratic victory for Woodrow Wilson that year, California gave two of its electoral votes to Wilson but otherwise went along with the Roosevelt-Johnson "Bull Moose" ticket. Johnson was back on the campaigning platform two years later, gaining 1914 gubernatorial re-election as a Progressive. He was the first California executive to be accorded two consecutive four-year terms at the polls.* Such is the fickleness of California voters that this feat was equaled only twice in the ensuing fifty years. Evidently discontented with this triumph and driven by unceasing aspirations, Johnson tired of the governorship in the middle of his second term. In 1916, he won a seat in the United States Senate where he settled down for the next twenty-nine years. He died in office in 1945. But the forceful, competitive, oftentimes cantankerous old battler did not settle down willingly. He contended in 1920 for the Republican Presidential nomination. He lost, of course, along with Frank Lowden, General Leonard Wood and other favorite sons and front-runners, when the deadlocked Chicago national convention's notorious "smoke-filled room" produced Warren G. Harding. With the odds clearly against him, Hiram tackled a sitting President, Calvin Coolidge, for the White House nomination in 1924, and failed again.

Johnson's real reputation in public life unquestionably rests on his years and many-sided endeavors as governor. His long record in the Senate, like his mercurial personality, was contradictory. He

* John Bigler, California's second American civil governor, was elected twice, in 1851 and 1853 when the gubernatorial tenure was only two years. Like Johnson, Edmund G. Brown won two four-year terms. Earl Warren was elected three times.

continued generally liberal on many domestic issues; he turned iso-
lationist in foreign affairs. He was the chief sponsor of the great
Boulder Dam (later Hoover Dam) project. But he also became an
outspoken ally of the Lodge contingent in the fight against Wilson
and the League of Nations. Republican Earl Warren, three times
governor and widely regarded as Johnson's most distinguished successor, was a schoolboy of nineteen when the redoubtable Hiram
"threw the Southern Pacific out of politics" and declared war on
California special interests generally. It is a fair guess that had there
not been a Hiram Johnson, with his marked impression upon political procedures and California voting mechanics—plus his nullifica-
tion of many of the powers of party bossism—there might not have
been an Earl Warren, or at least the opportunity for Warren's development along the independently progressive lines he pursued for
eleven years as chief executive some three decades later. A clear
pattern in California's swerving political attachments has often been
hard to discern over the years, but in an examination of the early
times of both Johnson and Warren some glimpse of parallelism and
a sense of logical continuity reward the onlooker. The merits of
both of them as administrators and their mastery of a volatile electorate stood out, in their respective periods, as exceptional. When
Warren's immediate predecessor, the late Democratic Governor
Culbert L. Olson, remodeled the California Capitol's executive
quarters in 1939, he retained just two oil portraits of earlier governors, one Democrat and one Republican, in his private office. "I
kept Peter Burnett," said Olson, "because he was the first governor
after California reached statehood; Hiram Johnson because he was
the most progressive."

Along with a certain pre-New Deal brand of liberalism which
featured his two gubernatorial terms, Johnson had the important
governmental faculty of running a "tight ship"—with a loyal and
disciplined crew assembled from the veterans of his battles of 1910,
1912 and 1914, and with himself, of course, prominently on display, nervously pacing the bridge. The late State Senator Herbert

W. Slater of Santa Rosa liked to recall that on the eve of the 1911 Legislature, Johnson, his lieutenants and a bloc of progressive legislators gathered in a downtown Sacramento hotel and hammered out the basic projects of that remarkable lawmaking session at an all-night conference, carefully measuring the need for each item against its political attainability. Slater, ultimately dean of the Legislature, had been elected with Johnson in 1910, and continued to serve, first as an assemblyman, then a senator, until his death in 1947. That useful career, like Johnson's, covered a long span of California political history, the more unusual in Slater's case since, for many of his productive years in the Legislature, he was completely blind. It also used to be said of Johnson's administration by other contemporaries that each of the Governor's subordinates was required not only to handle every state departmental assignment capably but to be ready, at the drop of a hat, to defend the whole gamut of Johnsonian programs with unswerving allegiance. Nothing was left to chance. The haphazard, self-serving "palace guard" type of operation, stumbling block of so many other administrations, state and national, was not tolerated for an instant.

In the political wars and campaign aspects of his affairs, though, Johnson, as often as not, seemed to be another man entirely. Unless placated by the role of leadership, he tended to turn rebel. Justly or not, he gained a name for being variable in his likes and dislikes, suspicious, alternately cocksure and gloomy, easily disgruntled, ever ready to hurl the thunderbolts of his wrath at all who disagreed with him on the smallest matters. Assorted stories of the so-called "snub" of Johnson by Charles Evans Hughes in 1916, and its repercussions in a Republican schism which landed California in Woodrow Wilson's lap, have become a part of political folklore, possibly exaggerated by the Governor's detractors. At opposite poles in an ideologically disturbed Republican party, Governor Johnson and Presidential nominee Hughes chanced to be housed briefly that summer of 1916 in the Virginia Hotel in Long Beach and went their separate ways again without meeting even for a ceremonial handshake. Hughes had brought his Presidential campaign to California and, as William Allen White describes the incident briefly in his *Autobiography,* Hughes's "conservative managers had managed his exits and entrances so that he slighted, indeed openly snubbed, Hiram Johnson—who was not a man to be snubbed." Johnson subsequently gave at least nominal support to the GOP national ticket, without, however, attacking Wilson. On election night, Hughes went to bed a winner and woke up to learn he had lost California and the Presidency. At the same balloting, Republican Johnson was elected to the United States Senate overwhelmingly.

As a Senator, the fiery Johnson once more bolted Republican party regularity, favoring Democrat Franklin Roosevelt in 1932 just as he had Bull Mooser Theodore Roosevelt in 1912. For reasons never thoroughly delineated, he developed a coolness toward F.D.R. in a relatively short time after the New Deal program began to unfold. Toward the end of his life, the driving, contentious, bristling warrior of 1910, now a strangely aloof and lonely little giant of insurgency, appeared to become embittered. To some it seemed as though, while still touchy on points of prestige, he had almost forgotten the magnitude of his early victories and accomplishments, as well as his assured place in the history of California, and had fallen victim to an unhappy feeling that destiny had somehow passed him by. If that is so, perhaps uncomfortable hindsight and an old frustration gnawed at him. Between 1910 and 1920, Johnson had run in almost every election—except the right one from the standpoint of his greatest ambition. In 1920, he had sharply turned his back on a suggested Republican Vice-Presidential nomination. He refused to play second fiddle a second time. But for that, when Harding died in San Francisco in August, 1923, Hiram Johnson and not Calvin Coolidge would have been President of the United States. It is perhaps not surprising that the only serious competitor against President Coolidge for the GOP nomination in 1924 was Senator Johnson.

8

CULT OF THE INDIVIDUAL

The preoccupation of present-day California with political party affairs, along with incessant factional bickering within the two major parties, is a far cry from the spirit of nonpartisanship which prevailed for so many years. Or so it appears on the surface. Yet the political habits of fifty years are hard to break and, even to this day, the state is suspected around the country of unpredictable skittishness and an election-time tendency toward prankish disregard for strict party regularity.

The long era of cross-filing, lasting through the incumbency of eight governors after Hiram Johnson, had the reputed effect of eliminating party bossism, in the generally accepted sense of that term, but it likewise lessened party responsibility for the behavior of affiliated nominees and encouraged the cult of the individual. The system minimized public concern with such differences as existed between the platforms of the principal parties, the more so because a large part of the population was new to California and, except when some issue of tremendous consequence came to light, found it difficult to become aroused over the state's intricate and generally unfamiliar problems. The cajolery of a persuasive office seeker, usually simplifying his pitch to lure votes across party lines, even at prima-

41

ries, seemingly proved much more enticing for many than the prosaic manifestoes of platform drafters. This attitude was not, and is not, confined to California, but few places encouraged it for so long a time. The strongly held belief of thousands that they served democracy best by voting for "the man," regardless of his party or how closely he adhered to its principles, inevitably led to personal "image-building" in California on a large scale long before Madison Avenue experts made the practice a television commonplace of American politics. This was substituted, quite often, for the more inflexible party authority long the rule in many Eastern states where, in the words of one old-time Pennsylvania boss, the leadership could wreck the party and still own the wreck and much preferred to lose an election, if need be, than to forfeit party control. Originally nurtured in the century's second decade by the Progressive movement as a means of seizing statehouse control for reform purposes, political independence appears to have lasted longer in California than elsewhere. A lot of it still lingers on. The inclination of Californians to shift allegiances erratically has given political managers sleepless nights for a good many years. Quite recently, in fact, California campaign directors have continued to count heavily on the vacillating nature of an ever changing electorate, tempting large numbers of conservative Democrats to the Republican camp and, to a somewhat lesser extent, progressive-minded GOPers to the Democratic side.

Before passing to the post-Johnson governors, it may be appropriate to note some of the state's odd gyrations in Presidential politics. After ranging from Lincoln to McKinley in the nineteenth century, California veered to Teddy Roosevelt and the Progressives in 1912 and to Wilson and the Democrats in 1916. In the latter year, although the state's voter tables were predominantly Republican, California actually swung the election away from Hughes. In 1920, characteristically enough, the state was back with the GOP and Warren Harding. California gave a 1924 plurality to Calvin Coolidge although nearly half of its northern and north central tier of counties favored Progressive Robert M. La Follette. That partial defection from the Republicans and the Democrats was a striking regional example of "the man, not the party" philosophy. By a freakish provision of election law, La Follette was obliged to appear on the California ballot that fall as the Socialist candidate. Next time around, the wayward state helped send Herbert Hoover, an adopted Californian, to the White House in the bizarre 1928 campaign against Alfred E. Smith and "Rum, Raddio and Romanism." It changed sides again in 1932, rejecting Republican Hoover and endorsing Democrat Roosevelt in the face of a still-substantial GOP margin in statewide registered voters. With unusual steadfastness, California stayed with F.D.R. until his death, and gave Harry Truman an edge of some seventeen thousand votes over Tom Dewey in the political upset of 1948. It is worth noting that more than 190,000 California votes were cast that year for Henry Wallace and his leftward-leaning Independent-Progressive slate of electors.

Meantime, beginning in 1934, California's enrolled voter strength had been drifting from the Republicans to the Democrats. Registration trends repeatedly have proved an unreliable indicator of election results, however, merely emphasizing on many occasions the degree of California's perversity. The state rallied warmly behind Republican Dwight D. Eisenhower in 1952, even though Democratic nominee Adlai Stevenson, who had been raised to the governorship of Illinois, was a native son of vote-heavy Los Angeles and might normally have been expected to cut deeply into that city's mounting array of Democrats. The Californians supported Ike again in 1956. During the 1940s and in 1950, by the way, while California was firmly behind the Democratic national regime, it maintained Republican Earl Warren in the governorship for an unprecedented three consecutive terms. Where party loyalty at the polls was in question at the half-century mark, organizational leaders threw up their hands; no reasonable design was apparent. As recently as 1960, native-born Richard M. Nixon, Eisenhower's Vice-President, squeaked through to a long-count state victory in his losing Presidential race with John F. Kennedy. Only two years later when Nixon, trying a political comeback, sought to unseat Democratic Governor Edmund G. (Pat) Brown, the state turned cold on him and handed Brown a second term. Eastern politicians and pollsters were much amazed in June, 1964, when California favored Barry Goldwater over Nelson Rockefeller in its Republican Presidential primary, clinching the nomination for the ultraconservative Arizona Senator. Followers of California's intricate political history were not surprised to find the state solidly behind Lyndon Johnson in November.

California's cross-filing played no part in the national primary elections, of course, nor in state campaigns after 1959. But acceleration of population undoubtedly did. Apathy toward public affairs, prevalent in many other localities, appeared to be magnified in California by the rootlessness of its surging hordes of new arrivals. For instance, in 1950, when the state went heavily Republican, the state superintendent of public instruction, elective nonpartisan head of the school system, was opposed by one Bernadette Doyle, "organizer and educator" and an avowed Communist. This Communist party affiliation was widely publicized. The incumbent superintendent was Dr. Roy Simpson, a registered Republican originally appointed by Governor Warren. He won re-election a second time with 1,771,245 votes that year and went on to hold the superintendency longer than any other school man in California history. For whatever combination of reasons—an illuminating voter indifference certainly among them —605,393 Californians marked their ballots for the Communist to the accompaniment of much eyebrow-lifting east of the Sierra Nevada.

California heads into the final third of the twentieth century not only as the most populous American state but also, in the judgment of many, as the most complicated American state of mind. This opinion is voiced mostly by outsiders. The resident population, old and new, is largely enchanted by the place and extremely proud of its every distinction. There is no evading the conclusion, nonetheless, that California's history, its political history in particular, is something of a scrambled jigsaw puzzle. While it has settled down much closer to national conventionality in recent years, the state has always had a soft spot in its heart for new ideas, new movements, good and bad, and new personalities. The 1966 emergence of Ronald Reagan is the latest manifestation of this fondness. California is still capable of jolting surprises. That is why political strategy doctors, national and local, busy themselves so mightily nowadays trying to evaluate each fresh West Coast development. Nobody knows for sure what strange pirouette may come next.

9

THE SWINGING PENDULUM

The California governorship passed back and forth between rival Republican forces—first progressive, then abruptly conservative and finally progressive again—in the fourteen years after the 1910–1916 reign of Hiram Johnson. The pendulum of public sentiment, during that whole period and for some time afterward, swung in jerky, agitated cadence. The mantle of Johnson, which was to become increasingly tattered as time went by, first fell on the plump shoulders of William D. Stephens, a placid but essentially liberal-minded congressman from Los Angeles where he had once been mayor. He had been sent to Washington at the 1910 election which landed Johnson in the governor's chair and was an appointive lieutenant-governor when Hiram moved on to the United States Senate.

California, as detailed chroniclers of the time like to say, was on the move in the years just before and after World War I. Population, only 2.3 million in 1910, was up 44 per cent by 1920 and had advanced another 65 per cent by 1930. The latter ten years represented an era of ferment and intensive, though somewhat random, growth. For California, to an even greater extent than in many other regions, it was the jazz decade of expansion, frenzied finance, get-rich-quick real-estate schemes, talking movies, phony prosperity, boundless optimism and, in the end, economic collapse when the depression struck. In a little more than 160 years since colonization, California found itself back among the hardships with which it had started. Indeed some Californians whose ancestors may have sold trinkets to the Indians faced the expedient of selling apples on street corners. That unhappy evolution and all the distress that went with it were scarcely dreamed of when Johnson concluded his term and a half as governor. The state's approach to America's first war in Europe and to the 1920s was cheerful, carefree and unsuspecting.

Governor Johnson, craving new honors, his reform program largely realized in the opening years of his first term, had been as busy as the proverbial cranberry merchant in the next several state and national election campaigns. After his national ticket flutter as a Progressive in 1912 and his governorship re-election in 1914, he was touted by some of his California adherents for the Presidency in 1916, or the Vice-Presidency at the very least. This turned out to be a flattering local ploy, repeated even more noisily in later years. Charles Evans Hughes won the 1916 Presidential nomination of the Republicans, and Johnson switched back again from Progressive to Republican to run for United States Senator. Meantime, the Progressive movement, as a dominant factor in California, had just about run its course. It had flashed like a new star in the political heavens of 1910. Six years later its brilliance was beginning to fade. Its active life was comparatively short, although the overall effect of its exploits was felt, from time to time, for many years. Now, however, the world was heading in new directions. The European war had begun in 1914, with new issues engaging public attention. There was a switch in emphasis to compelling international and domestic economic questions, as distinguished from the civic reforms and governmental regulatory functions with which the California version of Western Progressivism had been preoccupied in large measure. Governor Johnson's cherished plan to make the election of all state officials nonpartisan, as city and county elections were by that time, was defeated by statewide vote in 1915. Some of the Western and California Progressives had become Democrats; others had drifted back to the GOP. Johnson himself endeavored, with considerable agility, to keep both his feet in all three camps.

California labor troubles of the 1910–1916 period undoubtedly had an immense effect, indirect though it may have been, on the state's politics, and certainly on the voting inclinations of many people. Trade-unionism had an important foothold in the state, where it had made itself felt in strikes and other manifestations for years past, even though, at that stage of affairs, it lacked both the legal recognition on any broad basis and the regulatory mandates which were to influence its development around the country later on. The labor-management clash became increasingly bitter, resulting at times in California acts of frightful violence and climaxing in the Los Angeles *Times* dynamiting of October 1, 1910, in which twenty-one lives were lost, and in the San Francisco Preparedness Parade bombing of July 22, 1916, when ten persons were killed and forty more injured. The evident reaction of a great body of conservative-minded citizens, as well as numerous middle-class liberals, was to condemn laborites generally for such terroristic outrages, with a fairly inevitable tendency in some quarters to carp a bit at the progressive political vogue as partly responsible for the prevailing conditions. Among those arrested for the Preparedness Parade atrocity were Tom Mooney, a labor radical, and Warren K. Billings, who had a previous criminal record, having been imprisoned some years before for the illegal transportation of explosives. While they loudly professed innocence of the 1916 bombing, Mooney and Billings were convicted of murder. The Mooney-Billings case was to become an international *cause célèbre* and a thorn in the side of the next six California governors.

San Francisco's Preparedness Parade, involving 115 marching divisions, was conceived by the city's business interests and a broad representation of industry and other walks of life as a huge patriotic demonstration, not surprising in the summer of 1916, less than a year before America's involvement in World War I. In terms of trained military might, the country was seldom if ever so ill-prepared for a major war. Labor, as such, was not assigned a place in the Preparedness Parade line of march. On the eve of it, in fact, various of the city's labor leaders took part in a rally, protesting the event and denouncing militarism. San Francisco, at the time, was entangled in labor-management turmoil over efforts to unionize a great many establishments and the determination of numerous employers to operate on an open-shop basis. Amid these turbulent conditions, a suitcase full of explosives was ruthlessly set off in one of the parade staging areas. Demands for immediate apprehension of the criminals were quickly followed by the arrest of Mooney and Billings, admittedly in the left wing of labor, and some of their associates. After their conviction of murder and for more than two decades, Mooney and Billings remained in prison, persistently maintaining they were innocent "frame-up" victims.

The San Francisco bombing took place only three weeks before Charles Evans Hughes brought his ill-fated Presidential campaign to that part of California. This circumstance was not a factor in Hughes's loss of California, of course, but the disturbed state of the public mind assuredly did nothing to facilitate his electioneering. Californians emerged from the Hughes debacle of that November variously shocked and elated at this national display of their political muscles. They have been prone to flex them enthusiastically ever since. For his part, Governor Johnson, with his eye evidently on the senatorship or even higher national goals as early as 1912 and 1914, had picked John M. Eshleman as his second-term lieutenant-governor running mate and ultimate successor. But Eshleman, an old hand in the Progressive movement and a former member of the Lincoln-Roosevelt League's executive committee, died in office in the spring of 1916 while Johnson was preparing his successful bid for the Senate. With some signs of reluctance, Johnson appointed Congressman Stephens to the lieutenant-governorship vacancy, which meant the governorship in a matter of months. Then followed one of the oddest episodes in a truly odd career. Having won the office of

United States Senator in November, 1916, Johnson proved unexpectedly reluctant to give up his precious governorship. He stubbornly stayed on as the state's chief executive for four long months, even though Congress and the Legislature of California were beginning their 1917 sessions. His enemies accused him of arrogantly seeking to be governor and Senator at the same time. Finally, Johnson resigned his state post in March, on the eve of America's entrance into World War I. He departed for Washington with a seeming distrust of the capabilities of those he left behind him to fight "the forces of reaction" in California. Soon Johnson was girding himself for a new and quite different crusade on the national scene as an implacable foe of Wilson's League of Nations.

The doings of Stephens and those who immediately followed him as governor are primarily interesting as a reflection of the plight of men who, in California or other places, come to authority after the prolonged incumbency of a brilliant, self-centered, hard-hitting reformer. The ebb and flow of power struggles almost inescapably come on the heels of a strong regime of rugged individualism, whether of the political left or right. It may appear laughable to classify the Johnson of governorship days as even left of center, in the light of today's world and its sharpened concepts of such things. Yet the headstrong old scrapper—a "give-'em-hell" campaign performer long in advance of Harry Truman—was angrily berated, in his own time and place, both for "freak legislation" and "socialist tendencies." To Governor Stephens fell the thankless task of carrying out Johnson's California policies. It is worth noting that, after Johnson, a divided California, oscillating between political extremes as they then existed, elected six governors in a row and summarily dismissed each one of them at the end of a single term.

Assuming gubernatorial duties at long last, Stephens, with his receding silky gray hair, his black bow tie and his back-bench Roman-senator manner of courtly diffidence, seemed colorless, after the ebullient Johnson, and altogether the epitome of dignified routine. A victim of the times, heavily pressured by warring points of view, he defended the achievements of the Johnson years as best he could against a recurring wave of conservatism in California. Despite an ill-concealed show of distaste by Johnson, who still kept a finger in California politics, Stephens served out the short balance of the Senator's unexpired executive term and gained a regular term of his own in 1918. That same year, at the urging of President Wilson, he commuted Tom Mooney's death sentence to life imprisonment. The new governor was caught in the beginning of two decades of endless furor over Mooney and Billings, the former in San Quentin Prison, the latter, a recidivist, confined at Folsom, the state's maximum security penitentiary. Against the firm conviction of many that the two laborites were guilty of the vicious San Francisco bombing was arrayed the equally insistent contention that they had been "framed" on insufficient evidence.

Stephens likewise was harried by a dilemma common to rulers, royal and democratic, since the beginning of time—a shortage of revenue to meet expanding governmental commitments. California's state government was chiefly financed at that time by a tax on the gross receipts of privately owned utility companies, the railroads, the light and power corporations and all the other industrial giants falling into the category of regulated monopolies. The growth of California, especially its population-spread from the very rich to the extremely poor, resulted in mounting demands for more and more public services: more schools, to which the state granted local subventions, more colleges, more intensive regulation of business, larger mental hospitals and prisons, scores of other governmental facilities. The utility companies naturally resisted the periodic tax boosts which all these things entailed. While California's revenue system underwent drastic revisions with the passing years, so did its population and needs, with the result that treasury deficits became a repeated threat and often a reality. Governor Edmund G. (Pat) Brown faced one when he assumed office in 1959. Ronald Reagan inherited severe fiscal problems as recently as 1967. Back in 1921, Governor Stephens, opposed by "a gigantic corporation lobby" which he called the largest the State Capitol had seen up to that time, managed to obtain a legislative increase in utility gross receipts levies. In those days, the state tax system in California was so closely geared to utility corporation income that percentage-graded levies on the gross earnings of such firms were the primary source of revenues to balance state government expenditures. The Stephens administration, confronted with the mounting costs of a rapidly growing state after World War I, insisted on an overall utility tax hike and sponsored the King Tax Bill to bring it about. The opposition of the joint lobbies of the utility companies, among California's most powerful corporate entities, was monumental. Among the legislative tax authorities involved in this conflict was Republican Senator Lyman M. King of San Bernardino County. Although King, in later years, became a top figure in the State Finance Department, his name assumed a permanent place in California political annals more particularly because of its association with the tax increase legislation of Governor Stephens' incumbency. Some of the utilities, notably the railroads, fought in the courts, though unsuccessfully, to escape the rate boost for seven or eight years after the revenue measure had been enacted in 1921.

The King Tax Bill fight of that year is still recalled, after four and a half decades, as one of the most acrimonious parliamentary struggles in California annals. It marked, as seen in retrospect, the growing role of special-interest lobbies in the exercise of political influence which, not in California alone, soon was to fill a power vacancy caused by the diminishing manipulative leverage of outright party bosses. The outcome of the 1921 tax fight had a predictable bearing on Stephens' ouster the following year. On a slogan of "efficiency and economy"—which somebody has cynically said can be made to work successfully about once every ten years—State Treasurer Friend W. Richardson, a blunt Quaker of great shrewdness and strong conservative leanings, made a winning run for the executive mansion in 1922.

A one-time editor, Richardson was vigorously supported in his

52

campaign by the state's "country press," given credit in many quarters for his triumph. There was more than a little political naïveté in this. So huge a domain, with such regional rivalries and diversified viewpoints, is not ordinarily handled so easily. Many of the really big money sources, most of the corporate interests hardest hit by the King Tax Bill, were sentimentally or actually in Richardson's corner. It was a time of political reprisal. The already badly divided Johnson-Stephens forces of old-fashioned Progressivism were thoroughly trounced. Almost at once, at the 1923 session of the Legislature, came concerted efforts under the new Richardson administration toward wholesale budget trimming, an erosion of the state's business regulatory operations, a harassment of education and appropriation cutbacks for what, in the Johnson days, used to be called the government's "humanitarian functions." Although Governor Richardson was a Republican originally brought into the state service as an administrative official under Johnson appointment in 1911, he had since moved some distance to the right of his mentor's stance, and, in his new role, he speedily became the darling of reaction—at least where slashing Johnson-Stephens programs was concerned—and anathema to the scattered adherents of the Johnsonian tradition. Political and legislative battles raged over these considerations for four years while California, temporarily at any rate, changed its governmental face. As early as 1923, the left and right of the Republican party were staging a noisy California dress rehearsal of what took place nationally in the 1960s.

While their differences on governmental and economic theories appeared to be as pronounced as day and night, Richardson and Johnson closely and curiously resembled each other in strong-handed political organizing ability, in appetite for power, in cunningness of maneuver and in relentless attack on all who stood in the way. Richardson may even have surpassed Hiram in gritty self-confidence and biting sense of humor. Where governmental disbursements were involved, he liked to pose as the boy with his finger in the dike, holding back the "spendthrift" flood. Although California had been a state for seventy-two years when Richardson was elected to the governor-ship in 1922, that year marked the first authorization of an executive-drafted state budget. The new governor sent the Legislature what he termed a "net budget" of $79 million for two years, his administration critics maintaining actual expenditures would run closer to $150 million. Undoubtedly Richardson would have been astounded and outraged if he could have foreseen that, in a little more than four decades, California would have a YEARLY budget of approximately $4.6 billion, larger than that of many independent countries. He carried the fetish of "economy" to a point where even his public pronouncements often were handed to the press on tiny strips of onion-skin paper, single-spaced and loaded with sharp denunciations of his political foes. He was too busy fighting extravagance to provide California with very many new governmental enterprises. Nonetheless, a politician is judged by his fellow professionals on his savvy and operational acumen no less than on the desirability of his objectives. Granting the mediocrity of Richardson's affirmative programs, he was regarded, without question, as a canny individual in his homespun way and a much more forceful occupant of the California gubernatorial chair than many who came before and after him.

He was, of course, a figure of perpetual controversy. He had a heavy, somewhat lumpish build, affected a sandy, drooping mustache and wore his hair in a curling ducktail, not unlike William Jennings Bryan's. He used to read aloud from a little book of I.W.W. marching songs in sardonic ridicule of the continuing hubbub for a Mooney-Billings pardon. If this involved something of a non sequitur in logic, the same could not be said about his paraphrases of Machiavelli. He studied the writings of the old Florentine with vast admiration, finding use, now and again, for some of the more ruthless bits of advice on the political conduct of efficient princes. Richardson's reign was brief. But for four years he stopped California Progressivism cold in its tracks.

The remnants of the old Johnson crowd, bolstered by sympathizers who had stomached as much of Richardson as they could, rallied for one last fling in 1926. They elected as Governor Clement Calhoun Young, a progressively-oriented Republican who had spent something like a quarter of a century in California legislative and other political work, quite a lot of it as Speaker of the State Assembly and as lieutenant-governor. It was, in a sense, a return of the Johnsonites to power, but without the reform fervor and consuming drive of 1910. The new governor was well-intentioned, knew government thoroughly as an experienced technician and proved to be one of California's best administrators. It was said of Young that his knowledge of intricate public affairs was so far-reaching he could have taken over any one of California's huge departments and directed it with practiced skill in a couple of weeks. In that respect, he has occasionally been compared to Herbert Lehman who, in orderly managerial ability, frequently outshone some of New York's more spectacular governors. On close issues of controversial policy, however, Young was a trifle cautious at times and inclined to vacillate a little. In today's political jargon, he would be termed a careful GOP "moderate."

Governor Young, profoundly impressed with the value of an informed civil service and with the British tradition of governmental careerism, is best remembered for a long-overdue reorganization of California's wildly scattered and overlapping state agencies and for the inauguration of a cabinet form of government, patterned after the federal plan. It was also during the Young administration that California adopted a revised scheme of legislative apportionment, basing representation in the lower house on population and membership in the upper chamber on geography. This gave Senate veto power to the small counties of rural California. Though "balance of power" and various other reasons were assigned for this arrangement, one factor undoubtedly was apprehension over labor influence in the steadily growing urban population. This system was to affect legislative enactments for nearly forty years until the "one man–one vote" redistricting decision of the United States Supreme Court.

55

Unlike some of the older states, California regularly reapportioned legislative and congressional districts after each decennial census. But the urban-rural division of power loaded the dice where the Legislature was concerned.

A conscientious man, Governor Young launched the most complete re-examination of the Mooney-Billings case ever undertaken by California's executive department. At one time a huge vault in the Governor's office was stuffed to the ceiling with documents on this amazingly complicated disputation. Special hearings, presided over by Lieutenant-Governor H. L. Carnahan, were marked by recantations of testimony given in the murder trial some ten years before. This merely led to further argument over what could be depended on as the truth—the prosecution's original evidence or the repudiations. It is not the purpose here to harp unduly on the Mooney-Billings case; yet, as an ever present issue before half a dozen governors, it cannot be ignored. For many years this complex affair stirred contradictory opinions around the world and plagued the thoughts and consciences of public men in California as, later on, the Sacco-Vanzetti case was to do on the other side of the continent. It dragged on for so many years and became so beclouded with political considerations that many unbiased persons despaired of ever reaching the unvarnished truth. After all his research, Young eventually left the case about as he found it. He often complained that just about the time an independent investigator, pouring over the mountain of transcripts in the tangled litigation, arrived at a tentative judgment, some new aspect invariably popped up, inclining him to an opposite conclusion. Meantime, the two convicted murderers remained behind bars, refusing to seek paroles and insisting they were entitled to full and complete pardons. The troubled temper of the times also was reflected, incidentally, by stern California action against members of the radical Industrial Workers of the World, a number of them landing in prison as "Red card" carriers in the early 1920s.

Governor Young, the orderly governmental technician, tried for re-election in 1930 but failed. He tried again in 1934 with the same result. California changed governors and political styles in those days as airily as a *nouveau riche* matron throwing away her dinner dress after one wearing. The state was newly rich indeed. The flow of gold had been succeeded by the flow of petroleum. Broad and varied industrialization was beginning. Business and commerce were booming in the 1920s. The state's agricultural products, notably specialty crops flourishing under irrigation in a hot, dry climate, assumed rank with the nation's leaders in volume and worth. On the coast, San Francisco, reborn from the ashes of 1906, was gaining wider and wider recognition as one of the three most charming cities in America, while, at the other end of the state, Los Angeles continued the interminable population increases which were to make it one of the nation's largest urban complexes. The south and south-central coast was being likened to the French Riviera, along with the claim of whiter, more spacious pleasure beaches and brighter sunshine. California was beginning to boast. For good measure, there was Hollywood, too, the world's new mass entertainment capital. It was the golden age of the big studios and of filmland's gods and goddesses. Both to the natives and the multitudes of new arrivals, there seemed to be abundant reasons for California's self-satisfaction. The state's harbors were crowded with the world's shipping. Money was plentiful. Stock prices were climbing. Everybody, or nearly everybody, was happy. Then came the market crash of 1929, followed by prostration of the country's economy. The Great Depression's rain, cold and drenching, found California with too many people and too few umbrellas. The shock of financial dislocation rocked the state almost instantaneously, as Governor Young's administration neared its conclusion. To lead them in these conditions, the voters of 1930 chose the picturesque and almost unclassifiable James Rolph, Jr., of San Francisco.

10

Governor James Rolph, Jr., long the mayor of San Francisco, often reminded one somehow of Otto Soglow's Little King. He was a round, twinkling little man who combined urban sophistication, or the surface aspects of it, with wide-eyed innocence, or at least a good imitation. He was unquestionably the most colorful figure who ever lived in California's old Victorian executive mansion which, over the years, had housed some dandies. There was a strong strain of pixy in Rolph. A generous-spirited, debonair and altogether improbable man in many ways, badly miscast for days of depression, he experienced a frustrating administration after his gubernatorial election in 1930 and died in office during the final year of his term.

Although California's economy was crippled and the unemployment rolls were mounting, the Rolph inauguration in January, 1931, was a round of elaborate ceremony and cheerful merriment. Sacramento enthusiastically celebrated the new governor's arrival. Bands blared sprightly tunes, especially "Smiles," which Rolph had adopted as his official song. A semimilitary reception was included in the gay doings. A contingent of the San Francisco Grays, garbed in what closely resembled the dress uniform of West Point, circled the rotunda of the old Capitol of the 1860s as an honor guard, while a

58

sword-bearing aide marched close on Rolph's heels as the new executive graciously received his friends and well-wishers. The pomp and ceremony obviously delighted him. This formal display and other jubilant festivities launched Rolph on a career which was another small example of a very old and unaccountable political phenomenon: the periodic emergence of a scintillating, effervescent personality who, for no easily discernible reason, enlists public acceptance and even a measure of genuine affection. In this, to some degree, Rolph rather paralleled New York's Jimmy Walker, though many clearly felt that, for sheer gaudiness, California's Jimmy outdid New York's hands down.

Rolph's high-domed head was nearly bald and he wore a closely clipped gray mustache. Perhaps his lack of height suggested Soglow's diminutive monarch. He dearly loved to play the role of governor and painstakingly dressed it with stately old-fashioned formality. He was in morning coat and striped trousers at the slightest provocation. Always there was a full-blown pink or white camellia in his buttonhole. Even with evening dress, however, he sported a shiny, modified version of the boots of the old Forty-niners. He was reputed to own something like forty pairs of them.

From the very outset, the buoyancy of Rolph's disposition and his unorthodox mannerisms seemed to cast a pleasant spell on Californians, or at least on a good many of them. They recognized him as an incurable romantic and helped spread the legend that he was a descendant of Pocahontas. When the hard-pressed new state administration and the Legislature had to revise the California revenue system and imposed the state's first retail sales tax, the equally hard-pressed taxpayers, with agreeable forebearance for those bleak times, half-joked about shelling out their "pennies for Jimmy." The public laughed tolerantly when, on the eve of a national conference of governors in California, Rolph, feverishly preparing for his role as host, directed that a large section of the Capitol Park lawn be torn up and the soil replanted with a profusion of red, white and blue flowers, so arranged as to spell out "Three Cheers For The Good Old U.S.A."

59

It was amused, too, by the story that when the nation's governors crossed the state's border, their jubilant greeter met them in the dead of night in the high eastern mountains, cheerily crying out, "Welcome, strangers! Welcome to California!" This warmhearted salutation to the sleepy and understandably astounded governors was facilitated by the vigorous swinging of a railroad signal lantern to stop the Overland Limited.

The Governor's press conferences in those days were a riot of the unexpected. Once he personally ordered a bottle of whiskey for a condemned murderer who had written him saying he was not interested in a reprieve from his San Quentin Prison death cell but certainly was "mighty thirsty." After a triple lynching growing out of a vicious sex crime, Rolph impulsively announced he would be happy to pardon the lynchers if the police ever caught up with them. This advance promise of clemency drew national protests, including some critical observations from the White House. Recalling the bonus march of war veterans on Washington, Governor Rolph undertook to silence President Hoover with the tart reminder that California's government at least had never ordered the postwar military to "shoot our brave soldier boys."

The Governor was at his glowing best on other more pleasant social occasions. He cut ribbons and dedicated highways, public buildings and even private supermarkets from one end of California to the other. One day, on a sudden thought, he ordered a set of expensive blankets in the official blue and gold of California for a Hollywood movie starlet who was about to serve as a winter festival queen in the high Sierra Nevada. It occurred to him that she might have to sit for some time on a throne of ice. The Governor himself emerged from his private office that morning attired in a silver-painted top hat and a long overcoat which reached to his booted heels and was completely covered with cotton. He was headed for the festival, too, he said, and intended to be King Snow.

Critics of Governor Rolph pictured him as something of a benevolent but rattle-brained Nero, fiddling at his executive job while California lay about him in economic ruins. Actually, there was precious little he could do about a depression on the scale of that which ravaged the nation in the early 1930s. He could and did join in a revamping of California's tax structure, eliminating the exclusive state taxation of utility companies and returning the properties of all such corporations to the county tax rolls to broaden the local tax base and ease the plight of ad valorem taxpayers. And he could, of course, along with other governors, yell for federal help. Barring foolhardy extravagances on a big scale, though, few state executives can be blamed with any telling logic for the governmental results of general business collapse. Nonetheless, governors and Presidents, almost without exception, are held politically responsible in such circumstances, as Herbert Hoover was in that same era. The very nature of Governor Rolph—his restless enthusiasms, his bouncy flair for showmanship—was ill-adapted to the troubled, topsy-turvy world in which he found himself. He was having the time of his life and at the same time, an extremely sentimental man, he fumbled for ways to lighten the lot of the hungry and jobless. The State Treasury general fund, like treasuries all over the land, was fast running dry, however. For even the most brilliant and best-trained state executive, which Rolph was not, the situation at the depression's worst was hopeless. He erected Christmas trees in his office, with toys for the children of the unemployed. He flew about the state in his airplane, dispensing optimism and good cheer. "I wish I could have been governor in Governor Young's years," Rolph once said wistfully. "I'd have shown them how to entertain!" There was no cynicism in this attitude. Here was a completely unorthodox governor, fascinated by the social and ceremonial glitter of high public office, relatively unprepared for many of its more intricate problems.

This singular man had finally been elected governor in 1930, twelve years after he first sought the office. He had run back in 1918 against Republican Governor William D. Stephens, but, true to his strange and wondrous ways, he somehow managed to win the wrong nomination. Rolph also was a Republican—whether basically progressive or conservative nobody could say with any great confidence—and he had cross-filed in 1918 on both major party primary tickets. The Democrats nominated him. He was disqualified because his own party did not. After the celebrational fanfare of Rolph's 1931 inauguration, he found himself leading, or trying to lead, a weary, downcast California, financially prostrate and seething with unrest. Because of impressive westward migrations, California suffered during the depression more than many other sections of the country. Newcomers, suddenly thrown out of work, were far from their original homes and family ties, destitute and largely without friends to whom they could turn for help. Hard times always hit a population such as California's with smashing immediacy. Soon thousands were subsisting on charity and the public dole. Businesses were failing. Installment payments fell delinquent. Homes were lost. The almost empty State Treasury had to pay its bills with registered warrants, interest-bearing I O U paper. Mobs of unemployed, frequently prodded on by radical leadership, moved on city halls and the State Capitol in organized "hunger marches."

There was never a dull moment in Rolph's hectic, turbulent term of office. He was a freewheeling political rarity who, even in the most trying circumstances, made up his own rules as he went along. Once, when an ugly, unruly crowd of hunger marchers pressed to the very Capitol doors, the beleaguered Rolph met the demonstrators on the front steps with a characteristic display of smiling charm and a cordial address of welcome. While half a dozen rival speakers simultaneously harangued the ill-tempered mob on the Capitol lawn and armed peace officers stood by to prevent violence, the merry little center of all this hullabaloo climaxed his remarks by waving aloft a handful of *honorary* trade-union membership cards as an evidence of his sympathy for the working man. These and many other equally original performances enlivened the Rolph years immeasurably and prompted the Governor's detractors to charge him with a demonstrable inclination toward eccentricity. Wholly unperturbed, he continued to mix solemn, studied formality with unpredictable, apparently irrepressible prankishness. Oddly enough, Californians seemed to like him that way. Even the national advent of Franklin Roosevelt and the New Deal did not appreciably embarrass the jolly and comparatively haphazard administration of California. Although the voters marked their ballots for Democrat Roosevelt and against Republican Hoover, Republican Rolph was forever being showered with gifts, good wishes and other evidences of attachment. True enough, some disenchanted observers of the jaunty antics and continuing popularity of "Sunny Jim" found this only a disheartening proof of the old Roman formula for hard times: Give the people bread—or a circus. There must have been a little more to it than that. The depression governor's puckish unconventionality may have had a perverse entertainment value of sorts in days when there was little enough to laugh about. Moreover, many seemed to sense that behind the façade of merriment there was a reservoir of good intentions. At all events, people had a much warmer spot in their hearts for Rolph than for many other sober-sided governors with much more impressive records.

For all his gay insouciance, Governor Rolph probably wrestled with his problems more effectively, at that, than many were ready to admit at the time. Not only did the years of his office-holding produce the so-called Riley-Stewart Plan for complete state taxation renovation, bringing in the sales tax followed by the income tax a couple of years later, but Rolph, in 1933, gave the state its first reduced budget expenditure program in a decade. That same year he signed the vitally important Central Valley Project Bill. California, considered as a whole, is a semiarid state. Water always has been among its greatest needs. There are plentiful rains and broad rivers in the north and areas of serious water shortage in the south. A comprehensive public program for the conservation of water, flood control and hydroelectric power development had been advocated for many years. This involved the harnessing of northern streams, particularly the Sacramento River as a starter, and the construction of state dams and other works for the redistribution of northern waters. The realization of such a plan and its expansion later on were to entangle California politicians in controversy during the succeeding five state administrations.

After long opposition by determined special lobby interests, who claimed the undertaking would put the government into improper competition with privately owned power companies, the first phases of the Central Valley Project were authorized by the 1933 Legislature and $170,000,000 worth of bonds approved to start construction. Continuing the fight, the private utilities carried the bill to a statewide referendum. Out of a bitter ideological campaign, centering on the concept of public ownership and the state's role in the control and development of natural resources, finally came California voter ratification of the program in December, 1933. This was a large state enterprise for depression times. It was difficult to market the bonds. Ultimately Washington came to the rescue; in 1935, the federal government moved in to help and the United States Bureau of Reclamation took over the building and management of the Central Valley Project.

But Governor Rolph did not live to see the great Shasta Dam on the upper Sacramento and the rest of the CVP become a reality. Stricken by a cardiac ailment, high blood pressure and aggravated complications, he died in office in June, 1934, on the very eve of the next state election campaign. Partly because of this, fifteen men ran for the California governorship at the 1934 primary—a Communist, a Socialist, a Progressive, three Republicans and nine Democrats, a number of them bidding for multiple nominations, one of them filing on four party tickets. Considering the chaotic situation which this brought about, many people found themselves speculating afterward on whether, if Rolph had lived, a floundering but fascinated electorate might not have retained him in office. Looking back at what actually happened, it must be admitted that such a surmise was certainly not without some basis. The Democrats, just reaching California voter registration superiority for the first time in many years, chose that moment to nominate a lifelong

Socialist. And a Republican much less personable than Rolph ultimately won.

Something indefinably pleasant and a little precious, perhaps the last breath of California's carefree early days and confident, swaggering pioneer mannerisms, died with Jim Rolph. He was an elfish spirit of vivacious, uninhibited optimism, serving a people in the depths of dejection; a man of sunshine, elevated to power in a period of dismal storm. The times were wrong for him, but, all things considered, perhaps he was peculiarly right for them.

11

THE "SOCIALIST INTERLOPER"

The five California months of 1934 immediately following the death of Governor James Rolph, Jr., belong peculiarly to Upton Sinclair, the novelist. The harsh violence of those five months is probably without exact political parallel in California or any other state. It was a tumultuous period of grim and vituperative charges and countercharges and of attempted character assassination. The inhibitions which customarily govern civilized behavior, even in political contests, were largely tossed overboard.

Republican Lieutenant-Governor Frank F. Merriam had automatically become governor after Rolph's sudden death. It was election year, however, and Merriam had to stand for a full term of his own almost immediately. Novelist Sinclair was among the fourteen candidates who challenged him. With full allowance for the alarming impact which Sinclair's quixotic political adventure undoubtedly had on the power centers of California's financial establishment, the savagery of the response was excessive beyond anything comparable which readily comes to mind. Governor Merriam was an ultraconservative from Iowa who had worked his way up through the Legislature of his adopted California to the lieutenant-governor's office and finally to the titular leadership of the GOP. As a personality, the new governor was regarded as dull as Rolph had been colorful. A Socialist turned Democrat, Sinclair was fifty-six, energetic, a confirmed reformer and intellectually rambunctious when these two men, previously worlds apart, found themselves heading toward inevitable collision in the summer of 1934.

As Lyndon Johnson was to do exactly thirty years later, Sinclair, abruptly getting up from his writing table in southern California, trumpeted a crusade against poverty. He did so in a burst of uncompromising words and without the cautious Johnsonian strategy of striving to link his proposals in advance to a broadly prepared public consensus. If Sinclair enjoyed a consensus of sorts in the early phases of his venture into Democratic politics, the miserable conditions of the Great Depression provided it. The author of *The Jungle, The Brass Check* and almost countless other muckraking, crusading books and pamphlets attempted to win the governorship and simultaneously to change the economic setup of California radically. Failing in both undertakings, he stirred up local opposition of record-smashing ferocity. In his earlier California days, Sinclair had run before for governor and for other offices too, always as a Socialist, a sort of ideological token candidate, whose response from the voters had been comparatively meager. Now, in the darkest days of the depression, he became convinced that "production for use," as distinguished from production for profit, was *The Way Out,* as he titled a hurriedly prepared little book on the subject. He followed this, in October, 1933, while Rolph still was governor, with the publication of what must be unique in the annals of American political statements. Before even committing himself to a 1934 gubernatorial candidacy, he wrote *I, Governor of California, and How I Ended Poverty*. While this was intended at first as a work of the imagination, a dramatic expression of the author's economic notions, its reception persuaded Sinclair to reregister as a Democrat and try to make the fiction a reality.

As an aftermath of Franklin Roosevelt's national victory in 1932, California had swung by 1934 into the Democratic voter registration column. Old-line Democrats lost no time in branding Sinclair a "Socialist interloper." The *I, Governor* book, which became the gospel of an enthusiastically mushrooming "End Poverty League," proposed sundry tax reforms and welfare measures but concentrated principally on an "EPIC (End Poverty in California) Plan." First, as a proposed method of removing the unemployed as a taxpayers' burden, this sweeping plan called for the establishment of state land colonies on which the jobless would live and become self-sustaining through agricultural production. Second, the program envisioned the authorization of state-sponsored factories and production plants— "a complete industrial system"—in which other groups of unemployed would produce "the basic necessities" for themselves and the land colonies. Third, the scheme contemplated the issuance of state bonds for the purchase of agricultural and industrial machinery and urged an elaborate arrangement of barter and credits for the exchange of products within this publicly operated economic contrivance. Sinclair's advocacy of a statewide industrial-agricultural system for the depression's unemployed, paralleling, or actually within, California's privately conducted free enterprise system immediately engendered a battle royal from the Oregon border to Mexico.

No stranger to controversy, Sinclair blithely predicted his nostrum not only would cure the ills of California's underprivileged but likewise might "end poverty in civilization." The mildest rejoinder was "rainbow chaser." The nominally reconstructed Socialist was called everything from crackpot to Communist, with a full-colored spectrum of other epithets thrown in for good measure. The tempo of this was stepped up sharply when the Democratic Party, infiltrated by an almost fanatically devoted body of EPIC Plan supporters, nominated Sinclair for governor over eight Democratic primary election opponents, prominent among them the writer George Creel. Governor Merriam carried the Republican primary against a smaller field, including former Governor Young. And Raymond Haight, temporarily defected from the GOP which he later served as California national committeeman, won the nominations of the Commonwealth and Progressive parties that summer, assuring a three-way general election runoff. There were Communist and Socialist nominees, too, but their bearing on the outcome was admittedly negligible. California had eight political parties that year. In those days, the Communists had a place on the state ballot. The birth of the John Birch Society was still far in the future, of course, yet ultra right-wing conservatives already were plentiful in one guise or another. Unsettled by the depression, California was a heady mixture of varying political inclinations, strange prophets and crusading splinter groups.

Aside from the goal of reducing or eliminating poverty, there was little similarity between Lyndon Johnson's 1964 blueprint for the "Great Society" and Upton Sinclair's "End Poverty in California" plan of 1934. Whereas President Johnson's initial campaign pronouncements were sometimes criticized for a tendency toward generalization, Sinclair's were fairly bursting with specifics. He scared the California business community half to death. Organized efforts to smother him and his doctrines were set in motion with alacrity. For sheer malice and abusive fulminations, the Merriam-Sinclair-Haight governorship contest was, for a single campaign, undoubtedly the most vicious political imbroglio in California's modern history, not excepting some of the well-financed electioneering efforts mounted against "that man" Roosevelt. It was a field day for hired political sharpshooters and professional propagandists, with little or no apparent limit to the excesses indulged in. Sinclair was the obvious target of those convinced he was guilty of economic heresy and a threat to the established order. In the general uproar, Merriam and Haight often seemed to be of secondary importance, except as alternatives to Sinclair, in his fright wig of radicalism, and the actual Communist and Socialist nominees for governor were generally ignored.

In calm afterthought, it would seem enough for the novelist's detractors to have underscored the shortcomings which alarmed them in his program and his demonstrable lack of administrative experience for the public post he sought. That approach proved too mild for fear-ridden 1934. The personality of the man himself became the overriding issue—the things he had written, his many years of commitment to socialism. Public relations experts were engaged to pore over the entire output of Sinclair's long literary career, searching out suitable quotations to disparage the author. He protested in vain that these were often taken out of context and twisted out of meaning by strategic deletions. Sometimes the words of Sinclair's fictional characters were represented as his own beliefs. It was proof positive of the old saying that he who writes books is usually in poor position to run for public office. The results of all this relentless literary "research" were widely circulated and plastered on billboards from Eureka in the north to San Diego in the south, from San Francisco on the west to Nevada on the east. The so-called United for California League and kindred anti-Sinclair campaigning agencies were as active in attack as the End Poverty League was in hopeless defense. Sinclair himself scribbled rebuttals and elaborations of his embattled platform in a series of feverishly composed pamphlets. One of them, rather anticipating instant coffee, was called *Immediate EPIC*.

Religion as well as economics played a part in the frantic vote hustling, occasionally providing the campaign with high points of shabby, unintentional humor. One confused political orator called Sinclair an atheist, picturing him as standing in a church pulpit and, watch in hand, challenging God—"if there be a God"—to strike him dead within the next three minutes. The speaker had mistaken Upton Sinclair for Sinclair Lewis. Sinclair recalled this incident in writing about the election later on, but he did not mention another story of the day involving one of his own devoted rally chairmen. After an eloquent address by the Democratic nominee, this enthralled but befuddled master of ceremonies was reported to have wound up the proceedings with a hearty "Thank you, Mr. Lewis." All in all, Sinclair may have wished more than once that summer that he never had written *The Profits of Religion* back in 1917. This old volume

was combed for words and phrases which could be used or misused
to bolster the thesis that the novelist was a thoroughly godless man.
One resulting leaflet termed him a "defiler of all churches and all
Christian institutions."

Another favorite subject of anti-Sinclair pamphlets and roadside
posters depicted a huge, ugly, bewhiskered figure waving aloft a
red flag while trampling California. A broad phalanx of official and
unofficial political organizations waged the fight all summer with
tireless energy, oftentimes with unexampled venom. Governor Merriam personally conducted a rather lackluster campaign, leaving
smear techniques largely to his bellicose well-wishers. Almost all the
California daily press arrayed itself against Sinclair, most of it in
Merriam's corner, a small percentage favoring Haight. With the
Democrats badly split, many of the conservative adherents of that
faith were recruited into temporary campaign committees for the
Republican incumbent. Victory for Sinclair was portrayed as a disaster which would lure the unemployed of the whole nation to California in hope of a handout. After the primary, Sinclair conferred
with President Roosevelt and other New Deal leaders, but received
no endorsement of "production for use." He realized, he intimated
later, that California's Democratic nomination of a former Socialist,
something of a sensation around the country, had its points of em-
barrassment for the New Deal regime, intent on holding together
an uneasy Democratic party coalition for the national election of
1936. The New Dealers were not in the slightest danger, as it turned
out, but still indisposed to tempt fate by embracing Sinclairism.

In the closing weeks of California's general election campaign,
Raymond Haight, whose family had produced a California governor in earlier years, became a political headache to both major party
camps. Nobody could be sure from whom he might draw votes. He
had a Republican background, somewhat to the left of Merriam's;
he went around the state making progressive speeches, somewhat to
the right of Sinclair's. Both sides wanted him out of the race. Haight
claimed more than once that he had been offered high public office,

future political support and even financial considerations if he would step aside in favor of Merriam. On one occasion, he charged a substantial amount of political money had found its way into the Merriam campaign coffers as an aftermath of the National Guard having been called out in a San Francisco waterfront labor dispute, and offered to quit the campaign if the Governor could establish the falsity of this allegation. Merriam commented that a lot of lies were being told about him. An attempted understanding between Haight and Sinclair also fell through. Although less convinced than most that the Democratic candidate was Satan's handyman in disguise, Haight evidently felt that if anybody was to make an eleventh-hour gesture of withdrawal, it ought to be Sinclair. The latter took the position that it would be impossible for him to deliver his army of intensely loyal followers to Haight or any other candidate on the eve of the election, even if he wanted to.

So they went to a November vote. Merriam polled 1,138,620. Sinclair got 879,537. Those unwilling to mark their ballots for Merriam or Sinclair went to Haight—302,519 of them. The minor Socialist and Communist candidates mustered fewer than 9000 votes between them. Merriam had retained the governorship by less than a majority. This amazing campaign, which all but reduced California to a political shambles, was an early demonstration of the power of handsomely financed sloganeering propaganda to unleash a spirit of grim vindictiveness and create a species of public panic. As often is the case with writing men, Sinclair managed to have the last word. Three days after the election, he was back at his desk, composing a 215-page analysis of the campaign, complete with still another recapitulation of his politico-economic beliefs and a resume of the infuriated and infuriating attacks made upon him. He concluded that, had the balloting gone otherwise, he would have brought a considerable flair for concentration to the job of governor but might have suffered "acute boredom." He published the book himself in Pasadena and called it *I, Candidate for Governor, and How I Got Licked.*

Shortly after the election, Albert Einstein sent Sinclair a note, suggesting that the novelist was well out of "this rude business" and might with good conscience leave direct political action in the future "to men with tougher hands and nerves."

12

For eight years after the Merriam-Sinclair election battle of 1934, control of California's government veered crazily between the Republicans and the Democrats, the ultraconservative and ultraliberal wings of those parties dividing nominal power during the period almost evenly, without the emergence of a particularly strong administration in either case. The state itself was indecisive and leaned toward experimentation. Voter majorities shifted restlessly from the Republican right to the Democratic left, but neither group generated enough political momentum to realize very many of its goals. These were the years of Republican Governor Merriam's incumbency and of Democratic Governor Culbert L. Olson's—the irresolute interval just preceding the advent of Earl Warren.

It used to be said of Frank Finley Merriam who, from June, 1934, through 1938, served as California's twenty-eighth governor, that you can take a boy out of Iowa but often it is something else again to take Iowa out of the boy. He was not exactly a boy when California first knew him. In fact, he was reputed to be the oldest politician to reach the state's executive mansion in the first half of the twentieth century. He had matured politically, so to speak, in the Midwest and had been an Iowa state official before heading west to win new fame, and fortune if possible, in California. With thousands of new settlers flooding the Far West, even before the Dust Bowl days and the influx of the Okies and Arkies, there was no special political premium on California birth. Between Hiram Johnson's 1910–1917 administration and Jim Rolph's election in 1930, no California native son managed to capture the governorship. None did, even after Rolph, until Warren came along in 1942.

Everything considered, Merriam has to be classed as one of the luckiest men in the story of California politics. After a checkered career as Iowa State auditor, he made a new beginning in California and parlayed infinite patience and shrewd caution into the topmost position of his adopted state. Starting as a Republican assemblyman of decidedly conservative stripe back in 1917, he slowly climbed the ladder to Assembly Speaker (under the sponsorship of Governor Friend W. Richardson), then to state senator and finally to lieutenant-governor. Upon inheriting Rolph's governorship, he experienced the almost immediate good fortune of a Democratic split following that party's gubernatorial nomination of Upton Sinclair. It was no trick at all to mount a scare campaign against a Democratic standard-bearer who candidly admitted he never before had voted for anything but the Socialist ticket. It was possible to devise a sweepingly triumphant GOP operation which was basically anti-Sinclair rather than pro-Merriam. Fate rarely deals anybody such a pat political hand.

Stout and completely bald save for a fringe of gray around the ears, Governor Merriam was in very late middle years when he came to executive power, and might readily have been typed by Hollywood Central Casting for the role of a deliberately jovial, slightly pompous minor bank official. He had, indeed, played some such part in real life at one time in his varied career. That was after he had left the Midwest and settled in Long Beach, sometimes referred to in those days as California's "New Iowa." In the Legislature, back in the 1920s, he often favored a black-corded pince-nez, with gates-ajar collar and white piping on his vest. Politically, then and afterward, there was little attempt made to conceal his devoted alignment with the Republican Old Guard, an affiliation of long standing.

Merriam was a shade touchy and mysterious about his age. In 1934, so Sinclair claimed cattishly at the height of their political rivalry, the governor was nearly seventy-four. Evidently alarmed at the dedicated following which Sinclair's flashy program seemed to be recruiting among depression sufferers, Governor Merriam spoke warmly of aid to the aged and destitute, applauded the Townsend national pension plan for the elderly and undertook otherwise, upon occasion, to wrap himself in a temporary cloak of "progressivism." For the most part, though, the Governor pursued his usual plan of studied caution. In his concluding radio address of that memorable campaign, he contented himself with generalities and a hearty endorsement of the preservation of fish and game, an unlikely appeal in a period of mass unemployment. Nonetheless, despite the fears, uncertainties and susceptibilities to improvised cure-alls which characterized those difficult times, the Governor's careful posture of sober dignity and unswerving orthodoxy was crowned by victory.

Under fundamentally conservative auspices, a 1934–1938 reign of routine and uneventful government-as-usual ensued. Thousands were still on state unemployment relief. California's State Treasury was in bad shape. Venturing nothing very spectacular, Merriam called a number of statewide study conferences to consider the vexatious conditions. A state personal income tax was imposed in 1935 to supplement the retail sales tax adopted two years before during Rolph's time. The Riley-Stewart Tax Plan, as noted earlier, had abandoned state dependence on a percentage of utility corporation gross receipts for State Treasury needs—largely, so some maintained, because of the determined resistance of the utilities to increasingly heavy levies on their earnings. So new and different sources of treasury income had to be provided to keep the state solvent, or at least within hailing distance of solvency. The local governments, meantime, were allowed to tax utility property holdings along with other common property. While this was designed to ease the revenue problems of California's political subdivisions, the hard-pressed local governments, only a few years later, were renewing their appeals for additional state financial assistance. Very soon more than half of the rapidly growing state budget was going for local aid. This situation still obtained almost three decades later, constituting one of the major stumbling blocks to state budget balancing.

In his dealings with news media, aging Governor Merriam was extraordinarily watchful. A wintry smile and a brusque "No comment" constituted his frequent answer to pertinent press conference questions. He argued stubbornly—though unsuccessfully—that such official silence on public issues ought to go unreported. Once his native caution actually led him to attempt what he called an "off the record" observation in the midst of a statewide radio address. Another time his Midwestern background overcame him at the microphone while he was hymning the praises of California's annual agricultural and industrial exposition. "Come, one and all," he cried, "to the Iowa State Fair!"

The 1934–1938 Republican administration, to put the case as generously as possible, was not very distinguished either in style or accomplishments. The Democrats put an end to it at the next election with their first gubernatorial triumph since the 1890s. California elected only four governors in the next twenty-eight years—two Republicans and two Democrats, all in varying degree to the left of Merriam. Right-wing movements made their appearances from time to time during those years, but Merriam was the last California governor—as of the end of 1966 anyhow—whose usual policies were unabashedly in the tradition of Old Guard conservatism.

Governor Merriam's successor, Culbert L. Olson, was a dedicated, unwavering, even dogmatic Democrat, the first member of that party to enter the Capitol as chief executive in forty years. A tall, striking and dignified figure, he was conceded, even by his enemies, to "look like a governor at least." The admiration of many, in fact all, the supporters of the outgoing Merriam regime, stopped right there. Olson quickly turned out to be a confirmed liberal in his views on virtually everything. With extravagant esteem for the national record of Franklin Roosevelt, he promised, at the state election of 1938, to "bring the New Deal to California." A lawyer and former Utah state legislator, Olson had gained the state senate seat for population-bursting Los Angeles County in 1934 and become a leader in the Democratic legislative minority which survived Sinclair's ill-fated gubernatorial campaign against Merriam. Olson went on to unseat Merriam in a stunning right-left political switch. A widely known campaign management "specialist," who had searched the Sinclair novels from cover to cover for material which could be turned against the former Socialist four years earlier, observed with some regret that Olson, after all, "never wrote any books."

If the Merriam years could be said to have moved at a stately trot, the Olson administration started off at a headlong gallop and came many a cropper. Into office with him, Olson carried a slim majority of Democrats in the State Assembly, causing a good many politico-financial interests to shudder at the prospect of an ultraliberal take-over. From their special standpoint, well they might, for Governor Olson immediately fired a series of messages at the Legislature, not only endorsing the tenets of the federal New Deal but recommending a long list of California reforms and innovations. These included rehabilitation of the state's regulatory and humanitarian agencies which had suffered personnel and money cutbacks under Merriam. Moreover, Olson advocated a tax-supported program of public health insurance, the signal for uproarious controversy. In the parliamentary fights that followed, the Democratic executive achieved few of his objectives, though it was generally admitted, years later when the battle smoke had cleared away, that few California governors had equaled him in the scope of his arguments for liberal goals or in the stubborn persistence with which he battered his head against an unyielding legislative wall.

Three major courses of strategy in the opposition to the administration of 1939–1942 were deftly mapped to frustrate Olson's New Dealish proclivities and put him behind the political eight ball. The first was to split the Assembly's Democratic majority. The second step was to organize a well-disciplined antiadministration coalition. The third was to assail management of the State Relief Administration, an aid agency for the depression's destitute, and so center public attention on it that the rest of Olson's program could be quietly chloroformed. All three procedures worked to perfection. The thin voting advantage of the Democrats in the State Assembly was readily broken by siphoning off ten conservative Democrats and realigning them with a "nonpartisan" but Republican-dominated group which called itself an "economy bloc" and promptly took over lower house control. The State Senate already was Republican and had been for many years. Within twelve months, Olson's legislative support, shaky to begin with, was cut to ribbons. The State Relief Administration then became the big target. Most of California's regular state employees had by then been placed under civil service, leaving the new administration relatively few positions to hand out to job-hungry Democrats. The Relief Administration was an exception, a temporary agency to which the merit system of appointments did not apply. Some of the Olson regime's foes wasted little time in launching a species of Communist hunt. The Governor's patronage appointees to supervisory SRA jobs were closely scrutinized for mismanagement and leftward leanings. A watchful eye was turned, in some instances, on the relief recipients themselves. This highly efficient political operation spawned much vituperation and many a sensational headline. Amid the general outcry, Olson's other major legislative proposals, for the most part, were expeditiously sent down the political chute to oblivion.

In no small degree, Governor Olson contributed to his own unhappy dilemma. While unquestionably he could pose a progressive issue with extraordinary clarity, he was basically a legislator rather than a seasoned executive and not always the best judge of men or of methods to gain his desired political ends. No compromiser, he pursued his purposes with a blunt obstinacy which enabled his lawmaking opponents, while blocking him at every turn, to accuse him of "dictating to the Legislature." It has been called unfortunate that so many governors, and even occasional Presidents, come to power without the helpful background of legislative experience. Governor Olson's trouble may have been the very opposite. Too little familiarity with executive responsibility can raise equally insurmountable obstacles. On top of determined Republican opposition, this stiffly independent chief executive was confronted by friction between his own liberal followers and the more conservative "regulars" of the Democratic party itself. There was a wide gap between these Democratic elements which continued to be evident in California politics for many years and indeed played a part in the gubernatorial election of Republican Ronald Reagan as late as 1966. It certainly helped defeat Olson nearly a quarter of a century earlier. Then too, intensely loyal to his friends, Governor Olson may have been misled sometimes on fundamental political tactics by the flattering but amateurish advice of the "palace guard" sycophants almost inevitably to be found on the steps of every executive throne.

At all events, the usual pretenses of political politeness between the legislative and executive branches of government were missing in the California of the late 1930s and the opening 1940s. Animosities were undisguised. Olson was unable to patch up a truce with his bipartisan coalition adversaries in the Legislature even when the attack came on Pearl Harbor and Japanese craft, shortly thereafter, lobbed shells into the Goleta coastal area near Santa Barbara, the first American mainland bombardment of its kind by a major power since the War of 1812. In domestic affairs, the effect of the Roosevelt Presidency naturally reached California, in the construction of the Central Valley Project, in federal aid and in numerous other ways, yet Olson's endeavor to "bring the New Deal to California" as a motivating political factor in state government affairs was an utter failure. The drumfire of propaganda against practically everything Olson stood for was overwhelming. In 1942, following a rip-roaring campaign, the Republicans won the governorship back from Olson with the election of Earl Warren, not comprehending for a moment the intrinsically progressive nature of the man they had chosen.

"I am pleased, of course," Olson said sometime after his defeat, "to see that Warren is trying to get some of the same things done that I tried to do. He will find himself up against the same legislative stone wall that I faced."

Years later, in political retirement and moving into old age, former Governor Olson made his last public appearance in the Capitol to express his opposition to a little piece of legislation intended to revise the Great Seal of California and substitute "In God We Trust" for the old state motto "Eureka." As usual, he was forthright to the point of bluntness. It was reasonable to expect he might have defended "Eureka" as a unique and traditionally appropriate motto, dating back more than one hundred years to the days of California's Gold Rush. Instead, Olson talked about the civil rights of agnostics, stressed the importance of separation of church and state and chose to oppose "In God We Trust," for California anyhow, on the ground of religious freedom. "Eureka" remained on the Great Seal, but not, so far as could be observed, because of favorable legislative committee reaction to Olson's sentiments. As had been his fate for a lifetime, the old fellow came in for adverse publicity and seemed to be marked down by his critics as some kind of politico-spiritual apostate.

13

"THIRTY DOLLARS EVERY THURSDAY"

Disturbed and badly divided California probably led the nation, during the 1930s and at that decade's end, in dazzling displays of economic mumbo jumbo. In the depression days, before the federal social security system was inaugurated or the idea of it generally accepted, there was tremendous emphasis, particularly in southern California, on elaborate and often fantastic old-age pension schemes. The region also abounded in religious mystics and exalted originators of cure-alls for financial ailments as well as spiritual. A number of the pension promoters, some well-meaning, others cynical, made personal careers of these movements, with widespread political repercussions, at a time when many citizens of the Golden State were desperately short of gold, and even silver, shelter and groceries. It was argued, with some cogency, that the day when the average man could frugally lay aside a "nest egg" for his old age had long gone by. What with growing urbanization of the population and the temptations of runaway credit buying, fear for survival of the established economic order was gravely expressed unless some measure of security could be provided for the elderly after their years of productivity had ended.

Nobody gave tongue to these misgivings more noisily than the professional promoters. And nowhere were they more in evidence than in periodically eccentric Los Angeles County, the retirement haven of thousands of old people from the Middle West. Other areas farther east also provided their quotas to California as well as Florida. It was no accident that California, somewhat earlier, had become one of the country's pioneers in public aid to the aged. Some of the original pension enactments, financed in routine budget fashion out of ordinary state revenues, came with the support of fraternal organizations and similar welfare-oriented groups. Compared with the aid grants which commonly prevailed by mid-century, however, these first old-age assistance payments were tiny and predicated oftentimes upon a showing of almost utter poverty.

Something new was added to promotional techniques with the emergence of Dr. Francis E. Townsend. He was a retired Midwestern physician who, like Merriam, had settled in Long Beach. In 1934, Dr. Townsend discontinued the intermittent sale of southern California real estate and turned to the sponsorship of a spectacularly alluring "national" old-age pension program. He proposed a pension of two hundred dollars a month for every citizen of the land who had reached the age of sixty. It was part of the idea that every cent of this would have to be spent within thirty days. Dr. Townsend predicted this huge turnover would prove to be a financial shot in the arm not only for the understandably hopeful and elated old people but for the whole national economy. The program was to be financed by a 2 per cent federal sales tax on the nation's business.

This project caused an immense stir in California, with varying echoes elsewhere in the land and the lively organization of dues-paying "Townsend Clubs" and an active propaganda apparatus. The appeal was not hard to comprehend. Many depression victims of advanced years were near destitution. Even later in the decade, United States Senator Sheridan Downey, a pension-dedicated California Democrat, wrote *Pensions or Penury?,* a book about the paltry allowances which his own state and others had voted for "oldsters" no longer fitted for regular job holding. He was a one-time Townsend Plan advocate who had been Sinclair's lieutenant-governorship running mate in 1934 and whose attitudes had enabled him, in 1938, to take the senatorship from conservative Democrat William Gibbs McAdoo, an adopted Californian and former Woodrow Wilson cabinet member. In 1939, Downey reported California as topping the old-age pension payments of the states with an average grant of only $32.33 a month, while Mississippi, at the bottom of the list, paid a mere average of $4.79.

The Townsend Plan was objected to on the ground that its financing feature, a national sales tax, would invade a revenue-raising field upon which the several state governments were depending, in increasing numbers, as a principal source of income. It was argued, furthermore, that the addition of a broad and perhaps pyramiding transaction tax on the country's business easily might throw the shaky economy of the times into further disruption. While Dr. Townsend's proposal never really got off the ground insofar as gaining congressional approval was concerned, it caused a loud uproar, exercised no little influence in election politics, primarily in California, and lingered around for quite a span of years. Its California supporters actually established the Townsend party as one of the ballot-qualified splinter groups of that state's peculiar political machinery. In the gubernatorial primary election of 1938, many politicians flirted with the Townsendites and three major candidates were sufficiently impressed with the old people's vote to cross-file for the Townsend party nomination. It went to Republican Governor Merriam who filed on three party tickets that year but lost his governorship anyhow.

Old Dr. Townsend, meanwhile, became something of a national personality, adored by hundreds of thousands of the country's elderly citizens and credited with a kind of misguided sincerity even by many others who regarded his complicated national pension plan as fairly preposterous. It is hard to judge Dr. Townsend's remedy for hard times in terms of today's welfare standards. That is true perhaps even of some of the much more bizarre pension movements and fund-raising promotional operations which paralleled or followed the Townsend undertaking. They were the outgrowth of a nationwide dilemma of such magnitude that extraordinary economic jugglery sometimes was grasped at as entirely reasonable. The California situation certainly encouraged this. The migration westward had included a massive contingent of old people from colder climates, intent on spending their declining years in the southern California sunshine, caught up by unexpected hardships even in this "promised land" and unhappily wide open, all too often, to the attractions of odd economic panaceas and the wiles of charlatanism. It is barely possible, from a political standpoint, that some of these agitations may have paved the way, by happenstance and quite indirectly, for an improvement in the lot of the needy elderly as time went on. Thoroughly frightened politicians react very nimbly. By the 1950s and 1960s, the size of the old-age pension, funded by regular budgeting methods and with joint federal-state-county financial participation, had increased in most jurisdictions and had more than trebled in California, with substantial public aid, too, for underprivileged children, the blind and the otherwise physically handicapped. By that time, in fact, California's legislators had voted very nice retirement pensions for themselves, too, and, on a financially contributing basis, for other state officials of long service, both elective and appointive.

Near the end of the 1930s, in the yeasty ferment of numerous depression and post-depression "isms," however, the gradually fading Townsend Plan was rivaled by a new and infinitely more explosive pension promotion which soon was bidding for the enthusiasm of old people and their contribution dollars. Two shrewd brothers, Willis and Lawrence Allen, helped by the planning of an "engineer-economist" and a few self-styled social reform specialists, dreamed up what was known as the "Ham and Eggs Plan." Its charming slogan was "Thirty Dollars Every Thursday." With a keen eye to the competitive market in old-age assistance movements, the Allen brothers cut down their proposed pension eligibility age to fifty years.

As a starter, they limited this gaudy program to California. The "Thirty Dollars Every Thursday," as it quickly turned out, was intended to be paid in scrip, or "state warrants," rather than in actual money. The elderly were assured that this I O U paper would be redeemed in apple-pie order, every single piece of it, by means of a number of thoughtfully planned fiscal gimmicks. There would be, the promoters explained, a stamp tax, linked up with a state bond issue, the sale of stock to the public and a new 3 per cent gross income tax on all Californians and California enterprises. Meantime, campaign contributions were briskly solicited from the proposed beneficiaries.

The widely publicized benefits of the Ham and Eggs program were to be provided through an initiative measure to be submitted to statewide vote. Literally hundreds of thousands of California's aged took this rather astonishing proposition with great seriousness. After a period of utter disbelief, so did thousands of public officials, businessmen and reasonably impartial observers of California affairs, all of them alarmed lest this strangely winding path to the promised salvation of the elderly develop into a broad road to ruin for the entire state. The idea of a stamp tax on scrip, coupled with a bond issue and a general revenue levy on personal earnings and transactions to support this projected flow of printing-press paper, was denounced as an addlepated venture, endangering the economy of a state struggling back from depression, and also was assailed as a cruel fraud on the aged. In no time at all, argued the plan's critics, California's bonds and state credit would be worthless around the country. The promoters were more than happy, though, and those being promoted evidently were delighted.

The loudly reverberating Ham and Eggs campaign was waged in 1938, coincident with the Merriam-Olson governorship election which, in some degree, it confused. Republican Governor Merriam already was a psalm-singing advocate of the Townsend Plan and presumably had the votes of the Townsendites in his pocket. State Senator Culbert L. Olson, the Democratic nominee, flirted with the

Ham and Eggers, though a little shamefacedly. If Olson openly attacked "Thirty Dollars Every Thursday," according to the worried reasoning of some of his campaign lieutenants, he would have neither group of elderly voters on his side and almost certainly would lose the election. It was perhaps surprising that this consideration should have disturbed the stubborn-minded Olson, since even then he had committed himself to the controversial murder case cause of Tom Mooney and Warren K. Billings, promising a pardon which he delivered as soon as he came to power. At all events, he refrained from condemning the pension plan and won the governorship. At the same election, the brothers Allen, though defeated with Ham and Eggs, polled well over one million votes for their involved proposal.

Encouraged by this, and supposedly by the huge sums gathered in contributions from the faithful, the Ham and Eggers made ready for a new initiative drive in 1939. An aroused California business community exploded in angry opposition. Political right-wingers and left-wingers alike joined in. The whole offbeat scrip pension deal was damned as a cold-blooded, money-grabbing hoax. Even the White House became interested, President Roosevelt calling the proposal "fantastic." Upton Sinclair paused in his southern California literary efforts to assert the plan "would not work." Olson, the new governor, veering from his more or less noncommittal position of the previous year, concluded the scheme would retard rather than help California's economic recovery. The professional promoters, well organized on a statewide basis, whipped their hopeful supporters to a fever pitch of excitement. It was a spectacle of carefully nurtured mass hysteria in which the old people, full of righteous indignation, were hustled to the political barricades. It is not too much to say that studied malevolence was deliberately encouraged among ordinarily well-meaning elderly citizens as an electioneering tactic.

After the election, in which the Ham and Eggs Plan again was rejected, somebody sized up the whole promotion as an exploitation of "economic illiteracy." One national magazine called the amazing movement a compound of "moonshine and larceny." Certainly it would have been hard to find a more extraordinary proposal offered in any other part of the country, even in those far-off days of fiscal exhaustion and slowly contrived recovery. Yet, despite California's harrowing experiences of 1938 and 1939, an inclination to follow false prophets, phony soothsayers and promoters in such fields as religion, welfare and social reform persisted for a long time among an appreciable segment of the state's expanding and giddy-paced population. Looking back at the dubious situation three decades ago, it is something of a wonder, perhaps, that California turned out so well. Part of the reason may have been provided by an old-time political writer who once said of the democratic process: Never overestimate the public's intimate knowledge of the situation in the first blush of changing political events nor underestimate its ability to act intelligently once it has been adequately informed.

14

THE PHILBRICK REPORT

If the *Autobiography* of Lincoln Steffens can be called, as it often is, a thoroughgoing exposé of municipal graft methods, the 1938 *Legislative Investigative Report* by H. R. Philbrick, to give it its official designation, had a claim on California public attention as an equally searching inquiry into financial machinations on the state legislative level. It was the by-product of an exceptionally high-flown California exhibition—an open-door grand jury session, probing, with no holds barred, into allegations of legislative corruption. The effect was an updating of the accepted "procedures" in such squalid escapades. The peculiar genesis and ramifications of this curious business had never before been duplicated in California, or possibly anywhere else.

The temporary invisibility of an alert young public servant, a member of the State Assembly in the closing years of the Merriam administration, indirectly set this affair in motion. The "invisible man" was freshman Assemblyman Samuel William Yorty of Los Angeles County, a Democrat who later went to Congress, tried more than once for the United States Senate, became the mayor of Los Angeles in the 1960s and ran for governor in 1966. On May 14, 1937, Assemblyman Yorty was in the Assembly Chamber washroom and, according to grand jury and court testimony, was "concealed" in a cubicle from two other legislators who visited the same premises. In these accidental circumstances, so Yorty said later, he heard suggestive talk of bribery, actually overhearing one assemblyman tell another that "there was money for anyone" who would vote for a certain tideland oil-field drilling and leasing bill. Assemblyman No. 2, according to Yorty, thereupon agreed to vote for the measure, regarded as a major oil bill, "tacitly accepting the offer of money." The record shows that Mr. Yorty subsequently "described the incident" to some of his highly incensed colleagues and that things then began to happen very rapidly. It also discloses that, later that same day, a mysterious envelope was seen to change hands, subsequently disappearing. As for young Assemblyman Yorty, the general run of citizens read of his exploit in the newspapers with possibly confused interest and appeared to mark him down, by common consent, as a hero of the occasion.

Before the resultant political shooting was over, the affairs of about twenty legislators and lobbyists had been investigated either by the Sacramento County Grand Jury or by private inquiry agents engaged by District Attorney Otis Babcock. Under a unique California law, the District Attorney obtained court authority for an open grand jury airing of legislative affairs with press and public free to attend. Most of those interrogated are now dead; all of them have long since departed from the governmental scene. At this late date, it seems useless to clutter these pages with a long list of their names, their questioned financial records and the various peccadilloes attributed to each of them, although their doings were meticulously discussed in the extended public grand jury hearings. More to the point is the pattern which this unusual investigation established, its recitation of the "money pressure" maneuvers by which the course of legislation, not necessarily in California alone, can be damned up or otherwise drastically affected.

Much attention was given, for instance, to "cinch bills," introduced to extort money for their ultimate defeat. California lawmakers had undergone a frustrating experience investigating that sort of thing back in the 1920s. A bill had been offered demanding strict American medical educational standards, as a health safety measure, for Chinese herb doctors, many of them middle-aged and originally trained in Asia. Whatever its merits, it would have forced most of the older herbalist practitioners out of business. At about this time, a lively traffic in solicitation of funds to kill the legislation was reported in San Francisco's Chinatown. A full-scale special legislative committee probe into all this fizzled out when several of the key witnesses, rather ancient Chinese, would not or could not testify in English. Now, in the 1930s, a busy legislator had sponsored a proposal which would have harassed the makers of a certain soft drink of worldwide fame by prohibiting the California distribution of beverages containing a series of specified ingredients. Enthusiasm over this "health measure" evidently carried him too far. He unwittingly made the provisions of his bill so drastic as to forbid the California sale of tea and coffee. Involved in the impending grand jury investigation, this particular statesman popped District Attorney Babcock on the nose one evening in a fit of spirited indignation.

One of the two legislators overheard by Yorty in their washroom conniving over money matters was indicted by the grand jury and twice tried on a charge of bribe offering. The accused assemblyman escaped conviction by a surprising defense. The mysterious envelope which he was seen passing to a fellow lawmaker after their reported conspiratorial talk had really contained no money at all, he solemnly explained, but merely a proposed amendment to a pending bill on employment agencies.

The grand jury inquired deeply into the politically connected "legal fees" of lawyer-legislators, the contention being that retainers for attorney services, rather than outright bribes, had come into popular use in some circles as a convenient and non-incriminating means of compensation for legislative favors. While one lawmaker with a large and varied legal practice was on the witness stand, vigorously denying the slightest association with wrongdoing, a grand

91

juror propounded this rather involved question: How was it that a bill was introduced in the Legislature to restrict commercial sardine fishing; that a group of affected fishing interests authorized the spending of $2500 to help kill the bill; that the secretary of this group conferred in the State Capitol with a certain legislator who often did legal work for the fisheries; that this legislator thereafter took a leading part in defeating the bill before committee, and that, eventually, a series of checks totaling exactly $2500 found their way into the lawyer-legislator's bank account? Suggesting that this was much more than a hypothetical inquiry and that the bank account in question belonged to the man on the witness stand, the grand juror went on to demand, "How *was* that, Mr. Assemblyman?" The witness squirmed a little, flushed a bright red and then blurted: "God bless you, sir, I wish I knew!" Another witness, this one a state senator, broke into tears on the witness stand under a bombardment of embarrassing queries about his fiscal practices.

In the full glare of publicity, which seldom attends grand jury deliberations, there was much examination of banking records, attentive study of legislative "conflict of interest" behavior and considerable scrutiny of California's growing corps of professional lobbyists and the roles played by some of these "advocates," as they preferred to be called, in influencing legislation and elections. Among those called to testify was Arthur H. Samish, the kingpin lobbyist of the liquor industry who, according to the District Attorney's investigators, "received, controlled and disbursed" more than $496,000 during the years 1935 through 1938. Once when Governor Merriam authorized state funds to help Sacramento County finance a continuation of the expensive investigations, this quotation was attributed to Samish: "I'm the governor of the Legislature. To hell with the governor of the state!" All in all, a lot of soiled linen was publicly washed and, while nobody went to prison, at least not just then, a number of the officeholders whose conduct underwent examination were retired to private life at subsequent elections. Although it is only fair to say that average members of California's army of lobbyists and the overwhelming majority of California legislators have usually been completely innocent of improper intrigues, and were in the 1930s, the political fireworks of that decade provided the public with an early blueprint of corrupt lobby-lawmaker manipulations and the many-sided techniques of such shenanigans.

The grand jury sessions produced something else, too: the sensational 1938 résumé report of Howard R. Philbrick, the District Attorney's chief special investigator, which documented the tricks of legislative irregularity in unvarnished language. The famous Philbrick Report was, in fact, so intensely forthright and embarrassing to some in its discussion of shady and unorthodox influences on lawmaking that many politicians have shunned all mention of it for more than a quarter of a century. Howard Philbrick was a former FBI agent and an energetic private investigator hired by the Sacramento County District Attorney to dig up facts and ascertain patterns of cupidity and avarice around the State Capitol when the whole question of misbehavior in the Legislature was taken before an open grand jury. A relatively young, blondish man of disarming geniality, this inquiry specialist had a distinct flair for smelling out intrigue and considerable ability at generalizing from his specific findings. Later on, he became State Director of Motor Vehicles under Governor Olson and reputedly a kind of advising undercover-man-in-residence during part of that troubled regime. After the Olson administration ended, Philbrick was associated for some years with the motion-picture industry. It goes without saying that he was long remembered in legislative circles as a figure of controversy.

In his exhaustive summary report, when the Sacramento Grand Jury's work was concluded, Philbrick drew the conclusion that, in early twentieth-century politics at least, "open-and-shut bribery" and outright shakedowns had become largely outmoded by more subtle approaches to the influencing of legislative results. The cruder types of corruption, he found, were "limited to a small number of venal lawmakers." Wholesale pre-election contributions, pressure on prospective legislators in the form of "tangible personal favors," and the

93

payment of "legal fees" to lawyer-legislators, "employed because of their legislative influence," were described as more sophisticated and obviously safer courses of action in much more general use. Supplementing the grand jury transcript with page after page of "retainer fees" and other financial transactions, the report was an enlightening compendium of assorted shoddy stratagems.

"The weight of evidence," wrote Philbrick, "makes impossible any finding other than that lawyer-legislators have solicited and accepted, or have been offered and accepted, employment predicated upon their legislative influence. For the most part, the lawyer-legislators investigated could make no showing of legal services performed for the clients, apart from the Legislature, commensurate with the size of the fees. . . . After accepting such employment, lawyer-legislators have shown a marked tendency to vote for and otherwise act in the interests of their clients, as distinguished from impartial representation of the interests of the public."

Beyond that, a number of lawyer-legislators were found practicing law before state boards, commissions and other regulatory agencies, where their representation of individuals and special interests, according to Philbrick, commanded "favorable attention because of their official position." This sort of thing was noted both before and after Philbrick's day, the point often being made that such attorneys, as members of the Legislature, passed on the budget requests of the very state departments before which, in spare time, they practiced law. Later on, during Earl Warren's administration, efforts were made to restrict that kind of operation, with determined and successful opposition from influential legislators who were members of the bar.

The Philbrick Report said it was a different story with certain legislative types who were not practicing attorneys. "Evidence accumulated in this phase of the investigation," it observed, "leaves no possible interpretation other than that unscrupulous legislators have offered their votes for sale, haggled for the best price, and actually accepted money. . . . Certain legislators boldly have taken the position that their election meant not an opportunity for public service or political career, but for private enrichment. . . . Individual legislators with no material source of legitimate income, other than their legislative salary, have been able to accumulate substantial sums during a session of the Legislature."

As for pre-election political contributions and favors, especially those dispensed by professional lobby interests, Philbrick called it obvious that such financing generally carried with it "some degree of implied obligation—both in the mind of the contributor and in the mind of the recipient." The investigator dealt in some detail with the efforts of lobbyists upon occasion to "acquire influence" with legislators through "contributions and other favors" and then to "sell that influence" to industries and other moneyed interests concerned with legislation. Conceding that only a few lawmakers might be subject to such influence, Philbrick emphasized that, in a closely divided roll call on a controversial issue, "a small number of 'influenced' votes can prevail." In such operations, his report went on, the lobbyist of the kind pictured was typically "a middle-man" between legislative and business interests, such middlemen constituting "a powerful, if secretive and unofficial, 'fourth branch' of government."

There was much more in the 185-page report, including recommendations that lawyer-legislators file a yearly list of all clients having any interest in legislation; that lawmaking attorneys be barred from practicing before state regulatory agencies; that all legislators be required to maintain full and complete income records; that lobbyist regulations be tightened; that all contributions to California political campaigns be publicly reported both by recipients and donors. Twenty-eight years later, only a few of these proposals had been enacted into law, although a general mandate against "conflict of interest" activities was adopted in 1966 as part of a reorganization program calling for a higher-paid, full-time Legislature.

In summation, the Philbrick Report caused as big a stir as perhaps any comparable document in California legislative history. Naturally it was unpopular with quite a few in and around the legislative halls and, in its bold tendency to call a spade a spade, may have astounded numerous others whose consciences were clear and whose knowledge of such carryings-on as Philbrick described were minimal. The report appeared briefly in one legislative record and then vanished in an overnight revision. Later, on December 28, 1938, after Olson had defeated Merriam for governor, it was produced in book form, only to become an extremely rare item. A few months after the investigation, it was almost as invisible around the Capitol as vigilant young Assemblyman Yorty had been at the investigation's inception. It is a good guess that few of California's present-day legislators have ever seen its pages.

15

THE LAST NONPARTISAN

Earl Warren, invariably ranked on a par with Hiram Johnson as California's most distinguished governor in the first half of the twentieth century and, in fact, classed by many as a cut above the restless, sometimes capricious Hiram, was elected for his first term in November of the war year 1942. For many years before that, he had been the district attorney of Alameda County, across the bay from San Francisco, and latterly the state attorney-general. He was a native Californian, an unusual circumstance in the gubernatorial line rather than the rule. He and Jim Rolph were the only California-born politicians to reach the governorship in the twenty years after the Johnson-Stephens regime ended. Richardson was born in Michigan, Young in New Hampshire, Merriam in the Midwest, Olson in Utah. California's habit of electing governors of out-of-state origin persisted long after Warren. In fact, only three native sons have lived in the state's executive mansion in the last forty-five years. The latest occupant, Ronald Reagan, started life in Tampico, Illinois.

It has been suggested that the state election code system set up by Governor Johnson paved the way, to no small extent, for Governor Warren's election successes more than thirty years later, or at least the manner of them. Johnson more or less invented nonpartisanship as a way of California political life when Warren was still a student at the University of California. Warren revived the nonpartisan approach in a spectacularly effective style to win the four-year California governorship three times in a row. As Chief Justice of the United States and a moving spirit in the Supreme Court's school desegregation decision, among many other important ones, Warren went on, of course, to become one of the nation's great and sometimes controversial figures. In consideration of his earlier California years, he has been called the state's "last nonpartisan." In view of his long string of campaign triumphs, he may have been exactly that, especially since the election laws under which he ran were revised sharply only a few years after his retirement. Perhaps he would have been endorsed and re-endorsed at the polls in any case, but certainly the institution of cross-filing facilitated the result.

Warren was a fifty-one-year-old Republican, and by no means a hidebound or narrow-minded one, at the time he challenged Democratic Governor Culbert L. Olson. A seasoned political veteran, he had long participated in the state GOP's Presidential year activities, though in California's own governmental affairs he had been more particularly concerned, up to then, with law enforcement, in which he had gained a wide reputation. When Olson won the governorship in 1938, Warren was elected attorney-general. It is fairly significant, in the light of later events, that Republican Warren gained the state's top legal post, to all intents and purposes, at the 1938 primary. Cross-filing on several tickets, he received the Democratic and Progressive party endorsements as well as his own Republican nomination. He accomplished this in a Democratic year, marking California's first Democratic gubernatorial sweep of the century.

Governor Olson was a lifelong Democrat and a staunch, unswerving partisan. To establish the situation accurately, it needs to be re-emphasized that, with President Roosevelt in the middle of his second term, the Democrats had moved well ahead of the Republicans in number of California voters. Offhand, it looked as though they could anticipate reasonably smooth sailing as the Olson administration began its four-year struggle to foster New Deal principles in California government and reinstate unified party rule. Faced, however, with a Legislature which, despite the registration tables, remained predominantly Republican, the Democratic establishment was almost constantly in political hot water, and the press of the state was heavily against it. Whether entirely with justification or not, Olson was an unpopular governor by 1942. Re-election odds were against him in another respect, too: The fickleness of California voters was notorious; in the state's election history up to that time, only Governor Johnson had been granted a second four-year term. Many minor state officials had been re-elected, but not governors. With two strikes on him, Governor Olson stubbornly insisted on running strictly as a Democrat in 1942. He was against the practice of primary ticket cross-filing on party principle, although he had personally resorted to it at times in the past. It was a habit to which almost all California politicians were addicted in those days. This time Olson decided to depend on his own majority party alone. On the other hand, Attorney-General Warren appealed immediately to all voters, regardless of political affiliations, and cross-filed for both the Democratic and Republican nominations. So the Warren-Olson campaign was not only a clash of two strong-willed, independent politicians, both of Scandinavian descent as it happened, but a battle between an exponent of California's traditional free-for-all nonpartisan technique and an advocate of the strict partisanship more common elsewhere in the country.

The 1942 state primary result made Warren's ultimate election to the governorship readily predictable, if the trend continued. In a six-man field, including several splinter-party aspirants, Olson captured Democratic renomination handily with more than 500,000 votes. But for every five votes which went to Olson, four other Democrats marked their primary ballots for Warren as a cross-filer. For the Republican nomination, Warren amassed above 600,000. Olson, who had declined to put his name formally before the Republicans, received only 3504 GOP "write-ins." In the November runoff race, Warren stepped up his nonpartisan style of campaigning, while Olson continued to be bluntly partisan, presumably hoping to reunite the already badly split Democrats. Laborites likewise divided between the two candidates, however, even though Governor Olson had started out with endorsements from all the principal state labor organizations. The rank and file obviously did not follow labor's leaders. The Democrats enjoyed a statewide registration bulge of nearly 1,000,000 as the campaign terminated. Yet Warren mustered 1,275,287 general election votes against only 932,995 for Olson. Thus, after only four years of uneasy power, the Democrats lost the one California governorship they had been able to win since the 1890s. Clearly hundreds of thousands of California's 2,300,296 enrolled Democrats had ignored party labels and deserted Olson.

The personalities of the two contenders—Warren, the epitome of appealing friendliness; Olson, self-contained and undemonstrative—were unquestionably factors in the outcome, and so was the manner in which their rival attitudes were projected to a wartime electorate. Nonetheless, it was a revealing demonstration that California elections, at that period anyhow, could not be foretold by party numerical strength alone and that prophecies so predicated were undependable. The lack of solid party involvement, as such, on the part of a huge segment of California's population baffles the imagination of many out-of-staters. Those relying on mathematics alone were due for another surprise in 1966, though the political attractions of Earl Warren and Ronald Reagan could scarcely be more different. It simply proved that California's delight in eye-popping alterations of direction had not diminished very much in twenty-four years. Warren's sweeping victory of 1942 and the circumstances of it affected the state's political modes for nearly two decades and kept nonpartisanship alive as a dominant pattern for election conquests during most of those years. There was a corollary effect, too: the Republicans stayed in State Capitol administrative power until 1958. They clung to Warren's coattails tenaciously, even after the coattails had moved to Washington.

Unlike many of his predecessors, Warren continued to function in a generally nonpartisan manner after the 1942 election was over and he had been sworn in as California's thirtieth governor. Perhaps this was the measure of his staying power in a state celebrated for tossing governors overboard. He proved to be not only a shrewd politician but an able administrator. He appeared to choose his cabinet and chief departmental patronage appointees on the basis of fitness and capability, largely ignoring whether they were Republicans or Democrats. His first and, some thought, his most influential appointee, Executive Secretary William T. Sweigert, later a federal judge, was a Democrat. Warren's postelection behavior along that line made standpat GOPers unhappy, but the Republican county committees, and even the state committee, soon discovered that the new governor was a difficult man to pressure. While Warren was exceedingly amiable, friendly and expansive in his personal relations, he made his own governmental decisions and seldom delegated basic authority in important matters. He quickly gained a reputation as an independent who listened politely to the inevitable flow of advice which comes to all governors but kept his own counsel. In certain quarters, he was viewed with alarm as something of a political loner.

To many politicians, of course, Governor Warren was indeed an enigma. He seemed to draw a line between his role in state politics and his position in national affairs. In spite of the prevailing nonpartisanship of his posture on numerous problems in California, Warren headed his state delegation to every Republican national convention save one for a decade and a half. He became California's GOP favorite son at the wartime convention of 1944, as he previously had done technically in 1936 while still a district attorney. In both cases he made it clear he was not a serious bidder for the Presidential nomination but simply a Presidential primary rallying point, as it were, for free and uncommitted California Republican forces. The Republicans of California invariably chose such nominally favorite son delegations, avoiding party-splitting primary

101

fights and the invasion of the state by outside aspirants, during the Roosevelt-Truman years of Democratic White House occupancy.

New York Governor Thomas E. Dewey, first nominated for President in 1944, tried repeatedly in the behind-the-scenes negotiations of that year's Republican convention to obtain Warren as his Vice-Presidential running mate. The California leader refused the honor, though without any public display of having done so, and Ohio Senator John W. Bricker, a substantially more conservative man, was eventually chosen. Whether Warren sensed that the GOP had a lost cause that season and that President Roosevelt still was unbeatable is beside the question. After all, he had wartime duties of his own to keep him busy back home. California went Democratic again that fall, as it had in F.D.R.'s three previous Presidential elections, but without any loss of home state stature by the Republican governor.

In fact, two years later, once more on the California campaign firing line, Governor Warren scored a nonpartisan triumph which still is regarded as little short of a political miracle. He won his second gubernatorial term at the 1946 primary election, a feat never accomplished before or since by any other Californian, even under the now defunct cross-filing system, and seldom, if ever, managed by a governorship candidate in any other two-party state. Running against Attorney-General Robert W. Kenny, a brilliant and sophisticated Los Angeles Democrat, who conducted an unaccountably inept campaign, Warren swept the field with comparative ease at the nomination balloting in which he was endorsed by the majority Democrats as well as by his own minority Republicans. It was the fashion among some Democrats and a few left-wing labor leaders, at that relatively early stage of Warren's long tenure, to denounce the Governor's advocacy of progressive legislation as a phony gesture, indulged in only to recruit votes. At first, Democrat Kenny started out a little differently, posing the proposition that it was fine for a Republican governor to espouse progressivism but rather futile in view of a conservative Republican Legislature which, in any case, would block all liberal programs. This approach evidently was forsaken as a bit too subtle for general voter consumption, and soon the anti-Warren forces once more were shouting that the incumbent governor was really a kind of political faker. The election response with which California voters in both parties rejected this idea was deafening. It must be said for Kenny, who had been personally well disposed toward Warren in former years, that he undertook the 1946 gubernatorial candidacy with some reluctance, and seemed to some observers to wage the type of campaign which his followers insisted upon against the Republican executive with somewhat less effective vigor than might have been expected. On one occasion the Kenny camp charged Warren with neglecting the Central Valley Project, only to discover the Governor was currently recommending a larger congressional appropriation for the CVP than even its builder, the United States Bureau of Reclamation, had proposed. It may be that Kenny, ordinarily a shrewd judge of political movements, was a little ahead of his fellow Democrats in recognizing the unusual scope of Warren's election appeal.

Once more Governor Warren led the California delegation to the Republican national convention of 1948. There, though less than eager to enter national politics as a serious candidate, at least at that moment, he was finally prevailed upon to run for Vice-President on the second Tom Dewey ticket. President Truman concentrated his fire that fall on Dewey and the Congress, saying little against Warren whom he appeared to hold in some admiration. In Truman's upset victory, California went Democratic by a narrow margin.

In state elections, these were frustrating days for the California Democrats with their mounting registration advantage. From 1932 onward, they had been carrying the state in every Presidential year, each time losing the governorship campaign two years later, except for Olson's election in 1938. After Warren had spread-eagled them in 1946, in their own primary at that, they could only look forward hopefully to the day when he would ultimately retire. They were con-

103

fident that, by sheer numbers, they could prevail over whatever Republican emerged as his suggested successor. Meantime, the Democratic leadership discontentedly admitted, at least in private, that Governor Warren's attractiveness to run-of-the-mill Democratic voters, as well as to most Republicans, was undeniable and without state political precedent since Hiram Johnson's prime. This proved to be the case again in 1950 when James Roosevelt, F.D.R.'s eldest son, was trotted out in the Democratic hope that the magic of the Roosevelt name might somehow break the majority party's run of bad luck. Relatively a newcomer to California, though he later became a capable Los Angeles congressman, the Democratic standard-bearer was hardly a match for Warren either in the field of governmental problems or the intricacies of California politics. Winning a third consecutive four-year term, and incidentally breaking Hiram Johnson's campaigning record, Governor Warren polished off young Jimmy without working up a good political sweat. It was the old story again: thousands of people went to their registration places, signed up with the Democrats and then marched to the polls and voted for Republican Warren.

Cross-filing, according to the alibi offered most frequently by the thrice-defeated and somewhat benumbed state Democrats, was the overriding evil of this anomalous situation. Their determination to have the practice eventually prohibited developed into a No. 1 party shibboleth. The existence of cross-filing, they complained, enabled admittedly progressive Governor Warren to campaign actively among Democrats as well as Republicans even before the party nominations were made—and, furthermore, to have his name emblazoned on the primary ballots of both parties. Their boys had the same privilege, true enough, but not the same almost inconceivable non-partisan appeal. After the state election of 1950, the Democratic kingmakers endured three more years of Warren and then five years of Republican Goodwin J. Knight before they were able, at long last, to install a governor of their own.

16

A SUDDEN POT OF GOLD

The Warren administration, its middle and closing years in particular, coincided with an unusual period of plentiful revenue in California's State Treasury. This was the opposite of ordinary conditions which had previously prevailed for more than a decade, a time of acute money shortages and recurrent budget-balancing problems. California's state institutions, long preoccupied with the need for almost constant expansion, reconstruction and replacement, had ground to a virtual standstill in that respect during the Great Depression and World War II. The depression left public treasuries with little or no surplus cash for building work. There was a lack of both materials and manpower for such undertakings during the war. A long hiatus in the state government's physical improvements and those of its political subdivisions had become unavoidable.

While similar difficulties also plagued other states and most of the world, their crippling impact was conspicuously severe on California as the geographical end of the rainbow for one of the greatest voluntary mass migrations in history. The state's size, as well as the continuing influx of people, aggravated the situation. Over a long, narrow empire of more than 158,000 square miles, California had necessarily spread a complicated network of schools, colleges, penitentiaries, water projects, park installations, forestry establishments, youth reformatories, mental hospitals and numerous other institutions. Its highways were long and costly. Its number of motor vehicles topped the nation, even before its population did. The University of California alone had a variety of separate campuses scattered about the state, several of them with larger enrollments than many famous and long-established seats of learning in the East. It was beginning to be said that, in order to keep pace with population demands, the state ultimately would need to build the higher educational equivalent of "another Princeton" every year or two. And yet, from the market crash of 1929 through the end of the second global war, scarcely a hand had been laid to this huge institutional complex, save for temporary improvisations and patchwork repairs. Schools and colleges were rapidly becoming incapable of handling the student load. The highway system was inadequate to accommodate traffic. Prisons were overcrowded. So were the mental hospitals, a number of them extremely old and condemned as dangerous firetraps. Growth and time had outmoded the system. Notwithstanding this, the out-of-state pilgrims, in undiminished numbers, came in from the cold, perhaps with multicolored daydreams of California's vaunted beauty and "eternal sunshine," or something near enough to that to warm a man's bones. Most of them brought along their problems as well as their dreams—and their demands for increased public facilities and services.

Governor Warren's approach to this acute set of circumstances combined much common sense with considerable uncommon luck. It has always seemed to be feast or famine, somehow, in California's state finances. The initial luck in this instance was the development of a war production boom almost overnight, with aircraft factories and other military supply industries around the state thrown into expanded emergency operation. This around-the-clock production affected the state's economy immediately, incidentally rescuing the sorely strapped State Treasury. The state government had been depending primarily on sales and income taxes after its revenue plan reorganizations of the early 1930s. There were other levies, too, but, with the gasoline tax legally dedicated to highway purposes, these two were relied upon chiefly for ordinary governmental support. Since California's tax system was thus geared closely to fluctuating business conditions—to volume of sales and to personal and corporate income—the state coffers suddenly overflowed with wartime revenue. A deficit running back into the depression days was succeeded by the pleasant miracle of tremendous annual surpluses. The final budget year of Governor Olson's administration scraped through with an unexpected 1942–1943 showing in the black. Treasury accumulations under Warren were unprecedented. The state government, which had been obliged for a long period to pay its general fund bills with I O U paper, actually found itself with more money than it knew what to do with.

A bulging treasury is always a happy challenge to legislative spendthrifts. It was precisely in his opposition to any wartime circus of reckless spending that Governor Warren left his imprint on California governmental development. Any prolonged recitation of state fiscal affairs is just about as unglamorous as a romp through the telephone book. Nonetheless, some account of money matters in the early and middle Warren years is required in order to understand how California overcame its depression and post-depression retardations and readied itself for emergence as one of the country's most influential areas a little later on. As an alternative to haphazard disbursements, the Governor sponsored a policy of siphoning off into earmarked reserve funds every nickel of wartime treasury income in excess of the state's actual operating needs. These reserves, to which the Legislature assented, were intended to finance a vast postwar building and rebuilding program for the state's institutional network. Warren set up special wartime agencies to take inventory of California's accumulated needs, intelligently plan in advance for postwar reconstruction and indicate priorities for a multiplicity of scheduled statewide governmental building programs and public works expansions. Meantime, revenue poured into the treasury at such an unexampled pace that it was possible to authorize a temporary reduction in state tax rates. These were approved by the Legislature on a year-to-year basis, with the understanding the regular rates, or most of them, would be reinstated automatically at the first sign of a public income falloff. It goes without saying that such across-the-board tax cuts, with no treasury pinch whatever, had seldom been experienced in California and were not likely to be again for a long time.

This exceptional prosperity was strictly synthetic and war-created, something the administration comprehended and persuaded the Legislature to assess similarly. In a few years, revenues dwindled again and the old problems of budget-balancing for a wildly growing state reasserted themselves. By the middle 1960s, the budget of California had grown to more than $4 billion a year, larger than the spending programs of many of the world's smaller nations, and the politicians were busy once more devising means of raising the necessary cash without having a taxpayers' revolt on their hands. But in the middle 1940s, after Germany and finally Japan surrendered, releasing men and materials for nonmilitary use, the gigantic California melon was ripe to be cut. Hundreds of millions of dollars in reserve savings were appropriated for the rehabilitation of the state's long-neglected physical plant—the schools, colleges, prisons, hospitals and all the rest. Money was made available for district water projects. Wartime reserves made possible the retirement of most of the state's outstanding bonds. Governmental retirement systems were refinanced. Local political subdivisions shared to the tune of millions upon millions in state aid for city and county postwar programs. Enough amassed millions remained to create a special "rainy day" fund for emergency state budget-balancing use in the future, if and when hard times returned.

It took a world war to make all this possible. Like James Marshall's discovery of gold at Coloma in the 1840s, it was a thing unlikely ever to repeat itself, especially in the economy of peacetime. Without this unexpected pot of gold in the 1940s and the Warren government's careful hoarding of it for the renovation and enlargement of the state's run-down institutional system, California probably would have been helpless to cope with the surging growth and accompanying public service requirements which it was to experience in the 1950s and on into the late 1960s, with no signs of abatement.

17

EVOLUTION OF A PROGRESSIVE

To a greater degree than happens with most men, Earl Warren grew in stature and broadness of vision under the responsibility of increasingly high public office. It is almost as formidable a task to evaluate his many-sided development as it is to measure the often contradictory characteristics of the California which produced him. A strong sense of social conscience evidently was in Warren's make-up fairly early. It is equally incontestable, in the opinion of many who witnessed his spectacular rise in California, that his thinking clarified—or at least his expression of it—and expanded immensely as he was exposed to ever more complicated public problems. He was regarded as a much more progressive man when he left the governorship at the end of 1953 than when he reached it at the beginning of 1943. It used to be said that Governor Warren appeared to have a kind of built-in aptitude for political evolution, the faculty of thriving and maturing with each new experience. "If that is so," commented one observer long ago, "may the good Lord give Warren more experiences."

In his California years and even afterward, many Earl Warrens seemed to emerge: the big, smiling, friendly governor, carelessly pigeonholed by some as a genial extrovert; the conscientious, self-contained man who reached his important decisions in privacy and pursued his governmental purposes with striking determination; the jolly, inveterate football fan who seldom missed the California-Stanford Big Game, the San Francisco East-West Shrine contest or the Rose Bowl; the "master craftsman in the science of democratic government," as his biographer, Irving Stone, once called him; the courageous progressive who, for humanitarian goals, battled some of California's toughest special interest lobbies; the affectionate and devoted family man; the able and honest administrator whose eleven-year regime escaped even the hint of political scandal; the hunting enthusiast who, in his seventies, still loved to slosh around in a duck blind; the cautious, careful planner of legislative programs; the shrewd, successful "nonpartisan" politician; the Republican candidate for Vice-President and later for President; the figure of history, finally, who, as United States Chief Justice, wrote the school desegregation decision and helped produce many another controversial pronouncement of the "Warren Court." These are just a few of the many facets of what once may have seemed to some an essentially simple, jovial nature but proved to be, beneath this mild-mannered surface, a most serious-minded and complex one. The engaging visible exterior concealed, perhaps without any conscious intention to do so, a resolute, far-sighted, disciplined independence of spirit.

Beginning in 1919, after World War I army infantry service as a first lieutenant, Warren devoted his adult life almost entirely to public service. Starting as a clerk of the State Assembly Judiciary Committee, he became successively assistant city attorney of Oakland, deputy district attorney and later district attorney of Alameda County, state attorney-general, three times the elected governor of California and, after that, Chief Justice under Eisenhower appointment. He came to this long career as a first-generation Californian and a first-generation American as well. His father was a native of Norway, his mother of Sweden—both brought to America as infants. Warren was born in 1891 in Los Angeles and educated in Bakersfield and at the University of California in Berkeley where he was graduated in 1912 and took his law degree in 1914. He was first clarinetist in the university band and picked up the nickname "Pinky."

In considering Warren's eventual record, it is interesting and a little astounding to look back at the manner in which many California Democratic leaders underrated him when he first sought the governorship in 1942. It was their contention the Republicans had deliberately nominated beaming, husky, silver-haired Earl Warren as an agreeable and popular personality, a disarming "false front" in an Old Guard drive to regain State Capitol control. The Democratic hierarchy professed to anticipate, if he won, a restored reign of reaction, delicately seasoned with geniality. It took several years of experience with Warren's basically progressive policies and legislative proposals to convince the opposition party's chieftains of their error.

If the masterminds of the Republican Old Guard, on the other hand, had seriously counted on a California return to GOP ultraconservatism of, say, the Frank Merriam variety, they soon were subjected to an even ruder surprise. Both in governmental administration and policy-fixing, reactionary elements of the GOP quickly found themselves out in the cold, their advice listened to politely by the new governor but seldom followed. Warren proved to be a distinct individualist, a Republican in lifelong affiliation but a forward-looking independent in governmental practice. Not only at election time but between elections, his operational format was substantially nonpartisan. Republican conservatives of the Old Guard suffered their first apprehensive shudders with this realization.

But Warren was not much given to political labels or ideological nomenclature, especially in the opening years of his governorship. He was not very much impressed, or appeared not to be, when somebody urged an issue upon him with the argument that such-and-such was the accepted liberal stand while thus-and-so was the traditional reactionary position. He preferred to "pick up the issue by its four corners" and judge it after studying all the facts. When he did this, it was presently noted, his conclusions usually leaned toward the progressive side. Later on, Warren was to speak much more frankly of his middle-ground, non-extremist inclinations toward progressivism which both the state and the country came to recognize. Perhaps he recognized them somewhat more positively himself as he moved from the absorbing though restricted field of law enforcement, with which he had been primarily concerned for more than twenty years, to the broader areas of general governmental and politico-economic problems in which top executive leadership involved him.

It would be a mistake to conclude that the Warren governorship always enjoyed favorable winds and clear sailing. As Kenny warned and as Olson found out to his sorrow, a governor's programs rise or fall in terms of his dependable support in the Legislature. Lobbyism is undoubtedly as old as the legislative process. In California it had been expanding for more than half a century as industrialization widened and special interests became more varied, with a corresponding appetite for influence. Hiram Johnson had fought the railroad lobby; Governor Stephens found most of the utilities arrayed against him; educational forces plagued Richardson; the light and power companies threw their weight around before, after and during Jim Rolph's brief incumbency. Warren had his troubles, too, tangling with the lobbies of both the well-heeled oil companies and the medical profession.

Two decades before Medicare came into being as part of Lyndon Johnson's Great Society, Governor Warren was fighting an organized medical lobby in California in an attempt to establish a state system of tax-supported public health insurance. Liberal Democrats wavered between disbelief and amazement at the repeated efforts of a Republican governor to obtain such a legislative enactment, while cries of consternation were raised by many right-wingers of both parties. The private medical fraternity—or what Warren described as an "eloquent minority" of it—yelled "socialized medicine" and engaged the late Clem Whitaker and his Campaigns, Inc., an effective San Francisco political public relations and campaign management firm, to wage incessant and ultimately successful warfare on these administration proposals. Later the Whitaker organization linked up with the American Medical Association's national battle against President Truman's similar program for health insurance legislation.

Breaking ground for a number of other new projects, Governor Warren brought a good many of them to fruition. He reorganized half a dozen state departments, overhauled the entire California prison system and obtained liberalization of old-age pension, unemployment insurance and workmen's compensation insurance benefits. In an early display of opposition to racial discriminations, Warren advocated a state fair employment practices act, though it was some years before FEPC became a California reality. In cooperation with organized labor, however, the Governor sponsored legislation which made California the nation's first large state to inaugurate a sickness and disability insurance program for working people. The purpose was to provide benefits during periods of off-the-job illnesses and injuries, a counterpart of the long-standing plan of workmen's compensation payments for on-the-job industrial accidents. Up to this time, little Rhode Island was the only other state to have ventured into this expanded sector of social insurance.

Warren battled the oil interests in 1947 for gasoline tax increases to add an elaborate system of multilane freeways to California's already far-flung highway network. California's roads were all tax-supported and toll-free, except for San Francisco Bay toll-bridge crossings. It was a bit surprising that lobby groups, with considerable lower legislative house support, challenged the Governor on this question at the height of his personal popularity, less than a year after his 1946 re-election by double nomination. When oil lobby power blockaded the administration's gasoline and motor vehicle tax legislation in the State Assembly—where all freeway-financing provisions were summarily stripped from the program at one point —the aroused Governor took his case to the people in a statewide assault on "invisible government" in Sacramento. That was before the day of television hookups, but Warren's blistering radio attacks on entrenched lobby influence were sufficient to stir up wide public reaction and carry the vital freeway plan to enactment.

Long before Tennessee Senator Estes Kefauver's national investigation of crime conditions, Governor Warren took dead aim at gangsterism and created a special state crime commission to probe into efforts at underworld encroachments on California. Warren's warm advocacy of the Central Valley Project, plus at least a friendly attitude toward proposals for publicly owned and operated hydroelectric transmission lines to carry the federally developed CVP power, stepped painfully on the toes of some of the private light and power company interests. There were dozens of other important Warren undertakings, including an effective state fiscal management program. In fact, the stability of the kind of government offered in those years probably was a key factor in the acceptance of the Governor by an unusual majority of Californians without much regard for party ties. Obviously, Warren did not win with his proposals in every instance, yet the wide range of his interests and the unyielding perseverence with which he espoused each cause to which he committed himself produced, in the long run, an impressive array of achievements. Often faced by recalcitrant legislative blocs, he was accustomed to settle, if necessary, for half a loaf at one lawmaking session and then come back obdurately next session for the other half. His overall record in eleven years as governor, almost three full terms, was remarkable—and fundamentally one of practical liberalism.

As he neared the end of this precedent-shattering gubernatorial tenure, Warren enjoyed widespread public approbation in California: the admiration and reluctant good will of many liberal Democrats, the enthusiastic support of progressive-minded Republicans. It was inevitable, naturally, that he also incurred the frustrated displeas-

ure of some of the professional Democratic party-liners and election managers, along with the ill-concealed hatred of Republican reactionary extremists. All this time, Warren's national prestige was
on the upswing, to some extent among Democrats as well as Republicans. President Truman, not unfriendly to the Californian even
when technically opposed to him in the Dewey campaign of 1948,
once observed that Warren was really "a Democrat who doesn't
know it." Somebody else suggested, half-facetiously on another
occasion, that Warren, granted his progressive tendencies, well might
consider switching from the Republican ranks to the Democratic
party where, it was argued, he could at least be more comfortable in
his views. What the Governor may have thought about that kind
of talk, if it ever reached his ears, was never recorded. His party
background from the beginning, after all, had been Republican. And
his public career, which had covered more than thirty years up to
then, had been dedicated to the proposition that social progress under
the Republican banner was well worth contending for and plainly
attainable. As for changing parties, one of Warren's fellow progressives remarked wryly that if the Governor ever decided to leave the
GOP, "the Democrats would welcome him with open arms and
then probably start scheming the very next day to retire him to
private life."

18

VENTRILOQUIST AND DUMMY

California's phenomenal "million-dollar lobbyist," Arthur H. Samish, was, in his heyday, a singular and flamboyant combination of legislative procedural expertise, organizational skill, practical knowledge of political psychology and, so some contended, overweening though usually well-concealed tendencies toward vanity. Kingpin of the liquor lobby, he flourished for something like three decades. He was a fascinating, almost incredible figure who worked his little miracles in California politics for a very long time and left an indelible mark on those numerous phases of legislation in which he was hired to interest himself. Eventually he became, in his own strange way, a kind of celebrity, fawned on by some, feared by many and credited by all with immense power.

It is axiomatic that governors, and even Presidents, are fairly helpless without reliable backing in the legislative branch of government. In California, election law revisions running back to the Hiram Johnson days had technically eliminated the sway of political party bosses. Party leaders continued to exist, of course, but their strength as such was greatly diluted from the Johnson-Stephens period well into the 1950s, and their skills were no longer so highly regarded as formerly either in swinging elections or in rounding up legislative votes for a state administration or anybody else. The resulting power gap, at least around the State Legislature, was quickly filled by an augmented army of special-interest lobbyists.

The institution of lobbying is at least as ancient as the processes of democratic lawmaking. Lobby influence varies with the political climate in which it attempts to function and the malleability of the lawmakers. In twentieth-century America, and certainly in California, corporate combines and special interests of almost every imaginable sort have deemed it expedient to send hired spokesmen to every legislative session to encourage enactments considered advantageous to the employing agencies and to block, if possible, measures which are regarded, at least by such special pleaders, as potentially injurious. The methods of lobbyists differ widely. Some rely solely on reason and legitimate argument in their efforts to corral votes; others sometimes try to make their causes more palatable with elaborate and expensive entertaining and, upon occasion, with pecuniary favors. It has been said of lobbyists that when they are good, they are very, very good, like the little girl in the nursery rhyme, and when they are bad, horrid is too mild a description. At all events, when the authority of California party bosses decreased, the lobbyists multiplied and presently were known around the State Legislature as the "third house." After the first few "reform" years —from 1910, say, to the end of World War I—the political merry-go-round continued to grind along as madly as ever, with new hands clutching for the brass rings of authority and influence. And soon seated on one of the biggest horses of the wildly whirling machine was portly Mr. Samish.

Samish's basic *modus operandi* was to get the "right guys" elected. His influence flowed naturally from that. As an ambitious, personable and agile-minded young San Franciscan, he had prepared carefully for his career, learning as a minor legislative clerk every minute step in the lawmaking process and mastering the intricate make-up of the city-ruled Assembly and the country-dominated Senate. He studied election techniques with equal attention, interesting himself as early as 1922 in the Stephens-Richardson gubernatorial campaign. At the time, he may not have realized the eventual scope of his activities, but he was ready. Later on, as a practicing lobby professional, he was evidently not particularly concerned with how his political protégés voted in the Legislature, except where the welfare of his liquor and other "clients" was at stake. Those familiar with legislative matters came to classify certain officeholders as "Samish men," fairly predictable voters on subjects within Artie's deliberately restricted sphere of interests. In Samish's own fields of endeavor, however, even governors learned not to take him too lightly.

In the late 1930s, the grand jury investigator, Howard Philbrick, found Samish representing and attending to the lawmaking welfare of chemicals, beer, hard liquor, railroads, banks, motor carriers, horse racing, assorted other marginal interests, and even a national orange show. In the 1950s, the late Senator Kefauver, chairman of the United States Senate Crime Investigating Committee, reported discovering much the same "client" setup, plus the cigarette industry, taxicabs, restaurant interests and a few others. The "million-dollar lobbyist" tag was hung on the Californian by Kefauver who announced finding that more than $935,000 had passed through Samish's hands in his "labyrinthine operations" over a six-year period. The Tennessee Senator said he experienced great difficulty, though, in laying his hands on individual check stubs or cancelled checks.

"In both personality and physique, Samish is a remarkable figure," Kefauver once wrote. "Physically, he stands over six feet, two inches, in height, and must weigh better than three hundred pounds. He is bald with a monk's tonsure of gray fringe, and his face has the bland innocence of an *enfant terrible* about to light a giant firecracker under his nurse's chair. In manner, he is a combination of Falstaff, Little Boy Blue and Machiavelli, crossed with an eel."

Senator Kefauver, who once had Samish on the witness stand before his committee in San Francisco, also termed him a smooth, evasive, magniloquently-speaking "master lobbyist." A dozen years

119

earlier, the Philbrick Report had quoted descriptions of Samish as "the most powerful man in California," regarded with awe by many public servants and reputed to hold the Legislature "in the palm of his hand." Carey McWilliams, in his striking book *California, the Great Exception,* cited Samish's own estimate of himself as "the guy who gets things done." Lester Velie, in a 1949 series of articles for the old *Collier's* magazine, flatly called him "The Secret Boss of California."

Samish unquestionably exerted great pressure leverage. Oddly enough, though, he was not necessarily the most potent lobbyist in Sacramento in terms of effective, restrained operations or from the standpoint of huge and powerful special interests represented. Others were only too happy to let him have that reputation, while they went efficiently, quietly and usually more subtly about their own business. The legislative interests of the major utilities, the insurance companies, the oil corporations and other important financial concerns have seldom been poorly served by their lobby spokesmen, whether in California or other large states. Lobbying had become a well-paid and important calling in California by mid-century. Its growing influence was decried by many, but some legislators warmly defended the "third house" as a valuable institution, essential in providing them with useful and otherwise unavailable data on California's business and industrial affairs. Quite a few lawmakers, after termination of their public service, "graduated," so to speak, into lobby professionalism over the years, among them several former Speakers of the State Assembly. Almost every facet of California life and industry sooner or later was represented among the "advocates," as the better class of lobbyists preferred to be known—the railroads, the other utilities, the liquor interests, medical organizations, oil combines, cigarette manufacturers, labor unions, real-estate operators, banks, agricultural associations, savings and loan concerns, gas companies, billboard advertisers, schoolteachers, even spokesmen for cities, counties, public civil service, Christian Science and the race tracks. There was, however, a certain amount of gradualism in California's realignments of influence. The reform vocabulary of the sainted Hiram Johnson was not tampered with. Party bossism was officially "dead." A charming persuasiveness took its place. Arrogance and open manifestations of power were, as a general thing, scrupulously avoided. There is, as somebody recently said, an immense difference between political litany and reality. In a very few years after the downgrading of bossism as such, legislative lobbyists, in a vastly increased horde, were adroitly making their presence felt, some of them bringing as much weight to bear on public policy in their chosen realms as the outmoded party bosses had ever dreamed of doing. The overall effect on legislative elections, in which campaign contributions were generous as a rule, and on the course of legislation itself became tremendous in half a century.

While this bustling reorientation of political pressure fashions passed almost unnoticed by the general public, reaction set in among California party politicians around the middle of the century. They bestirred themselves to reinstate party "leadership." The Democrats, holding the governorship and a majority of the Legislature by the late 1950s, lined up the votes to abolish cross-filing and minimize nonpartisanship. There was neither criticism of the burgeoning lobbies, which naturally worked both sides of the political street, nor any praise, of course, for bossism. The old-time nomenclature was studiously maintained. The new dispensation was hailed as simply a restoration of "party responsibility." The power structure of California had thus swung almost full circle in five decades, leaving for future determination whether the forces of "party responsibility" and the entrenched lobbies and their employers ultimately would clash or negotiate an unofficial pact of peaceful coexistence.

Over the years, attorneys with experience in lawmaking procedures and other specialists in the problems of corporate entities usually were in attendance at legislative sessions as the astute lobby representatives of the major oil companies, "independent" oil, the railroads, the gas companies, telephone interests, horse racing, wine and whiskey distributors, financial institutions and comparable large business, professional and industrial concerns. In some instances, the good-fellowship of "wining and dining" and otherwise entertaining legislators of consequence was evidently regarded as a routine part of good public relations, often indicated in the size of periodic lobby expenditure reports. Other practitioners of the gentle art of political influence appeared to depend primarily on their gifts of persuasion at committee sessions. Among the former Speakers of the State Assembly who entered the field of lobbyism, some of them flourishing for many years, were Edward Craig, Walter J. Little, Charles W. Lyon, Sam L. Collins and Gordon H. Garland. Numerous lesser ex-legislators pursued similar careers. In a Baltimore address in 1967, after both California lawmaking branches had been placed on a population basis, Jesse M. Unruh, then Speaker of the Assembly, suggested that unicameralism—a single house legislature—might offer the best hope for survival of vigorous democratic processes in America. Nebraska, at that time, was the only state with a one-house legislative setup. Governors trying to further their programs in other states, Unruh said, can and frequently do resort to the "whipsaw technique" of pitting one legislative house against the other. Special-interest groups, he added, also take advantage of such a power vacuum.

"Lobbies are subversive to the extent that they undermine the general welfare by forcing attention to their own selfish interests," it was contended a few years earlier in *The Legislature of California,* a survey of lawmaking prepared for the Commonwealth Club of California under the supervision of former Governor C. C. Young. Lobby control regulations had improved appreciably toward the middle of the century, it observed, but there was still room for "a larger measure of ethics" in the profession of fashioning laws. However, the average legislator, the report concluded, was no longer responsive to a "tap on the shoulder" and peremptory instructions on how to vote.

Fairly coincident with the augmentation of lobby activities in Sacramento, a few new wrinkles also were devised to influence the nomination of state office candidates. Back in the 1910–1920 full flush of the Western Progressive movement, California had done away entirely with the selection of political candidates by party state conventions. It adopted a "free and open" primary system, heralded as the end of the hand-picking of office seekers by party bosses and their satellites in "smoke-filled rooms." Party conventions were outlawed save for the drafting of campaign platforms. The state's official party committees were even prohibited from distributing preprimary blessings to favored politicians. The new role of the party committee in this reform setup was to elect its candidates after the primary, not select them in advance. This worked splendidly for a while, but presently, without changing the law, means of circumvention were cleverly contrived. The state's Republicans, having enjoyed a distinct edge in number of enrolled voters for many years, felt their position threatened in the 1930s by the growing popularity of the Roosevelt New Deal and the abrupt climb in California Democratic registrations. In consequence, the California Republican Assembly was founded in 1934. Although complete candor was lacking, the fundamental purpose of this "unofficial" organization was, in effect, to short-circuit the prescribed open competition of the primary by an early endorsement of carefully selected bidders for each state constitutional office. The idea was to pick "a single, strong candidate" for every place on the Republican state ticket and discourage all other primary contestants. It was intended in this "unofficial" way to promote Republican "unity" and avert GOP intraparty primary contests, while the Democrats exhausted themselves in bloody and party-splitting nomination battles. This strategy was highly successful for a couple of decades. Then the slowly awakening Democrats, in the early 1950s, took a leaf out of the Republican book and formed the California Democratic Council, also "unofficial" but politically potent. The CDC likewise centered its efforts on preprimary ticket selections, its "endorsing conventions" eventually becoming larger, in sheer number of delegates, than a national Presidential nominating convention. Nostalgic devotees of the old direct primary reforms screamed from the housetops that the intended system of free-for-all nominating races was being deliberately undermined by these voluntary agencies of the two major parties. These minority voices of protest appeared to count for very little. A majority of the electors seemed apathetic, hoodwinked or totally unmindful of the "good old days." Even after cross-filing was repealed in 1959 and each party primary restricted to the candidates of a single political faith, the unofficial party organizations, a mere handful of busy politicians compared with the mounting voter registration totals of the state, continued to stage endorsement meetings and make preprimary selections. Each list of anointed candidates became known among less fortunate rivals as a "package deal." In modified form, with bright, new packaging, something very much like the old-fashioned convention system was flourishing again. So influential had these informal endorsing groups grown in a relatively few years, in fact, that zealous left-wingers were represented as eagerly seeking a foothold in the CDC while right-wingers of the John Birch Society ilk were accused of attempting to infiltrate the CRA and some of the other Republican associations spawned by that party's latter-day factional warfare.

At the State Capitol, meantime, Arthur Samish was probably the best-known name in the ranks of professional lobbyism, especially in the late 1930s and 1940s, perhaps epitomizing the general public's hazy notion of what a lobbyist was like. Around June, when the California legislative chips were down, Samish, almost invariably wearing a hard straw hat and a plain blue tropical suit, was often to be seen in the Capitol corridors, listening amiably to the badinage of his entourage of eager hangers-on and keeping a sharp eye on his manifold interests. Toward the end of his prolonged career, the king of the lobbyists made these "royal" appearances less frequently. He chose rather to hold court in his nearby hotel suite, while a corps of minor associates and runners brought him regular tidings of almost everything, big and small, which went on in the legislative halls across the street. Personally, Samish had the name of being charitable to the point of softheartedness with some and hard as nails with others. According to his own lights, this super-lobbyist was distinctly among the "good guys" of political influence manipulation and possibly had some difficulty figuring out why anybody thought of him otherwise. He liked to do favors for people, ranging from poor newsboys to prominently placed politicians.

The marvelous candor of Samish in his interviews in 1949 with Lester Velie for *Collier's* is generally regarded as the beginning of his prestige decline. For some reason never completely comprehended by politicians, who noted the incident with feelings which extended from dumfounded amazement to growing anger, Samish allowed his picture to be taken for publication holding a small puppet on his knee. The recognizable pose, whatever Samish intended it to be, was that of a ventriloquist with a dummy. "How are you today, Mr. Legislature?" said part of the text. If humor was intended, it was received as a bad joke, and a flabbergasting display of arrogance, around the Legislature. Samish was further represented as claiming some ability to tell whether a man yearned for "a baked potato, a girl or money," and as suggesting that the question of political cupidity might be effectively tested by dropping some currency of relatively small denominations in the rotunda of the Capitol. Velie reported him as observing that "two bucks" might be enough to "start a riot."

It is next to impossible to put one's finger on a single happening that is decisive in an eclipse of power, but Samish's reign of effectiveness definitely appeared to wane from that time on. Governor Warren sent the Legislature a message in 1949, pointing out that while honest lobbyists were "greatly in the majority," he wanted lobbying regulated to "control the few who flout decency." Samish's lobbying credentials were taken away "forever" by 1949 resolution, but a similar resolution failed in 1950. Other 1949 enactments required all lobbyists to register the details of their employment, called for monthly reports of their expenditures and made it a felony to cause the introduction of "cinch" or "shakedown" bills. After his United

States Senate Crime Investigating Committee hearings, Senator Kefauver expressed the hope, in his 1951 book *Crime in America,* that the federal income tax people would take up the task of probing liquor lobbyist Samish's fiscal affairs where he left off. Eventually, Samish did become entangled in tax irregularity charges and served a term in federal penitentiary. In subsequent years, though, there was no decline in lobbying as a recognized and well-financed California business. It was estimated that, in the 1960s, there were three or four lobbying professionals to every legislator in Sacramento during regular lawmaking sessions.

19

SWORDS FOR HIRE

Full-time public relations specialists and magic workers began to play an increasingly important part in California politics, both in ordinary election contests and in direct legislation campaigns, during the governorship terms of Rolph, Merriam, Olson and Warren, and continued to do so during succeeding administrations. The political press agent is an almost carelessly accepted commonplace in this day of supersalesmanship and organized propaganda, but generally unrealized is the massive influence which a relatively few expert technicians in this line have come to exercise in the last thirty-five years. Prior to that time, give or take a few years, the breed consisted largely of second-rate hacks, temporarily employed to get a reasonable number of blurbs into print about candidates or issues around election time. Their standing was often a cut below that of the advance man for a one-ring circus. All that has changed. Public relations operators have become, for better or worse, the indispensable masterminds of campaigning. Those who rely on them tacitly recognize this, yet, in the preservation of their own self-importance, usually pretend not to.

In California, as elsewhere, however, few ambitious politicians would think of launching a big-time project nowadays without first surrounding themselves with a full panoply of reliable policy advisers, press secretaries, ghost writers, campaign managerial authorities, gimmick thinkers and mass communication strategists. Such hired swords generally come high, but they are currently regarded as infinitely more useful than the typical old-time political boss. Topflight men in this comparatively new and highly profitable mid-century vocation are not infrequently smarter, at least in the wiles of vote-snagging proficiency, than many of the political figures they represent. They are careful, hard-eyed students of all the political techniques. They scorn amateurism. Self-effacing professionals, most of them, they map the moves of a campaign with the cold mathematical precision of chess players. Their aim is the manipulation of majority public thinking by a many-sided kind of subliminal cozenage, so unobtrusive that those influenced seldom suspect the cause or, better still, attribute revised opinions to their own acute comprehension of public affairs.

The practitioners of this subtle brand of political expertise are no longer simple "press agents" and generally abhor the term. In the larger states, dominated by urban, industrialized populations, they have become the "image makers" of would-be Presidents and governors, the advisers of powerful corporations, the "consultants" of legislative and other political aspirants, the commanding designers of overall strategy in election conflicts and ballot measure campaigns. Their keenly competitive "art" has grown into a lucrative business, upon occasion Big Business.

An imaginative California operator of concentrated efficiency in this field was the late Clem Whitaker whose Campaigns, Inc., and Whitaker & Baxter advertising and electioneering management firm of San Francisco flourished with a remarkable political clientele for more than three decades. Sometimes credited with introducing the so-called Madison Avenue approach into California politics, at least on an organized, full-time basis and with an efficiency which may have anticipated the East Coast in some particulars, he became as much a fixture in election contests as lobbyist Arthur H. Samish did

1. James Wilson Marshall, whose discovery of gold in 1848 brought American politics and statehood to Spanish-Mexican California within two years. (California Historical Society, San Francisco)

2. General John Charles Fremont, Military Governor of California (1847), United States Senator (1850-1851) and the first presidential candidate of the Republican party in 1856. (California Historical Society, San Francisco)

3. Peter H. Burnett, first American Civil Governor of California after statehood in 1850; a Democrat. (California Historical Society, San Francisco)

4.   Leland Stanford, Civil War Governor; California's first Republican state executive (1862-1863); later a United States Senator. (California Historical Society, San Francisco)

5.   Hiram W. Johnson, California's first Governor twice elected (in 1910 and 1914); later served as Republican U. S. Senator (1917-1945).

6.   Governor William Dennison Stephens, at the Salinas Rodeo, reading a World War I headline. Heir to Hiram Johnson's governorship, progressively inclined Republican Stephens served from 1917 through 1922. (San Francisco Public Library)

7. Governor Friend William Richardson, fiddling with the engine of his old National (lucky license 7) in which he covered some 50,000 miles in California campaigns of the "Roaring Twenties." He defeated William D. Stephens in 1922 and lost the governorship to C. C. Young in 1926. A GOP conservative, Richardson stressed the slogan of budget slashing in a manner unparalleled until Ronald Reagan's election forty-four years later. (San Francisco Public Library)

8. Clement Calhoun Young, Republican Governor (1926-1930); a temporary restoration of Johnsonian progressivism. (California Historical Society, San Francisco).

9. Republican Governor Frank F. Merriam (right) with Dr. Francis E. Townsend, the pension plan promoter, in the Los Angeles Coliseum to address the Townsend National Convention in 1938. Merriam lost the governorship that year to Democrat Culbert L. Olson. (United Press International)

10. Arthur H. Samish (left), the so-called "kingpin lobbyist" of California for many years, shown in the mid-1950s leaving the San Francisco Post Office Building on his way to the McNeil Island Federal Penitentiary to begin a sentence for income tax irregularities. With him is Deputy U.S. Marshal Herbert Cole. (San Francisco Public Library)

11. Vice President Richard M. Nixon (center), with Governor Goodwin J. Knight (left) and United States Senator William F. Knowland, the "Big Three" of California Republicanism in the middle 1950s. They are shown at a 1958 GOP rally. Later that year Edmund G. (Pat) Brown and the Democrats captured the governorship. (Wide World Photos)

12. United States Chief Justice Earl Warren, Governor Edmund G. Brown and the author, 1962. (Wide World Photos)

13. Democratic Assembly Speaker Jesse M. Unruh (center) huddling with majority Democrats in 1963 during a lull in a deadlocked inter-party battle over state spending bills. Later the Los Angeles speaker was to become a major critic of Republican fiscal policies after Ronald Reagan assumed the governorship in 1967. (Wide World Photos)

14. Ronald Reagan and his wife Nancy greet supporters at Republican headquarters, after his 1966 defeat of Pat Brown. (United Press International)

in legislative politics, though their methods and personalities were entirely different. Along with countless other campaigns, the Whitaker organization, as already noted, helped defeat Governor Earl Warren's public health insurance program in the early 1940s and later was engaged to direct the nationwide publicity battle against President Harry Truman's similar federal plan. Among old magazines in doctors' waiting-rooms at about that time were to be found colored reproductions of a familiar painting in which a kindly, bearded physician sat anxiously at the bedside of a sick child. The original title, if memory serves, was "The Family Doctor," or something quite similar. The substituted caption, rewritten for campaign purposes, read: "Don't Let Politics Enter This Picture!"

How far modern techniques in political persuasion have departed from the haphazard antics of the old-fashioned "press agent" is indicated in the elaborate operations of such organizations as Whitaker's and many others which later came into prominence. Upon acquiring a political "client," it was the preferred procedure to control the entire affair from start to finish, to blueprint the campaign in advance, scout the opposition through pollster ascertainment of political chances and "marketing conditions," plot the action and "pacing" of the campaign thoroughly and insist upon an orderly and centralized determination of the issues to be stressed. With this understood by the "client," it was the custom with streamlined agencies of this sort to assume direction over press releases and other publicity; placement of radio, television and advertising material; organization of allied interests into a temporary political machine, and development of the campaign's themes and slogans, with a judicious simplification of speeches and electioneering arguments to fit them. This, at least, was the operational ideal, insofar as it could be realized. Many thousands of dollars in fees and expenses, all meticulously budgeted, were involved in a statewide endeavor of this magnitude—the election of a high state official, say, or the passage or defeat of a controversial ballot proposition. The managerial firm undertook to run the whole show—and no sweat. The political front men, if they could be induced to stand still for it, were often shunted as quickly as possible, diplomatically and for their own good, into the role of cooperating but maneuverable puppets.

In the years after Campaigns, Inc., set the pace, so to speak, numerous other California individuals, companies and partnerships entered the lists as rival entrepreneurs in the scientific molding of public opinion. This offshoot of the managerial revolution prided itself on bringing a measure of effective orderliness to a process as old as politics itself. Whitaker was fond of quoting Abraham Lincoln as having said: "He who molds public sentiment goes deeper than he who enacts statutes or pronounces decisions." A talented and experienced idea man—half-romantic, half-pragmatist—the founder of Campaigns, Inc., spoke and wrote with considerable candor about his methods in "merchandising" men and measures. "You can interest him [the average voter] if you put up a fight," he once said. "If you can't fight, put on a show " It seemed to work. The Whitaker organization alone has claimed success in about 90 per cent of more than seventy-five campaigns over the years. It is a good guess that fewer than 10 per cent of the California voters had any idea of the part which campaign professionalism, "molding public sentiment" as discreetly as possible behind the scenes, played in these results. Possibly Lincoln would have been a little surprised, too.

Nowhere has the new breed of political publicists and scientific swayers of voter opinion been more active than in the field generally classified as "direct legislation." For more than half a century, California has had, as an inheritance of the Hiram Johnson days, three forms of direct legislation—the initiative, the referendum and the recall. Since California is the largest and one of the earliest "reform" states, it may be pertinent, and even mildly diverting, to consider the political sleight of hand by which the works of reformers are often made to disappear. Reassuring words, accompanied by practiced manipulative agility, can work wonders in political legerdemain. It is a continuing magic act in California and no doubt in other places of corresponding size, complexity and public gullibility.

Take the California initiative law, for example. A reform measure of the century's infancy, it was originally lauded as a means of state-wide voter action to achieve desirable governmental ends over the heads, if necessary, of do-nothing governors or deadlocked Legis-latures. Theoretically, it gave the people, through petition, the inde-pendent right of direct legislation at the polls. By rounding up a specified number of petition sponsors, they could originate, or "ini-tiate," a proposed new law or amendment to the state constitution and have it placed on the next election ballot for approval or rejec-tion by statewide vote. In similar fashion, an enactment of the Legis-lature could be "held up on referendum," if a sufficient number of qualified voters objected to its provisions, and its operation thus could be delayed until California citizens as a whole had passed judgment upon it. In like manner, the recall procedure permitted the removal of government officials by public vote. This, in essence, was the Johnsonian plan of direct legislation. At first it produced some striking results. California osteopaths and chiropractors, for example, gained independence and separate state licensing boards by initiative in the early 1920s, at a time when the influential medical profession frowned on drugless practitioners as a class. Over the years, however, the growing number of petition signatures necessary to place an initiative proposition on the ballot—a percentage of the vote total at the last preceding state election—sharply limited the availability of this instrument in California. In practice, only large and particularly well-organized groups or heavily financed move-ments could obtain the needed signatures in an increasingly popu-lous state. This led to the establishment of firms which made a regular business of petition circulating on behalf of any and all types of measures, undertaking to qualify them for the election ballot either for a flat price or a given fee for each solicited voter signature. Public apathy proved of great assistance in such enterprises. A sardonic experiment, conducted in the city of Fresno, once demonstrated the careless willingness of an astonishing number of citizens to place

131

their signatures on a street-circulated petition which, in fine print, expressly requested the death penalty for all signers.

While the circulation of petitions was developing into a highly specialized business, efficient campaign and public relations companies came into being at the same time as experts for hire in handling such propositions as managed to reach the ballot, engaging, often at the instance of the most free-handed bidder, to stir up public sentiment for their approval or defeat. So the initiative, though still hypothetically useful and the continuing subject of much eulogistic oratory, fell largely into the hands of political professionals, as likely as not to be more intensely concerned with their contracts than with the merits or demerits of the issues at stake.

Along the way some extraordinary enactments reached the statute books. In 1948, at the Truman-Dewey-Wallace Presidential election, for instance, George McLain, a latter-day Los Angeles pension plan promoter, managed to produce a little gem. He whipped the old people of California into something of a political frenzy and, while almost everybody else was absorbed with the White House race, gained adoption of an initiative which, by its specific terms, named one of the promoter's own organizational associates as director of the entire State Department of Social Welfare. Since the people had spoken, albeit not very thoughtfully, they had to speak again later on, through another expensive statewide ballot measure, to undo all this. Fifteen years later, the initiative was being used not just to supplement the legislative record but, in one noted instance, to nullify it. The State Legislature, in 1963, passed a law forbidding racial discrimination in the rental or sale of residential property. Real-estate interests assumed a prominent part in a successful and professionally-handled 1964 initiative campaign to wipe out this statute. Considerable bigotry marked the electioneering. A simple referendum movement could have been undertaken against the legislative enactment—an uncomplicated yes-or-no decision on its precise terms. The initiative was invoked instead as a means of prescribing additional prohibitions and restrictions on future legislation of like character unless authorized by statewide vote. Direct legislation, timed to coincide with the Johnson-Goldwater Presidential contest, was thus utilized to tie the hands of the Legislature in this field. The initiative in question was eventually invalidated on constitutional grounds by the State Supreme Court, though its approval at the polls had been overwhelming. In 1966 and 1967, the issue was involved in further threatened litigation. Amid opposition cries of "book burning," still another initiative, this one aimed at pornography, was rushed before the California voters in 1966. Because of its extremely far-reaching terms, the measure failed, but not before it had touched off a noisy battle from Oregon to Mexico and become an issue in that year's Brown-Reagan gubernatorial election.

By the mid-1960s, in fact, the gulf had appreciably widened between the emergency use of direct legislation for affirmative purposes, as originally intended, and the callous manipulation of the initiative process, in many cases, for special-interest causes, frequently negative in nature. There was no lack of legislative stalemates on pressing public problems during the 1950s and 1960s, yet their solution by the initiative method, once envisioned as a means of popular revolt against governmental stagnation, was attempted only occasionally. There appeared to be a tendency to think twice before resorting to a procedure fast becoming too cumbersome in an unwieldy, heterogeneous society, its requirements too imposing for effective use by ordinary unorganized and poorly financed groups, its results too readily controlled by "experts" who dealt in the pros and cons of ballot measures as a principal means of livelihood.

When one remembers that California was one of the first "direct legislation" states, thanks to the bubbling enthusiasm of the Hiram Johnson-period reformers, it was perhaps inescapable that the high art of political hocus-pocus in dealing with this manifestation should have developed in California somewhat earlier and more flamboyantly than in most other regions. At all events, the rationalization of professional "hard sell" management of initiative campaigns became artful and bland in California with the passing years. The practitioners of sophisticated persuasion were merely doing with real finesse what political novices and naïve bunglers had been doing badly for a long time, it was explained, and the people, in any case, still had a perfect right to vote as they pleased. If, indeed, the voting public was nudged a little, one way or the other, by skillful touches of campaign inventiveness, the result, according to the hired swords, was just one of the small miracles of modern technology. The launching of direct legislation, especially of a controversial nature, became an increasingly untidy and unpredictable business toward the middle of the century. More and more, election issues of this sort were being marketed like soap and cigarettes, with "scientific" reliance on mass psychology, appeals to group and regional prejudices and consumer-tested salesmanship gimmicks. To the often perplexed public, however, the make-up of a long and complicated initiative measure was a bit harder to evaluate than the ingredients of a detergent, even with the aid of simplified slogans and singing commercials.

20

MOBSTERS AND HANDGUNS

There was not very much Governor Warren or other California officials of his period could do about professional gimmickry in the promotion or wrecking of initiative measures—short of overhauling the whole sacrosanct system of direct legislation which had stood for some forty years—but professional crime was something else again, and to this Warren gave urgent attention. From its earliest days, the state had suffered recurrent manifestations of lawlessness. Even in comparatively modern times, outcries against "crime waves," real or fancied, often played a profitable part in election-year politics. The intensified westward movement of people to California—marked by a 1940–1950 increase of more than 53 per cent in the state's population, as compared with a gain of less than 15 per cent for the nation—brought in its predictable share of underworld elements.

Big, sprawling, sometimes boisterous, indubitably wealthy California was a rich plum of immense attraction to organized criminal enterprises and an obvious lure to mobster types with close and sometimes lurid past connections in Eastern gangland affairs. It is altogether probable that most Californians had little or no idea of this and entertained, at best, a somewhat hazy notion of what organized crime was all about. Many of them have been considerably more familiar with the legendary Western exploits of Joaquín Murrieta, Black Bart, Jesse James and Billy the Kid, in the previous century, than with the more recent and notorious escapades of, say, Al Capone and Frank Nitti in Chicago. This was, after all, some time before such dramatic contrivances as *The Untouchables* came to the country's television screens and Capone and his boys strode boldly through everybody's living room once a week.

There could be no doubt, however, that Benny "Bugsy" Siegel, reputedly a prominent migrating member of the Eastern gang, "Murder, Inc.," had been around Los Angeles for at least ten years before he was unceremoniously gunned down in 1947. There had been other acts of gangland violence, too, and other uninvited arrivals, with sinister antecedents and sharp jackets tailored to accommodate shoulder holsters. The emphasis on new rackets and the refurbishing of old ones, plus the spread of both in the underworld's years of readjustment and "retooling" after the gaudy prohibition decade, tended to make California officialdom extremely uneasy. This was clearly one form of endeavor in which California had no desire for national supremacy.

So, in an effort to minimize further mobster infiltrations and tighten law-enforcement machinery against gangsterism generally, Governor Warren appointed his first "Special Crime Study Commission on Organized Crime" in 1947, followed later by another which pursued its investigations until mid-1952. The United States Senate Crime Investigating Committee also devoted part of its attention to California, as a place, according to the 1951 conclusion of Chairman Estes Kefauver, "where mobsters thrive." There was, so the Governor's commission described the situation, an "invasion of undesirables," shady characters formerly associated with Chicago, New York and other Eastern operations, a number of them taking their ease at luxury retreats in plush Palm Springs, desert spa at the foot of southern California's Mount San Jacinto, and in the fabulous Reno and Las Vegas gambling towns of adjacent Nevada.

"There is reason to believe," the second state commission reported in May, 1953, "that California has great cause for concern when it views the numbers and importance of nationally known hoodlums who are actually crossing our state line to assume at least part time residence in California or to meet with hoodlums who are permanent residents of our state to plan strategy for future moves of the mobs."

The crime inquiry reports of those days were studded with accounts of bizarre doings and dealt as glibly as a paperback mystery thriller does nowadays with "trigger-men," "syndicate" disagreements, "enforcers," "rides," "Black Hand retribution" and gangland "rubouts." It took thirteen closely printed pages of the Warren commission's final summary report to cover a fifty-year record of "Gangland Killings" in the Los Angeles area alone. These murders, in vast majority, so the report said, were committed with handguns on the public streets. Los Angeles was pictured as a "favorite rendezvous" of undesirables from other states, and San Francisco as "a refuge for the organized underworld" from time to time when efficient law enforcement made other jurisdictions too hot for profitable vice practices.

This situation alarmed, if perhaps not complacent Californians as a whole, at least Governor Warren, the state's former chief law-enforcement officer as attorney-general, and many other authorities charged with crime prevention and the administration of criminal law. They redoubled and broadened the scope of their investigative apparatus. It was their collective judgment, in the long run, that vigilant poking into the intricacies of gambling rackets, organized prostitution, strong-arm "protection" operations, incipient gangsterism and other phases of vice and corruption, plus the enactment of a stiff felony anti-conspiracy law, had slowed down the criminal "invasion" considerably and maybe permanently halted the threatened encroachment of organized crime west of the Sierra Nevada. The Warren commissions unearthed enough odd and disquieting material over a six-year period, however, to keep California more or less on the nervous alert for the next decade or so.

It goes without saying that this sort of thing was far removed from the California advantages, actual and imaginary, which still brought millions flocking in from other states and countries. The official revelations understandably came as something of a shock to law-abiding Californians, native and adopted. They were a trifle bug-eyed, in fact, as they read the startling reports. But soon the average citizen of the late 1940s and early 1950s appeared to recover comfortably, rejoicing to learn that energetic investigations were under way, that the good guys evidently had stopped the bad guys on the other side of the mountains and that California, in the last analysis, was relatively safe after all. But only relatively safe, warned the crime commission authorities. Still "poised upon our borders" were the bad guys.

"There is an absence of big syndication and organization," said the 1953 commission findings, "but there is no absence of the hoodlums in our state nor of the seedbeds in which to nurture new rackets. . . . Organized criminal groups still exist, still extract their toll of extortion, corruption, assault and murder, and still remain to be reported and dispersed. These objectives can only be accomplished by a steady, persistent effort, stimulated by a high standard of public service and a growing degree of civil responsibility by the people of all communities. No lasting reform can be expected from temporary drives to 'close the town' which are only too often accurately assessed by the underworld as nothing more than insincere displays of force. Continued vigilance will always be necessary. . . . It is obvious that these racketeers have no intention of abandoning permanently such a rich and lucrative area as the State of California. It is only reasonable to assume that they will reorganize their forces and again invade our state at the first favorable opportunity."

Ten years later, new law-enforcement problems, not peculiar to California though certainly to be found there, were arising out of racial disorders, anti-Vietnam war demonstrations, college campus disturbances and other manifestations of social unrest which seemed to produce more public apprehension and, in some cases, louder

138

indignation than even the old-style underworld mobsters had managed to generate. This was especially true when California became the scene of one of the bloodiest race riots in the country's modern history. Six shocking days and nights of destruction, looting and street fighting in the Watts Negro district of Los Angeles in August, 1965, resulted in thirty-four deaths, 1032 injuries, 3952 arrests and property losses estimated as totaling close to forty million dollars. An anti-crime outcry against "violence in the streets" had already figured in the Presidential campaign of 1964 and added uproarious notes to the general hullabaloo of California's 1966 gubernatorial contest. Californians, in the closing 1960s, were still a little jittery and on the qui vive against the hazards of crime, organized or not, and against group violence of whatever kind, whether home-brewed or imported from the other side of the mountains.

21

CAMPAIGN FOR "SOCIAL PROGRESS"

Earl Warren was a serious candidate for President in 1952, as distinguished from his technical status as a favorite son at three previous Republican national conventions. It is well to look back half a dozen years before that, however, for first hints of the wavering course of California politics after his long governorship ended. With Warren riding taller in the political saddle than ever, 1946 proved to be an important year for five other Californians who were to assume increasingly impressive positions, some of them nationally, in the post-Warren era. Richard M. Nixon, a young Los Angeles County lawyer and former Navy lieutenant-commander, was first elected to Congress that year. Within six years this political unknown was to rise to the Vice-Presidency of the United States. Another young Republican, William F Knowland, won his first full term as a United States senator. Governor Warren had appointed him to the Senate in 1945 following the death of veteran Senator Hiram Johnson. Knowland was destined to succeed Robert A. Taft of Ohio as the Senate's Republican leader. Also in 1946, Thomas H. Kuchel, long-time Republican state legislator, was appointed State Controller and retained that chief elective California fiscal post with a Democratic-GOP double nomination. Eventually, he was to be-

come Republican whip in the United States Senate and an acknowledged leader in the moderate wing of his party. Edmund G. (Pat)
Brown, Democratic district attorney of San Francisco, chose 1946
for his debut in California statewide politics, losing a campaign for
state attorney-general. He gained the attorney-generalship at the
next election, though, and went on to the executive mansion eight
years later as the century's second Democratic governor. And finally,
in 1946, Republican Goodwin J. Knight, a politically-minded Superior Judge of Los Angeles County, gave up his judicial career to venture into statewide partisan competition. He became the second
lieutenant-governor of Warren's extended gubernatorial reign and,
at long last, Warren's successor. The affairs and ambitions of these
five men underwent complicated entanglement in California's disjointed politics over the ensuing decade or so, each of the five emerging, at one time or another, as a figure of marked controversy.

Fate first turned the spotlight on Goodwin Knight. There had
been a distinct political coolness in the 1943–1946 state administration between progressive Governor Warren and conservative Frederick F. Houser, his first lieutenant-governor, though both were
Republicans. Dissatisfied with his lot and out of sorts with Warren,
Houser went home to Los Angeles in 1946 and ran for a Superior
Judgeship. Judge Knight happily filed for lieutenant-governor. But
for this trade of jobs, as it was in effect, Houser and not Knight
might have inherited the governorship a few years later. One of the
peculiarities of California's election system under cross-filing was
that state candidates of the same party often ran independently
rather than as a ticket. This was invariably so in Warren's gubernatorial campaigns. Knight came to the lieutenant-governorship
under the impetus of his own energetic electioneering, but as an
outspoken Warren admirer. It must be remembered that 1946 was
the year in which Warren was re-elected at the primary with the
record-smashing endorsement of both major political parties. He was
undoubtedly in more complete command of California election poli-

tics at that moment than anybody had been in the modern annals of the state. His position was almost unassailable.

It was all the more astonishing that, only a short time after Governor Warren settled in for his second 1947–1950 term, elements of the reactionary wing of the Republican party began intriguing against him. He had carried a lot of their favorites into office on his coattails. But the Old Guard leaders detested his liberalism. They were disgruntled almost as much by their lack of influence with him. As the time for the next state election drew nearer, they started scheming at means to unseat him, some of them seizing upon Lieutenant-Governor Knight as the handiest, most available instrument for this purpose. Conservative-controlled Republican county committees openly touted Knight for governor in 1950. The dissident factions professed to see no particular ideological difference between Republican Warren and James Roosevelt whom the Democrats had trotted out against him.

For a time, Lieutenant-Governor Knight appeared to be flattered, as any eager politician might well have been, by all this sudden attention, and toured the state in tireless quest of new friends and supporters. It was an odd situation, especially since Warren had been the national choice of the Republican party for Vice-President only two years earlier. It amounted to a local right-wing attempt at repudiation, by no means the only one Warren experienced during a long career. The life of this little revolt within the GOP was extremely short, however. Warren backers contended, in the first place, that Knight could not beat the Governor at the Republican primary, and argued further that, even if he managed it, his nomination under fundamentally anti-Warren, ultraconservative auspices would ensure victory for James Roosevelt and the Democrats. Ambitious to be governor but evidently persuaded that the time was not ripe, Knight turned his back on the "oust Warren" movement and filed candidacy again for lieutenant-governor. From the viewpoint of his political future, it was just as well he did. Knight won 1950 re-election by double nomination. Warren disposed of Roosevelt with more than one million votes to spare.

Looked at in retrospect, this brief preprimary episode of 1950 was significant as a foretaste of tumultuous Republican battling to come in California, and later nationally, between the extreme conservatives and the progressives, or "moderates," as the latter soon preferred to term themselves. The struggle for power in the immediate post-Warren years was perhaps inevitable. But the party-splitting proclivities of the GOP's reactionary faction assumed an intensity which was little short of suicidal. On the eve of a national political renaissance for the Republicans under General Dwight D. Eisenhower, California GOPers headed toward a period of turbulence which, at its height, rivaled that of the state's Democrats in the mid-1930s. In one way or another, Nixon, Knowland, Kuchel, Knight and Brown all figured in the intraparty and interparty uproars of the next ten or fifteen years.

Governor Warren spoke out for "social progress" in his 1952 preconvention candidacy for the Presidency and warned the Republican party against "extremists of the Right" more than six years before the founding of the John Birch Society which was to denounce him with such fury after he became Chief Justice. Warren's last California campaign before he went to the Supreme Court was perhaps, in a special sense, his most gratifying. He met the opposition of the GOP ultraconservatives in his home state head-on and defeated it. The displeasure of Republican reactionaries over Governor Warren's increasingly plain tendencies toward political liberalism on a broad scope of issues had been evident for some time. In 1952, a coterie of them, forerunners of the right-wing extremists who were to become so active on the West Coast a dozen or so years later, undertook the task of eliminating Warren as a power in California politics. No sooner had Warren's name been put forward as a Presidential aspirant than the Governor's intraparty foes, eagerly and with considerable vindictiveness, presented a rival delegation ticket, technically committed to Thomas H. Werdel, a little-known but ambitious Old Guard Congressman. This contingent rallied around the myth that, if given a Presidential primary "choice," the voters, especially Republican voters, could be depended upon to endorse conservatism. It was a concept which was to reappear many times in the years ahead, in state and national politics, as the struggle over liberal-conservative theories continued to be waged, not in the Republican party alone.

In 1952, the disgruntled anti-Warren element of the state's GOP grumbled bitterly that the Governor's unexampled series of successes at the polls in fourteen years of statewide campaigning could be attributed chiefly to his deliberate flirtation with the Democrats. They were faced, as they had been for years past, with the curious fact that Warren maintained no discernible political machine, in the generally accepted sense, between elections, but customarily put together a temporary organization when campaign time came and launched himself on a highly personal and amazingly effective round of nonpartisan electioneering which might have made even the late Hiram Johnson green with envy. There was, of course, no room for nonpartisanship in a Presidential primary, no place for cross-filing or cross-voting. It was to be strictly a California Republican showdown. General Dwight D. Eisenhower and Ohio Senator Robert A. Taft did not formally enter the contest, though their lieutenants kept a close eye on the local row. Backers of the hastily assembled Werdel slate made war directly on Warren, loudly denouncing him as guilty of "Trumanism." The Governor sailed into battle full-tilt, pulling no punches. The Republican party, he declared, could not win the Presidency or hold it for any appreciable length of time unless it adopted a forward-looking and progressive attitude toward the great issues before the country and the world. The Republican right wing was to grow increasingly strong in California during the years ahead, but its take-over venture that summer of 1952 was ill-timed. Warren's delegation won the Presidential primary by a top-heavy majority, something like two to one.

At the 1952 Republican national convention in Chicago, Governor

144

Warren stood third in number of pledged delegates behind General Eisenhower and Senator Taft. Among his delegates were California Senators William F. Knowland and Richard M. Nixon, concerning whom there is much more to be said later on. Warren's chances for the Presidential nomination depended, obviously, on a Taft-Eisenhower convention deadlock, which did not develop. In October, 1953, Warren resigned the governorship he had held for eleven years to accept President Eisenhower's appointment as Chief Justice of the United States. His departure marked the end of an extraordinary decade in which California governmental and political supremacy was vested in a single strong figure to a greater degree than had ever been the case before. Every other year during that period, Warren stood before the voters either as a state office seeker or a nominal federal candidate, and each time his unorthodox manner of electioneering carried the day, except in his national campaign partnership with Tom Dewey in 1948. And even Warren's detractors held him innocent of the GOP posture of cocksure complacency which contributed to Dewey's debacle.

After Warren left state politics, the Republicans managed to hold the California governorship for another term, due to an admixture of circumstances, and then the Democrats, campaigning along strict party lines, finally polled their huge registration book majority and took over. In 1959, under Democratic auspices, the state's primary election cross-filing law of nearly half a century's standing was abolished, eliminating at least the legalistic basis for the nonpartisan "consensus" style of campaigning in which Earl Warren was a past master. Even so, nonconformist California persisted in the opinion that party loyalty rules were made to be broken. The Democrats lost the state in 1960, won it back in 1962, carried it again in 1964 and then took an unmerciful mauling in 1966 which cost them virtually all their State Capitol power, except in the Legislature.

When Warren announced for the Republican Presidential nomination in 1952, he had a lively apprehension of political dangers which vociferous right-wing extremism held for the GOP. At a San Francisco meeting of the Republican National Committee on January 17 of that year, he put it this way: "Our party has never had a radical wing, but we have our problems just the same, because we do have in it extremists of the Right—those who would freeze our nation to the *status quo,* with whatever inequalities go with it, and those who would have our country return to what they look back to nostalgically and affectionately call the good old days. I believe these extremists of the Right are not as numerous as they are vocal and influential. It is my deep conviction, however, that, unless there is a forthright repudiation of this thinking by our party, we will suffer again at the hands of the voters. . . . I am convinced the American people are not Socialists and will not tolerate socialistic government, but they are definitely committed to social progress. Any party which turns its back on social progress will be repudiated by the people."

For those with sense to see it, this was, in large measure, a summary of the thinking that had motivated Governor Warren in California, and perhaps an enlightening preview of what lay ahead in his farewell to partisan politics, less than two years later, and his elevation to the post of Chief Justice of the United States.

22

YOUNG MAN IN A HURRY

Richard Milhaus Nixon moved from political zero to the Vice-Presidency of the United States in half a dozen years. In California, where his electioneering techniques soon became widely known, and throughout the country, which came to know them later, this record aroused both envy and astonishment among the general run of politicians, accustomed to climb slowly up shaky party ladders to much less distinguished heights. Nixon showed an early and uncommon adaptability to political requirements, along with a sharp perception of how these were beginning to change with the increased availability and variety of American communications facilities.

In 1946, a group of southern California Republicans were looking for a likely candidate to unseat Representative H. Jerry Voorhis, a liberal Democrat of Los Angeles County who was proud of the fact a poll of House press gallery reporters had rated him "the best Pacific Coast Congressman." The GOPers decided to back young Dick Nixon, a Whittier lawyer and political neophyte, only recently returned from World War II service in the Navy. A southern California native, born in 1913, Nixon was a graduate of Whittier College and of the Duke University Law School. He was the author of *Changing Rules of Liability in Automobile Accident Litigation.* A shrewd, energetic, resourceful campaigner even in his first bid for elective office, Nixon was charged by Democratic leaders, then and for years afterward, with having directed a devastating anti-Red "smear" attack on Voorhis, insinuating, though never quite declaring, that the ten-year congressman had leftward political inclinations, or at least the support of left-leaning organizations. Congressman Voorhis, who was soundly defeated in an extremely well-organized Republican effort, complained later that the Nixon forces had unjustifiably pictured him as the endorsed candidate of "Communist-dominated" interests.

Certainly Congressman Nixon was a busy examiner into domestic radicalism manifestations during his early days in Washington. He was re-elected to the House of Representatives in 1948, the same year he participated actively in the Alger Hiss-"pumpkin papers" Communist espionage investigation, one of the high points of his public service up to that time. The Hiss case, the subject of wide press coverage and public attention in 1948 and immediately subsequent years, grew out of inquiries by the House Committee on Un-American Activities, on which Nixon served, into allegations of Communist infiltration of the federal Government. Hiss, a former State Department official, was accused of having been a Communist party member in the committee hearings testimony of former Communist Whittaker Chambers. A lurid tale unfolded in which Hiss contradicted the charge of Communisn and denied having removed restricted documents from the State Department, while Chambers, equally insistent in his statements, produced typewritten copies of State Department papers and, at one point, microfilm which he had hidden for a time in a hollowed-out pumpkin. This is not the place for an extensive review of the charges and countercharges of this complicated investigation to which Nixon, energetically concerned in the inquiry, has devoted some seventy pages in his autobiographical work, *Six Crises*. Chambers is now dead. Hiss, though protesting his innocence, was convicted of perjury in 1950 and served a term in federal prison. Years later, Nixon was to say that, as an aftermath of the Hiss affair, he personally was subjected to "an utterly unprincipled and vicious smear campaign." He cited estimates of friends that, had it not been for the Hiss case, he might never have become Vice-President in 1952 and later a candidate for President, and also that, had it not been for his role in that investigation, he might have reached the White House in 1960. He surmised, in retrospect, that there might have been "a grain of truth" in both calculations.

Figuring importantly in the chronology of Nixon's rise was the announcement of Democrat Sheridan Downey, a California United States Senator since 1938, that he would not stand for re-election in 1950. Republican Nixon, then nearing the end of his fourth year in the House, decided to try for Downey's job. So did Democratic Congresswoman Helen Gahagan Douglas of Los Angeles County, the wife of Melvyn Douglas, the actor, and herself a former stage-screen star and opera singer. In view of California election styles about a decade and a half later, it may be appropriate to note that Mrs. Douglas, a high-spirited New Dealer, was the first Hollywood personality to make the big time politically, although the practice of sending film actors to the State Assembly also started in the 1940s. After a bitter 1950 campaign, Nixon was elected Senator and the congressional career of Mrs. Douglas ended. Again the Democrats broke out in a rash of charges that Nixon and his electioneering organization, headed by Murray Chotiner, a southern California attorney and an astute and highly pragmatic campaign manager, had resorted to objectionable "smear" methods, subtly designed to pin a left-wing label on Congresswoman Douglas, an outspoken liberal. Indeed the California Democratic hierarchy appeared never to forgive Nixon for the Douglas campaign. It was about then that Nixon's detractors began calling him "Tricky Dick." But Nixon was comfortably in the Senate, and higher honors, as it turned out, were well within his reach.

Quite aside from Senator Nixon's subsequent role in national politics, his part in the California story and California's influence in

149

his are compellingly significant. For a very long time, California was necessarily the important home base of this unusual politician's varied activities. One scarcely can escape the feeling that Nixon, almost from his political beginnings, was a much more perplexing and inscrutable personality than his enemies ever realized. He was smart, articulate, inventive and farsighted, and not without his seeming periods of moodiness, alternating with high-strung restiveness. Undoubtedly, from the first, he was an adept practitioner of political realism—a briskly ruthless one, many said. He could be gracious and pleasant as well as irate and argumentative. He tore into his opponents with studied indignation, yet he was credited with the pronouncement that no man in politics can afford the luxury of losing his temper, except deliberately. An almost insatiable yearning for public acclaim and honors appeared to be seldom very far beneath the surface of a professionally polished political demeanor, but often Nixon discussed his talents and attainments with disarming modesty. Evidently accepting his controversial image as one of the hazards of public life, he extolled the art of turning a political "minus" into a "plus." Many saw him as something of an actor, a "quick study," a skillful professional, always "on." At times, to those who watched his tireless rounds with some amazement, he seemed to have the knack of switching his moods on and off like hot and cold water faucets. And always he was a young man in a hurry.

It was, of course, not until several years after Nixon's Senate victory that the country generally recognized in his quick emergence the development of a new breed of political operator, actually an authentic original in many respects. It was only then that certain observers of the national scene, a number of them with considerable hostility, began to picture Nixon as an ambitious supersalesman—rather than an actual producer—of assorted political ideas, with some of the modern advertising-man's flair for apposite slogans and mass psychology. By 1950 and 1951, though, the eager junior Senator was fully appreciated in his native state, and either adored or hated by a large number of people. Politicians and run-of-the-mill voters alike usually had strong feelings about Nixon, one way or the other. A cadre of devoted Nixonites had come into being, notably among Republicans in southern California. They were hard-working and dedicated, and continued to labor in Nixon's behalf for many years, some of them rising with him to posts of political prominence. On the other side of the California political fence, there was an increasing disposition to mark Nixon down as a freewheeling demagogue on the campaign trail and a master of adroit hints which suggested dangerous and intolerable flaws in the political character of his adversaries, and sometimes radical connections, without ever precisely saying so. But Nixon, apparently unworried by sniping of that sort, was on his way upward, as subsequent events abundantly proved, and 1952 dawned as a crucial year in his spectacular and contentious career.

In Governor Earl Warren's unsuccessful 1952 candidacy for his party's Presidential nomination, freshman Senator Nixon was a member of the Warren-pledged California delegation to the Republican national convention. He was, in fact, second only to senior Senator William F. Knowland, the delegation chairman, on the list of California representatives. All seventy of them were committed by the state's June 3 Presidential primary, and by their oaths of personal preference under the election code, to support Warren at the Chicago convention in July to the best of their "judgment and ability." The California law was specific on that point. Consequently, the California delegation vote was cast as a bloc by Senator Knowland for Governor Warren—along with a scattering of Warren votes from other regions—on the first and only convention ballot which resulted in the nomination of Dwight Eisenhower.

Nevertheless, a story spread, and gained considerable circulation among confirmed Warren followers, that Nixon had engaged in a flirtation with the Eisenhower camp, talking up the General's virtues among fellow delegates, and that this had a bearing on the young Senator's speedy nomination for Vice-President. It was recalled that

151

Nixon had joined Warren's California delegation train only after it was halfway to the convention city and that previously he had been in the East and Midwest, with ample opportunity to become familiar with the rapidly developing situation and the ins and outs of the major rivalry between General Eisenhower and Ohio Senator Taft. Nixon took cognizance of the unpleasant implications of this tale and stoutly denied them in his book, *Six Crises,* ten years later.

"This," wrote Nixon, "is perhaps as good a place as any to lay to rest one of the many myths regarding my selection as General Eisenhower's runningmate in 1952. It has been alleged that there was a 'deal' between [Thomas] Dewey and myself under which I was to receive the Vice-Presidential nomination in return for 'delivering' the California delegation to Eisenhower. There are two facts which completely demolish this allegation. In the first place, I was for Eisenhower long before I met Dewey at the New York dinner in May. And, in the second place, the California delegation was pledged to Governor Earl Warren and stayed with him to the finish. It did not shift to Eisenhower until he had already been assured the nomination by reason of a switch to him, over Harold Stassen's objection, of the Minnesota delegation."

The original story, or "allegation," as Nixon called it, died hard among certain pro-Warren California politicos, however. Some observers studied the political calendar and took the position that if Senator Nixon, as he reported, had been for Eisenhower "long before" a New York GOP fund-raising dinner on May 8, he probably had favored the General after becoming a California convention delegation candidate firmly pledged to Warren. The California Presidential primary was held that year on June 3, and the Warren-committed delegation slate had been chosen long before that. The would-be delegates, including Nixon, had filed their oaths of convention loyalty to Warren on April 7 at the California Secretary of State's office and had qualified as a primary ticket on April 10. It was noted, too, in that season's political calculations, that secondary support in the large California delegation might have proved of immense importance if the nomination contest between General Ike and Senator Taft had proceeded beyond the first convention ballot. The incident, regardless of the pro and con disputes about it, plainly irritated dyed-in-the-wool Warren adherents and was not forgotten by some of them for a long time.

Whatever the motivating reasons for his nomination may have been, Nixon headed into the fall of 1952 as the Republican Vice-Presidential candidate and was whistle-stopping through the West at a lively clip when the so-called "fund scandal" suddenly exploded around his ears. This was the revelation that a group of well-to-do California supporters of Nixon had provided the new Senator, after his 1950 election, with a special fund of some eighteen thousand dollars to help finance his political activities between elections on a year-around basis. The result was a noisy, coast-to-coast political uproar. Headlines called it Nixon's "secret fund." Anti-Nixon elements screamed wrongdoing from the housetops. It was one thing to contribute campaign funds to a candidate for office, they contended, but quite another to provide political money to a public office holder after the votes had been counted. The Democrats jumped on the issue jubilantly. Demands were made, some of Republican origin, that Eisenhower drop Nixon as Vice-Presidential nominee and choose another running mate. At first blush, the General evidently found it hard to decide. Some of his friends were apparently in disagreement on whether Nixon should stay on the ticket or get off. It was later disclosed that, at one juncture in the topsy-turvy affair, Senator Nixon actually had drafted a telegram of candidacy resignation but that campaign manager Chotiner, opposed to any such surrender under fire, had torn it up. All in all, this was undoubtedly one of the most trying experiences of Nixon's life, certainly of his first six years in public office. It was a measure of his remarkable political resiliency that he came out of it victorious in 1952 and 1956 and became the Republican party's candidate to succeed President Eisenhower in 1960.

The famous "Checkers Speech," a carefully pondered, emotion-laden national broadcast from Hollywood, saved the day for Nixon in 1952. It was probably as unusual an address as any Vice-Presidential candidate ever made. Nixon accused his accusers of smear tactics in questioning his integrity. The between-elections political fund, he maintained, was not in any sense morally wrong. He denied that any of the contributors got special favors for their contributions. The fund was administered by a trustee, he said, and "not one cent" of it had gone for his personal use. Nixon told his listeners he was baring his life to them. He offered a list of all his holdings and debts. Among his properties, Nixon included Checkers, a black-and-white-spotted cocker spaniel which had been presented to the Nixon family by a Texas admirer. Whatever the criticism, the nominee stated with some feeling, the Nixons intended to keep that little dog. He wound up with praise for Eisenhower ("Folks, he's a great man") and with a promise to continue fighting up and down America to drive "the crooks and the Communists" out of Washington.

It was, of its unique kind, an indescribably fascinating political speech. Nixon remarked later that Checkers came out of that campaign as the best-known dog in the land since Franklin Roosevelt's Fala. A short time after the broadcast, at a meeting of the two Republican standard-bearers in Wheeling, West Virginia, Eisenhower concluded that Nixon had completely vindicated his position and ought to remain on the ticket. "You're my boy," said the General.

23

KNIGHT'S GAMBIT

While Richard Nixon was being acclaimed as the new political wonder boy of the early 1950s, two other California politicians, with
whom he was to clash later on, were also catching the public's attention, though in a much less spectacular fashion. The 1950 election, which had elevated Nixon to the United States Senate, marked
a second-term lieutenant-governorship victory for Republican Goodwin J. Knight. Democrat Edmund G. (Pat) Brown was chosen state
attorney-general the same year. It is probable that both men, or
at least the forces back of them, already had their eyes on greater
honors, and were waiting as patiently as possible for the golden
opportunity which Earl Warren's retirement from the governorship
eventually would provide.

An unhappy thing happened to Democrat Brown at the very next
election, however. At a time when the Republicans were aglow with
hopes that the Eisenhower-Nixon ticket might be a formula at long
last for national revival of their party, the California Democrats celebrated the 1952 Presidential year with a comedy of miscalculations.
The Democrats assumed, with cheerful logic, that rosy days were
ahead; the state was booming and so were their voter enrollments,
now exceeding California GOP totals by more than 800,000, easily

enough to guarantee victory in a less volatile state. The luck of the Democrats in electing governors had been notoriously bad, yet they had been carrying California in national elections unfailingly since 1932. So, in the early spring of 1952, the Democratic state leadership casually set about preparing another national convention delegation, a "broad consensus" of party regulars, all dedicated to the renomination of President Harry Truman. This "Truman ticket" was all but qualified for the Presidential primary ballot when President Truman announced, almost as laconically as Calvin Coolidge had done twenty-four years earlier, that he had no intention of running again. That disclosure unceremoniously yanked the rug out from under the startled California Democrats. They hastily regrouped their embarrassed forces, a carefully selected assortment of the party's liberals, conservatives and middle-roaders, and decided, since no accepted substitute for Truman had yet appeared on the horizon, to form a California favorite-son delegation.

This makeshift arrangement made Attorney-General Edmund G. (Pat) Brown a technical candidate for President of the United States, much to his surprise. A Republican in his youth, Brown was one of those who, fascinated by Roosevelt, had not only voted with the Democrats but permanently joined them in the early New Deal days. A native of San Francisco and the long-time district attorney of that city, he had not always been a winner in his political beginnings. Once he had been beaten for the State Legislature, as a young Republican. Even as a Democrat, he had tried twice before finally capturing the state attorney-generalship and, in 1952, was getting into his second year in that office. As the only statewide constitutional official of the Democrats, Brown consented, with some reluctance, to head their abruptly reorganized national convention slate. It was really a Republican-type improvisation. With so stimulating a vote-getter as Earl Warren usually on hand to lead them, the state's Republicans had regularly resorted to the favorite-son dodge ever since Franklin Roosevelt's first election. It had enabled them to maintain at least the semblance of national convention independence and, incidentally, had the merit of discouraging California primary bids by serious GOP Presidential aspirants around the country who lacked the stomach to tackle Warren on his home ground.

The California Democrats were not so fortunate with this formula in 1952. Over the Sierra Nevada almost immediately popped the coonskin cap which Estes Kefauver sometimes wore for campaign picture-taking purposes in that year's political charade. The ambitious and mettlesome United States Senator from Tennessee was playing the preconvention primary circuit that spring, and vote-heavy California, with its Democrats in confused disarray, was too tempting a plum to pass up. California, always with a soft spot in its heart for showmanship, greeted the coonskin candidacy with open arms. Kefauver, sponsored by a quickly assembled ticket of proposed Democratic delegates on which enthusiastic political amateurs predominated, turned the California primary into a Tennessee waltz. It was a case of a seriously intentioned White House hopeful challenging a local favorite son whose candidacy was recognized to be only nominal. The Senator swamped Attorney-General Brown and the party regulars by an unexpectedly heavy margin of 1,155,839 to 485,578. It was a sad day for "Pat" Brown, providing little intimation that some day he would join Hiram Johnson and Earl Warren in the charmed circle of California's multi-term governors. It was an even sadder occasion for the party hierarchy, now thrust, temporarily at least, into outer darkness after having ruled the roost in California Democratic affairs for the better part of two decades.

The Californians were completely unprepared for the course of events at the 1952 Democratic national convention or, for that matter, the ensuing Presidential campaign. Senator Kefauver's big, seventy-six-member maverick delegation from the West Coast arrived on the convention scene full of dreamy enthusiasm and apparently without the slightest suspicion that their hero was headed for the skids. The group was bound under unit rule to front-runner Kefauver and, until lightning struck, many seemed to have only the vaguest realization of the magnitude of the drive to "draft" Adlai

E. Stevenson or of the impending bandwagon switches which were to sweep the Illinois governor to the nomination on the third ballot. Accustomed to relatively easy Presidential victories in their state during the Roosevelt-Truman days, the faction-split California Democrats were poorly equipped to cope with the rigors of this first Eisenhower-Stevenson general election campaign. Other strong Democratic voter bailiwicks had similar trouble, but it is perhaps not too much to say that dissention in California that fall played its part in keeping the Democrats out of state power for another half-dozen years.

In any case, despite his charm, wit and sophisticated good sense, native-born Adlai Stevenson found the going rough in California. He was born in Los Angeles, but that had been many years ago and thousands of California newcomers had forgotten the fact, if they ever knew it. The glamour of General Eisenhower's military record in Europe was infinitely more persuasive. Moreover, the Democratic regulars in California had lost control of their party machinery, for the time being, to the erstwhile Kefauver supporters whose first love was by no means Adlai. The final outcome was a stunning illustration of California's independent cross-voting. The Democrats came to the November election with a state registration book advantage of 856,000. The Republicans defeated them by 699,000. General Eisenhower was the first Republican Presidential nominee to carry California since Herbert Hoover in 1928.

Meantime, for Republican Lieutenant-Governor Goodwin J. Knight, 1952 was a year of eager anticipation, rewarded in 1953 by the governorship. A native of Utah, a Stanford University graduate, an attorney, a gold-mine operator and for many years a Los Angeles judge, Knight bounced upon the state scene near the middle of the century as one of California's most effervescent and colorful politicians. For a good many years, he provided the public with more personal drama than it had seen in a long time, running from light situation skits and political tragedy to gags, patter and election-year acrobatics, with an occasional trick of vote-getting magic thrown in for good measure. At times, Knight was almost as irrepressible and picturesque as the memorable "Sunny Jim" Rolph. He was also an ardent and well-informed student of political history. It used to be said of him that his eye had been on the governorship of California since boyhood.

However that may be, Knight certainly was long bedazzled by politics generally and Republican politics in particular. He was proud to recall that, as a youngster, he had distributed handbills for Hiram Johnson. He got his real political start in 1935 when old Governor Merriam appointed him to the Los Angeles County trial bench. Superior Judge Knight's timely shedding of judicial robes for the lieutenant-governorship campaign of 1946 already has been re-counted briefly in an earlier chapter. And so have the circumstances of his momentary 1950 notion that he could beat Governor Warren, a slippery position from which, with agile sure-footedness, he pulled back just in time. In any consideration of how California became the curious place it did shortly after mid-century, Knight's further adventures are appropriate. Their start almost exactly coincided with a mounting preoccupation in both major parties about where this unpredictable state was apt to drift when "strong man" Warren, sooner or later, relinquished the reins of political power.

South of the Tehachapi Mountains, Judge Knight evidently had been pondering this question with growing interest for a long time. He had been "building his image," furthermore, in a most inventive and unusual way long before he became lieutenant-governor. After a busy week on the bench, he used to travel in his spare time to San Francisco to appear on radio as a public affairs commentator. His canny purpose was twofold: to learn all about broadcasting and to become known as a political personality in the northern end of a state which extended almost two-thirds the length of the country's West Coast. In the long run, this chatty, extroverted jurist developed more comfortable ease before a microphone than perhaps any other politico of his day. Making himself what very well may have been the first

American politician deliberately pretrained in these mysteries, he was more than ready for television a bit later.

Sitting quietly in the shadow of well-entrenched Governor Warren must have tried the patience of so impulsively energetic a man as Knight. His decision to give up an eleven-year judicial career for that privilege actually affected the course of California politics, directly or indirectly, for the next decade—until 1958, in fact, when political misfortune finally beset him. Jovial, imaginative though relatively unknown "Goodie" Knight bounded on stage back in 1946, bubbling with animation and good will toward everybody, especially Warren. The buoyant Lieutenant-Governor spent the next seven years methodically preparing for a take-over of the executive mansion. It was estimated that during those years there was scarcely a city, village or crossroads in the state where Knight had not visited, dedicated a public facility of some sort, made a speech or otherwise exposed his friendly, vivacious and altogether charming personality to the citizenry. Plainly and happily, he was on his way to the governor's chair, but realistic about it and not disposed, at least after the quickly fading temptations of 1950, to foul up fate's timetable.

When the Republicans nominated Governor Warren for Vice-President in 1948, the new lieutenant-governor must have felt that the state's big prize was about to fall into his lap almost immediately. Jubilantly he led the railroad station cheering when Warren's campaign train took off from Sacramento on its national electioneering swing. He followed the train down the track a bit, in fact, calling hearty last-minute words of encouragement to Warren on the rear platform. Knight's hopes, along with Warren's, were dashed by Harry Truman's "give 'em hell" campaign. Again in 1952, after Warren's declaration of Presidential candidacy, Knight's expectations soared and took another painful tumble when the Republicans gave the nomination to Eisenhower. The state's No. 2 man faced a further anxious period of waiting for California's political champion to hang up his gloves, but this time he was cheerfully confident it would not be long. Governor Warren, after all, could not be expected to remain in California forever. The possibility that he might, though, caused sleepless nights in a good many political bedrooms, almost surely including Knight's.

The first year of the Eisenhower administration was a silly time of wild speculations in California. The 1953 political grapevine sprouted rumors by the dozens, some of them attributed to the hopeful Knight camp, about Presidential appointments for Warren. One day he was slated for ambassador to one of the Scandinavian countries; the next day it was Spain; Britain was mentioned, too. Once, at a cocktail party, Governor Warren, who preferred an occasional bourbon, remarked casually that he understood vodka left its consumer without an alcoholic breath. This mild observation was deliberately repeated to see what would happen and, sure enough, within minutes somebody ventured the surmise that the Governor might be the next American diplomatic representative in Moscow. In October, President Eisenhower finally appointed Warren to the Supreme Court as Chief Justice. After nearly two terms as lieutenant-governor, Knight was very possibly the most delighted politician in California. He had been smart, despite the many years of waiting, to relinquish a pleasant judicial position for the vicissitudes of statewide politics, and Frederick F. Houser, the heir apparent of the first of Warren's three administrations, had been too impatient, had quit too soon and missed the dreamboat.

With Warren gone, however, Governor Knight soon had other powerful leaders to reckon with, notably Republicans Richard Nixon and William Knowland. As Vice-President, Nixon continued to keep a sharp eye on California, his original support base. And California was never far from the thinking of Senator Knowland who had only recently been chosen Senate GOP leader to succeed "Mr. Republican," the late Senator Robert Taft. Then, too, there was the aspiring California Democratic chieftain, Attorney-General Edmund G. (Pat) Brown. These three men, among others, were to become key figures in the complicated California tangle which came about, with more than a few national political ramifications, in the years immediately following Warren's departure. But, in that short, harmonious lull of 1953, "Knight's gambit," as somebody called it, had paid off handsomely.

24

TRANSITION TO AFFLUENCE

The 1950s were years of helter-skelter transition for California, of growing urbanization and suburbanization. On many counts, the business of governing and winning the right to govern grew more and more intricate and difficult. A little like some of its post-Warren political leaders, the state was restless, ambitious and in a tremendous rush. Along with much of the world after the second great war, it was deeply concerned with instant security, status attainment, public and private, and the conventionally accepted physical symbols of accomplishment. The advantages and disadvantages of affluence jostled each other in uneasy balance during most of the decade.

The incredible river of incoming millions, sometimes running as high as 500,000 a year, hiked the California population by nearly 49 per cent between 1950 and 1960. But relatively few left Eastern factories, Midwestern farms or Southern villages simply to bask in rural California scenery and sunshine. Rather there was a new concentration of people in and around the larger cities, with a multiplication of the problems of urban sprawl. The Abundant Life arrived amid enthusiastic hallelujahs, with many benefits and much tinseled gadgetry. There were more schools and colleges, more home swimming pools, increased social conscience, higher bank balances, broader welfare programs, uglier billboard jungles along the highways, larger state budgets, better business conditions, more art galleries, parks, public works and two-car garages, more tourists, tax problems, housing shortages and "cookout" barbecue equipment. San Francisco, like Manhattan, found itself bursting at the seams and handicapped for expansion space. Situated on the tip of a peninsula, surrounded by ocean and bay, it depended increasingly on four or five adjacent "bedroom" counties. Suburbia became inevitable. Los Angeles, always a widespread metropolitan complex, continued to expand in all directions. So did San Diego, Oakland, Long Beach, San Jose, Sacramento and other urban centers, annexations periodically swallowing up what recently had been independent rural or semirural communities.

The nuclear age speeded and modernized California's industrialization and drastically changed the economy of some of its localities. Overnight the state found itself the center of varied electronics installations and the recipient of substantial government contracts. Scientific research ranged from the practical to the theoretical, from laboratories to busy testing grounds, from astronomy and oceanography to missile components and rocket engines. Some of the areas once panned for gold became the scene of feverish, hopeful preparations for man's conquest of space. With the state's more traditional industrial institutions also humming at peak capacity, thousands of ordinary workmen and highly trained scientists found places in these new pursuits.

Every step in this many-sided expansion was accompanied by magnified demands on the ruling politicians for greater and more diversified governmental services. California had always been a huge and difficult domain to govern, and each new decade was posing more involved problems. Annual state expenditures had passed the $1 billion mark in the 1950–1953 period; disbursements in a few more years ranged well above $2 billion; by the middle 1960s the State Capitol governing business was to become a $4.5 billion affair, with no assured limit in sight. With countless bond issues piled on top of the yearly legislative appropriation totals, California's expenses, including huge state subventions to the local governments, were frequently compared with those of many middle-sized foreign countries. Long ago, over the portal of a pseudo-Grecian temple in the growing Sacramento complexity of state government buildings, had been carved the words: "Bring Me Men To Match My Mountains." However, in the matter of hands to cope smoothly with the state's complicated concerns, the gods seemed disposed to grant this petition only occasionally. Professional politicians, especially the successful ones stuck with the job of governing, felt steadily mounting pressures for closer management of natural resources and conservation programs; for improved transportation, water supplies, education, smog control, highway safety and crime suppression; for better health and welfare standards and a lessening of racial tensions; for tax relief and, at the same time, intensified regulation of the business and industrial systems rapidly altering the texture of an earlier California. Modern officeholders indeed had a rambunctious Golden Bear by the tail and were far too busy to practice much of the gaudy boastfulness for which Californians had so often been reproached in the past.

This is not to suggest that the flavor of pretentiousness had altogether soured in the mouths of Californians. But their points of pride had changed somewhat. The state appeared, in the eyes of its natives anyhow, to be finally coming of age, without losing its irrepressible behavior habits or the exuberance of its youth. With no noticeable sacrifice of vigor, it was attaining a measure of imported and locally-contrived sophistication. And now it tossed with restless dreams of economic, political and even cultural empire and already had become the curious seat of a bustling and uniquely different manner of life, not to say a maverick regional civilization. As the century moved into its second half, it was pretty well agreed, of course, that California's potentialities and dilemmas would require the ingenuity of any and all such mountain-matchers as fate might happen to cast up.

Mobility, for instance, was a mid-century watchword. The face of California was gradually being changed by complicated transportation networks. Long before it reached national population leadership, the state had advanced beyond all others in number of motor vehicles. It was a place on wheels, confronted by the new crises of that condition. Its thoroughfares were glutted with traffic, running bumper to bumper in metropolitan district rush hours. Political warfare soon opened between highway engineering bureaucrats, intent on the crying need to break transportation bottlenecks with elaborate multilane freeways, and indignant community interests, clinging nostalgically to some of the few remaining vestiges of yesterday and adamantly opposed to the destruction of old landmarks and related "historical values" by the march of modernity. The broad, twisting ribbons of steel and concrete continued to remake the California countryside, nonetheless. At times, even the state's unique groves of mighty redwoods and other mountain and coastal regions of outstanding scenic attraction stood in danger. The unhappy choice, in many instances, lay between man's sense of beauty and his pressing awareness of a necessity, both commercial and otherwise, for the facilities of rapid movement.

Despite an urban huddling of new population, California still had no shortage of wide-open spaces and continued to rank among the nation's top states in volume and value of agricultural production. The key to the state's rural prosperity was the diversity of its offerings, the wealth of its specialty crops which were scarce, or could not be grown in commercial quantities, in most other sections of the country. With climate ranging from frigid to subtropical and rainfall varying sharply over its spacious area, California not only ranked high in its yield of wheat, corn, cotton, potatoes, barley and most staple crops which other states grew abundantly, but also provided the country with avocados, pomegranates, dates, artichokes, asparagus, cantaloupes, olives, nectarines, figs, rice, wine and table grapes and all types of citrus fruits. At its southern end, the Imperial Valley became famous for its winter lettuce and melons. By 1959, according to the United States and California Departments of Agriculture, the annual net income per acre of California farms was $26.70 as contrasted with a national average of $10.68. At the same time, small

166

farms, on a gradual but appreciable decrease since the 1920s, were making way, more and more, for large-acreage operations, in many cases corporation-owned. These, for the most part, were efficiently managed, highly mechanized and scientifically planned enterprises, sometimes pictured by labor interests and other critics as "factories in the fields." Such giants of organized production manifestly had a significant impact both on the overall agricultural industry and the nature of rural life in California. For one thing, the state had an acute and long-standing farm labor problem. Some of its aspects, with frequent political overtones, dragged on unsolved into a fourth straight decade. Native workers were ill suited or indisposed to assume the tasks of "stoop labor" in the fields, at least in sufficient numbers to meet critical harvest requirements. Foreign nationals were imported, especially Mexicans. The practice was controversial. Low farm wages were assailed and, in some localities, miserable farm labor housing conditions. Unionization, however, had been bitterly fought for years. Strongly established big commodity producers were, in many places, determinedly opposed to general organization of agricultural labor. On through the 1950s and into the mid-1960s, some phases of these persistent disputes recurrently affected the rural economy.

The years of transition were smoother in other respects. Recovered from the crippling effects of the depression and post-depression periods, business, big and small, was branching out in every direction. It was an era of chainbanking, chain supermarkets, group-organized production and distribution in numerous other fields and thriving growth in general. California's processed exports were approaching a record high—canned fruit, canned beer, canned soup, canned vegetables, even canned entertainment. Like almost every other industrial mammoth, Hollywood, the acknowledged world center of tinned amusement, found itself in the throes of adjustment to something new in the early 1950s. Television was hurting the motion-picture box office. The fabulous Hollywood days of Chaplin, Pickford and Fairbanks were long gone, and even such comparative newcomers as, say, George Murphy and Ronald Reagan were beginning to age a little. The new Movieland still ground out its quota of full-length features and historical superspectacles, but it shrewdly hedged its bets by making half-hour and sixty-minute TV series quickies, too. In no time at all, independent television factories were in full southern California production. The cinema crisis had turned into a new California industry. An old pro at entertainment improvisation, Hollywood came out of the menacing situation with prestige and bankrolls still intact. Presently the ubiquitous film capital magnates were peddling their old pictures to television's late, late shows. Hollywood, in fact, was only a few years away from still another new and scintillating expansion—the production of politicians.

California political fashions, as a matter of fact, underwent a transitional period along with the rest of the state in the 1950s, fumbling and tentative at first but unexpectedly violent toward the end of the decade. At the outset, there was not an actual, fully realized shift in political opinion, so it appeared, but rather a cautious, almost unconscious, revision of everyday political terminology. If California showed indications of uncertainty, of an uneasy change in political nomenclature and party shibboleths a little ahead of some of her more prosaic sister states, this was perhaps understandable in the circumstances. The Democrats had just lost California in a national election for the first time in a quarter of a century. The California Republicans, having helped elect General Eisenhower in 1952, were full of party jubilation but evidently in some doubt at first concerning whether progressivism or conservatism had moved into the White House with him. There was no question about the progressivism of Earl Warren or the strides California had made under his long governorship. That regime was ended, however, or nearing an end, and it was time for new faces and fresh political calculations.

The reaction of both California's major political parties was to move gingerly toward the middle of the road for a brief spell, after eleven years of Warren, while party leaders consulted pollsters and other accredited soothsayers for an inkling of the future. It was merely a temporary adjustment, as it turned out, but plainly discernible in a

168

softening of factional identification terms and a certain fuzziness in the political dialogue. With a wary eye on mounting right-wing influences, many Republicans of more flexible beliefs curiously put away their once-cherished "progressive" label, for the time being at least, and quietly began calling themselves "moderates." By the same token, confirmed political rightists within the GOP no longer drew so many resounding attacks as "reactionaries" but suddenly were spoken of much more politely as conscientious followers of "constitutionalism." Among many California Democratic regulars, immediately after Governor Knight took over from Governor Warren, there was a corresponding propensity to stress total "party unity" as a sacred way of life and more and more to soft-pedal, without quite abandoning, the Roosevelt-Truman era battle cry of "liberalism." The Republican Old Guard greeted the departure of Warren with undisguised rejoicing. They now expected a larger voice in Republican affairs and policy-making, but appeared momentarily confused on how to set about getting it. It was a state of politics not unusual in California where left and right factions, within the framework of both principal parties, had been jockeying for the upper hand over a span of forty or fifty years. The odd circumspection of political professionals simply covered a general bewilderment while they sought to gauge, as accurately as possible, which way the wind was really blowing and what precise tactics promised a safe voter majority in 1954, the occasion of the first post-Warren gubernatorial election.

25

THE WARREN AFTERGLOW

Earl Warren's successor, Governor Goodwin J. Knight, was a difficult man to dislike, although the Democrats tried to with sober partisan zeal and some of the leaders of his own Republican party eventually had a stab at it, too. Knight was nimble-minded and discursively charming. His quick friendliness, his bursting enthusiasms, his good nature and unquenchable spirit of optimism caused a good many cynics to class him as something of a political leprechaun. In California nobody really hates leprechauns, whether the citizenry actually believes in them or not.

The new governor's vivacious, almost elfin temperament covered up a deep-seated earnestness about his inherited job and a well-informed grasp of political realities. He sorely needed the latter quality as Warren's replacement in the opening 1950s. He had to face California's peculiarly divided voters only thirteen months after the former executive moved up to the Supreme Court. This 1954 situation was one which the registration-dominant Democrats had been avidly awaiting for years. Since 1942, Governor Warren's remarkable campaigning talent and the general esteem in which he was held had kept a majority of Republican officials cosily in State Capitol control. Few of them were so forward-looking as the electioneering wizard with whom they carefully allied themselves every four years. So the Democratic chiefs and most of their devoted braves were convinced that, with Warren safely out of California, they could easily beat any other candidate the Republicans had to offer. Governor Knight, after all, had neither the Warren nonpartisanship flair nor, of course, the renown of Eisenhower who had swept the state over Stevenson in 1952. With the Democrats topping the Republicans in eligible California voters by about three to two, Knight's chances of pulling another GOP rabbit out of the political hat, only two years later, appeared to be mathematically remote.

Looking back on it, 1954 represented a kind of Western hiatus in the rivalry of the conservative and neo-progressive movements which, in a very few years, were to be felt again much more sharply, both in California and the country. While the Democrats were regrouping, or trying to, after Stevenson's first national defeat, and at a time when President Eisenhower was being wryly credited with a "vague, unfocused idealism," the California leadership in both major parties appeared to be a little off stride, in political dialogue as well as in tactical judgment. Yet the opposed forces which brought John Kennedy to the forefront six years later, and led in a decade to the Barry Goldwater experiment, already were stirring. It may be that Knight, on his little California throne, envisioned some of these possibilities a bit more clearly than most of his fellow politicians realized.

Knight seemed to sense, at all events, that there would be no political profit for the Republicans, or for him, in allowing right-wingers to rock the governmental boat unduly. He subsequently recalled that he had warned President Eisenhower against the danger to the Republicans of antilabor measures, specifically so-called "right to work" proposals that threatened union controls, which some ultraconservative GOPers had begun to advocate. He contended the introduction of such issues in California, for instance, could be fatal. Knight also cautioned California Republicans, early and late, that conduct to ensure their continued State Capitol and legislative control was imperative during the next few years, lest reapportionments following the 1960 census move the Democrats into prolonged power. His apprehensions on both counts were justified, but his advice was largely unheeded.

Nonetheless, in 1954, unorthodox Governor Knight upset the California betting odds and boldly improvised a personal victory. The Democratic leaders, bemused by their huge voter enrollment, were a shade overconfident and shortsighted. More disorganized than they knew, after the long Republican reign under Warren, they miscalculated the Warren afterglow and the giddy disposition of California voters. Their one state constitutional office incumbent, Attorney-General Edmund G. (Pat) Brown, did not. The unsettled times prompted him to be patient. Moreover, he had scarcely recovered from his recent Presidential primary battering at the hands of Kefauver. Brown decided to run for re-election that year rather than for governor. This left the majority Democrats without a candidate of recent general experience in statewide electioneering, or at least without one on whom they could agree. So, as a challenger to Governor Knight, they finally settled on Richard Perrin Graves, an earnest, likable young man, well schooled in governmental problems, who for some years had been the influential, leading public lobbyist for the League of California Cities. Graves's ability in public affairs was widely appreciated around the Capitol and the State Legislature. To the generality of California voters he was almost a political unknown.

That alone gave the initial advantage to jaunty, peripatetic Governor Knight. Assessing the somewhat rudderless political situation with nice discernment, he played his cards accordingly. He courted the admirers of former Governor Warren devotedly. As a precautionary measure, he also kept the Republican Old Guard in a reassured frame of mind, although this was one element of support upon which he could count with virtual certainty. What Knight really needed in order to win was a dependable lure for the majority Democrats. As a compelling attraction to pull prolabor Democrats across party lines, the Governor flirted winsomely with the trade-union movement. There was a promise in advance that he would veto any "right to work" bill which might reach his desk as well as certain other types of threatened legislation unfavorable to labor. This maneuver, whether intended to improve the image of the Republican party or Knight's own, worked to perfection. The elated executive said afterward that labor campaigners, many of them Democrats, were more effective in his behalf that fall than almost anybody else.

Regardless of a Democratic state registration edge of over 850,000, Republican Knight defeated Democrat Graves by more than 550,000 votes. It was not only a notable feat of magic but another shining example of the utter uselessness of trying to predict, by any hard and fast rules, what California voters will do. The antics of California political party leaders in those days were just about as unforeseeable as those of the forces they undertook to lead. Only four years later, the Republican high command, in the full flowering of a latent conservatism, turned its back on this proven gubernatorial vote-getter. In the process, the GOP lost its principal Western stronghold after sixteen years of uninterrupted rule.

The development of GOP factionalism, as much personal as ideological, helped to pave the way for this. If the political affairs of California appeared to the rest of the country to be particularly disjointed in 1956, perhaps the capers of some of the state's newly crowned leaders had a lot to do with it. Republican Governor Knight, for instance, diverted the public with a long and stubborn show of reluctance to endorse his fellow Californian, Richard Nixon, for Vice-Presidential renomination. In the light of what happened later to California Republicanism, this incident may have marked the first open sign of discomposure in the GOP triumvirate which assumed the state power vacated by Earl Warren.

Goodwin Knight, fresh from his spectacular 1954 gubernatorial sweep, happily headed the state government. William Knowland, scion of the Oakland *Tribune* publishing family, was Republican leader of the United States Senate and a figure to be taken seriously in both state and national politics. Richard Nixon was riding high as Vice-President and was generally conceded a cinch to be retained as

173

President Eisenhower's second-term running mate. All three were freewheeling individualists, with less in common than might have been indicated by the alliance into which circumstances had shuffled them. It became evident fairly early that Knight was less than thoroughly enchanted with Nixon. Their personalities were quite different. The Knight camp indicated at times that political empathy also fell short of perfection.

Whatever the fundamental motivating factors may have been, the Governor of California stirred up a small hornets' nest by refusing for a long time to issue even a perfunctory endorsement cheer for the Vice-President from California. He explained, with bland reasonableness, that a choice of Vice-President was up to President Eisenhower, whom he loudly praised, and added that his own support of Nixon might be expected only if and when Eisenhower had made it crystal-clear and official that Nixon's renomination was desired by the White House. That desire may have been implied but was not voiced in altogether exact terms until the President arrived in San Francisco for the 1956 Republican national convention. Also in San Francisco was former Minnesota Governor Harold E. Stassen, staging a one-man "dump Nixon" drive. That Republican nominating convention, like some the Democrats had held back in the Roosevelt days, amounted to a Presidential coronation ceremony. What Ike wanted, Ike got. When the President's unequivocal blessing finally was conferred on Nixon, Governor Knight went along, though rather less enthusiastically than the rest of the California delegation. This little episode drew quite a bit of public attention in an otherwise uneventful convention, and managed once more to spotlight California's manner of political life as being incomprehensibly odd. More to the point, it helped to engender additional coolness among California Republican leaders who were to clash so vehemently only a short time later.

On the California Democratic side, meantime, Attorney-General Brown, with painful recollections of his favorite-son adventure and home state defeat in 1952, busied himself with organized ballyhoo for the renomination of Adlai Stevenson. California boasted it was the first state in the Union to unite Democrats in full-scale promotion of Stevenson for a second candidacy. "Pat" Brown was at least on the right side that year, well in advance of the Democratic national convention, but that provided little solace for him or his party when the Eisenhower general election bandwagon started rolling. A large segment of California's Democrats bolted their party that fall, as they had four years earlier, and the state landed once more in the Eisenhower column. All in all, though, the bustling and optimistic Democratic Attorney-General came out of the campaign in relatively good shape, his head already filled, in every likelihood, with exciting gubernatorial dreams. The California political scene was strewn with Democratic wreckage, but Brown, to all intents and purposes, owned the wreck. It remained to be seen whether it could be salvaged and, with an expert engine overhaul, remade into a good-enough machine to negotiate California's rocky election highways in 1958.

That test was two years away, of course, a lot depending on how the Republicans handled their steadily increasing state power in the interim. There seemed to be signs of preliminary disagreement at top GOP levels, with the question duly noted whether this could be afforded by a party which, though still winning, was really a California minority. Actually, the manner in which the California Republicans had set up their delegation for the Eisenhower-Nixon renominating convention established something of a record in the state's political annals. Nixon, Knowland and Knight each demanded a piece of the 1956 action. The Vice-President was understandably intent on making sure of home state loyalty. Senator Knowland, as it became abundantly clear later, had ideas of his own about the desired course of California GOP affairs. And Goodwin Knight had some claim to party titular leadership as the recently elected governor. None of these men was politically naïve or particularly trustful. Somebody, probably a Democrat who had read a history book, whimsically called the California Republican scrambling of the immediate post-Warren years a pretentious, minor-league version of the breakup of Charlemagne's empire. Everybody with the slightest claim to political inheritance wanted to be the new "emperor of the West."

At any rate, Nixon, Knowland and Knight proceeded to split up the state's pro-Eisenhower convention delegation representatives among themselves, one-third apiece. Their chosen spokesmen gathered in solemn conclave to accomplish this with meticulous care, making sure that exactly 33⅓ per cent of the proposed delegation was politically friendly and acceptable to each of these three aspiring statesmen. The endeavor, however, encountered a problem of simple arithmetic. The state delegation strength that happy Republican year was seventy, a figure which could not be divided precisely by three. So twenty-three loyal delegates were picked on behalf of each of the three leaders. By general consent, the seventieth place on the delegation was given to junior United States Senator Thomas H. Kuchel, a party "moderate" to whom nobody had any objections.

All this rigmarole soon had its tragicomic aftermath. Within two to four years, the "Big Three" of 1956 California Republicanism had been retired to private life, and only Kuchel, among the top-ranking GOP officials of the elaborate enterprise, remained in public office.

26

THE BIG SWITCHEROO

William Fife Knowland of California was the Republican opposite number of Lyndon Baines Johnson of Texas in the 1950s when the latter was Democratic leader of the United States Senate. Knowland went to the Senate in 1945. He became Republican majority leader in 1953 and was minority leader from 1955 through 1958. That latter year he was the moving force and central victim of one of California's recurrent election upheavals, the most devastating political earthquake the state had experienced in a decade and a half. It shook the Republican party to its foundations.

Knowland was an engaging, exceptionally able, straightforward and conservatively-inclined young man in his middle twenties when he first began California political activity as a state assemblyman in 1933. He was the son of Joseph R. Knowland, former congressman, conservationist, long-time Republican leader and the editor-publisher of the Oakland *Tribune,* the most influential newspaper of Alameda County in the San Francisco East Bay district where Earl Warren got his start in politics. Bill Knowland's advancement in legislative politics was steady and, in Republican party affairs, it could better be described as spectacular. He was forging smoothly toward the top at an age when most youngsters are just getting their careers fairly in motion. Having moved up to the State Senate in 1935, the vigorous young legislator reached the Republican National Committee in 1938 when he was only thirty. Two years later he was on that body's Executive Committee and its chairman in 1941 at the age of thirty-three. After Pearl Harbor, Knowland volunteered for the Army, serving first as an enlisted man, then as an officer, for more than three years, eighteen months of that time in Europe. He was still overseas in 1945 when word reached him that he had been appointed by Governor Warren to the United States Senate for the unexpired term of the venerable Senator Hiram Johnson who had died in office after having served continuously since 1917.

The following year, Knowland was elected for a full six-year Senate term of his own. He was re-elected in 1952 with 3,982,448 votes which, at that time and for many years afterward, ranked as the largest vote ever received by any public official in California election history. His prestige climbed further the following year with membership on the Senate Foreign Relations Committee. Concerned with the turn of Far Eastern affairs, marked by the perennial hopes of the Chiang Kai-shek forces ultimately to regain control of the Chinese mainland from the Communist regime, Knowland was sometimes dubbed "the Senator from Formosa" by hostile critics who, at that stage, evidently saw no prospect of American involvement in Asia aside from Korea. In the late summer of 1953, Knowland's stock mounted even higher with his selection as Senate Republican leader. Even then, the party's new floor spokesman was only forty-five. The California Republicans were in clover by the end of that year. One of them was Chief Justice. Another was Vice-President. They had both seats in the United States Senate, Thomas H. Kuchel having succeeded Nixon. Back home, they still held the governorship. All this and more represented their pleasant lot as politicians of a state where the Democrats, in theory anyhow, had the numerical strength to rule. National interest, in Knowland's case, continued to grow as he pursued the busy task of trying to match Senate stratagems with Lyndon Johnson. He was even among those talked about tentatively as a Presidential candidacy possibility in the uneasy days after President Eisenhower's heart attack in 1955 when there was fear, for a time, that the President might be unable or reluctant to run for a second term.

Toward the end of 1957, Senator Knowland, at the peak of his congressional powers, surprised his home state, not to mention political professionals around the country, with the revelation that he intended to give up his Senate Republican leadership and indeed his place in the Senate as well. Although he had ample evidence, on the basis of his last California popularity test, to believe that the voters there would keep him forever, he flatly announced well in advance of 1958 campaign time that he would not stand for re-election. One is tempted to wonder about Knowland's private reasons and to speculate on what his political future in national affairs might have been had he concluded to remain in the Senate where his rise to party leadership status and overall influence had been so swift. That would be idle, though, because it became clear with the opening of the 1958 California election year that the Senator, a quiet, self-contained political figure now approaching the age of fifty, had made up his mind, instead, to return home and try for the governorship. The California Republicans already held that post in the person of Governor Goodwin J. Knight. Furthermore, since 1934, they had made something of a fetish of avoiding intraparty fights, whenever possible, over positions of that magnitude. Nonetheless, Senator Knowland, an outspoken advocate of wide-open primaries, let it be known he proposed to wage an all-out campaign for the gubernatorial nomination, whether Knight sought another term or not.

That decision, coupled with the ensuing repercussions in both parties, produced one of the most acrimonious battles and amazing election upsets in the history of California politics. What the California Republicans did to each other in 1958 was, from the standpoint of election-year pragmatism, virtually unbelievable. If California itself was aghast at the sudden intraparty carnage, the rest of the country found the goings-on utterly inexplicable. One startled observer said at the time that the long-entrenched West Coast Republican party seemed to be undergoing a mass compulsion to commit political hara-kiri. It was, in some sense, a shattering preview of the reverberating collision of GOP moderate and conservative elements which was to come nationally only half a dozen years later with Barry Goldwater's bid for the Presidency.

Many may have been puzzled by Knowland's relinquishment of his party's highest place in the United States Senate to run for governor, but nobody could doubt the blunt sincerity of the conservative approach he brought to that enterprise. Nor could anybody fail to understand the perplexed and then resentful reaction of the more moderate Governor Knight who had established his vote-getting ability in 1954 and already was an avowed candidate for re-election. Senator Knowland set the pattern of the gubernatorial nomination challenge against Knight in his opening campaign tour. Assuming a frankly conservative posture on issues generally, he set off a whole package of political firecrackers by endorsing antilabor "right to work" legislation. This, in simplified form, was the concept that nobody should be compelled to join a labor union in order to hold a job. The effect, so laborites hastened to point out, would be to outlaw union shop contracts. Since labor leaders had fought for years for the union shop, with its contractual recognition of the right to unionize employees, they were quickly up in arms against any proposed measure which would nullify this by rendering trade-union membership unnecessary as a qualification for job-holding. It was the kind of proposal against which Governor Knight claimed to have warned President Eisenhower, calling it highly dangerous to the Republican party, particularly if sponsored by that party in California. Beyond that, it flew in the face of Knight's happy and effective political alliance with organized labor to retain the governorship for the GOP against the somewhat clumsily surging Democrats only four years previously. With strong feelings on the subject, Senator Knowland stood his ground on the issue stubbornly.

Angry at Knowland's invasion of his political domain, Knight said unequivocally that he had no intention of stepping aside for the Senator or anybody else. He fired off a number of other sharp blasts, too. In what was perhaps the harshest and longest-remembered of these, he accused Knowland of seeking the California governorship as a political steppingstone to a Presidential candidacy later on. Whereupon moderate and conservative Republicans, not to speak of the state's generally elated Democrats, promptly chose up sides for Armageddon. This encounter of determined personalities and ambitions developed, with peculiar timing, at a moment when the Republicans, though in second place numerically, held all of California's statewide constitutional offices except one. From the viewpoint of party-splitting possibilities, it was a hazardous business. With a wary eye on the Democratic vote potential, particularly in the circumstance of this threatened GOP division, the Republican state leadership began desperate maneuvers to avert a direct Knight-Knowland confrontation. The prevailing idea in some influential circles seemed to be that Governor Knight ought to drop his re-election candidacy. Unwilling to be pushed aside, Knight retorted with further lively bombardments of Knowland, roundly berating the Senator's campaign tactics and motives.

Senator Knowland said later, with some emphasis, that he had no personal part in efforts to bring about Knight's withdrawal. Noting his complete belief in the direct primary system, Knowland explained he had launched his candidacy with every expectation of contending at the nomination polls with the incumbent governor. Strong pressures, nonetheless, actually were brought to bear on Knight to bow out of the contest. These came from Republican sources obviously preferring the Knowland brand of Republicanism and certainly favoring the Knowland candidacy. The backing, financial and otherwise, which Governor Knight ordinarily could have expected in support of his renomination endeavor began to slide away from him. It soon appeared clear that his primary campaign, if he insisted on going through with it, would have to be made under a tremendous handicap. That spring was a trying time for Knight. He scurried around trying to mend his political fences. He renewed his fulminations against Knowland. From both camps, in fact, came an array of broadsides which continued to echo for the rest of the year. Perhaps Knight had a presentiment that California voters, in that political season at least, would shy away from the Knowland conservatism, even if the Senator achieved the GOP endorsement. In any case, Knight's own political future was on the line, and he was reluctant to give up the career he had built so carefully over so long a time.

The embattled Governor, beset with more headaches than his supply of aspirin could cope with, disappeared to a desert hideaway to ponder his mounting problems and, if possible, find a way out of his dilemma. It was not easy. Eventually, he took his troubles to Washington, D.C., for a talk with Vice-President Nixon whom he had been so slow to endorse for a second term only two years before. This consultation apparently provided him with very little comfort. Almost immediately, an astonishing solution was devised—a kind of political status trade. Surrendering to circumstances beyond his control, the Governor who had won so handsomely in 1954 was prevailed upon to give up his re-election attempt and accept a hastily improvised political accommodation which became known in California that year as "the Big Switcheroo." It amounted to a reluctant abdication. Knowland would be the unopposed Republican candidate for governor, insofar as a major primary adversary was concerned; Knight would run for United States Senator; the two would simply switch jobs, or at least try to. This arrangement was followed by speedy reports of endorsement by Vice-President Nixon. The rest of the Republican state ticket found itself in a state of more or less shocked confusion. Most of the GOP's constitutional office incumbents, whether friendly to Knight or Knowland, took care not to become involved with the Senator's controversial "right to work" position.

The Republican primary was held in an atmosphere of artificial harmony. Senator Knowland was nominated to run for governor that fall against Democratic Attorney-General Edmund G. (Pat) Brown.

Governor Knight, obtaining the Republican nod for the Senate over long-time San Francisco Mayor George Christopher, was matched against Democratic Congressman Clair Engle. The other principal Republican state officers, several of them State Capitol veterans, were renominated, each of them operating with canny independence in preparation for the autumn runoff election. There was such perfunctory politeness from all hands as party regularity seemed to require, but everybody, including Knowland and Knight, decided to paddle his own canoe through the dangerous waters ahead. With unspoken bitterness still rankling, the situation was as extraordinary as any California had witnessed, particularly in the Republican party, for several decades. Republicans elsewhere, remembering the West Coast victories of 1952, 1954 and 1956, not counting the impressive string of Warren successes before that, probably shuddered a little. As for California, the old GOP championship team limped toward the November showdown disorganized and in extremely bad shape. Republican morale had seldom been lower, with precious little time to patch up the wounds and repair the damage.

The Republican collapse of 1958 turned California over to the Democrats and started the long incumbency of Governor Edmund G. (Pat) Brown. When volatile California decides it is time for a political change, there is seldom much advance notice. It often comes with the unexpected violence of a volcanic eruption. Both in tactics and on issues, the Republicans of 1958 misjudged the temper of the state. Democrat Brown, then in his second term as state attorney-general, timed his campaign for the governorship perfectly. Though the Republicans had been living for years on the side of a smoldering mountain of latent Democratic vote strength, they had been winning elections comfortably—first under Earl Warren, then Knight—for a decade and a half, largely through an attractive show of reasonably progressive tendencies. They beat themselves in the Knowland-Brown campaign by abandoning that formula. Outspoken conservatism had had its California seasons, and would again, but this was not one of them.

Knowland's declaration in favor of a "right to work" enactment brought labor roaring into the fight on the side of the Democrats. Knight's reluctant withdrawal of gubernatorial candidacy to run for the United States Senate seat he only half wanted tended to tarnish the GOP "leadership image," as political technicians like to phrase it these days. There was sympathy for the repudiated Governor in many quarters, admixed with a feeling he should have damned his detractors a little louder and refused to capitulate. On balance, the switched candidacy "deal" hurt the Republican cause. Originally, of course, Knight had done quite a bit of damning, especially of Knowland. The Democrats had carefully preserved a record of these preprimary epithets and now replayed them full volume. It was not necessary for the Democrats to indulge in much general election name-calling. They simply publicized what the Republicans had been indiscreetly saying about each other.

Then, too, there was heavy stress on the allegation that Senator Knowland wanted to be President of the United States. Again drawing on earlier Republican utterances, the Democrats let no opportunity pass to suggest that the governorship was merely an intended brief stopping-place for the Senator, a kind of White House launching pad. Although the grim sincerity with which Knowland pushed his chosen issues was apparent, it was equally plain that, from the standpoint of the Democratic strategists, he was to be made the bête noire of the campaign. And lest there be a repetition of the Democratic vote defections from which GOP candidates had profited in past California elections, the conservative aspects of Knowland's pronouncements were singled out and heavily underscored.

Brown proved to be an excellent standard-bearer for the Democrats in this type of contest. He was untainted by either right-wing or left-wing extremist background. Like Earl Warren, he had emerged politically by the district attorney and attorney-general route. He was an old law-enforcement man and a devout Roman Catholic. In his youth, in fact, he had been a Republican. Brown and Knowland resembled each other somewhat in platform technique in that both were plain talkers, rather than oratorical spellbinders; both came through to their audiences as earnest, serious men, with little reliance on rhetorical witticisms; both projected considerable warmth of personality in private conversations, Brown rather more so before campaign crowds. The Democratic nominee offered himself as an exponent of liberalism, carefully qualified by the adjective "responsible." Conscious of having wound up on the short end so many times before in California, the designers of Democratic electioneering procedures that year were intent on steering a middle course as closely as possible, with perhaps an occasional judicious detour along the side roads of sensible progressivism. If they could hold together the wayward elements of their party's registered vote majority, victory was a certainty. If they could pick up a few disgruntled Republicans along the way, so much the better.

These, meantime, were hectic days for the Republicans. Some of their major candidates were privately at loggerheads with others. The Knight adherents were unenthusiastic about Knowland. The old-line conservatives were fervent in their response to the governorship candidate's delineation of issues, but the bulk of the party's lesser nominees seemed to want no part of Knowland's "right to work" proposition and side-stepped the subject as gracefully as possible. The party was grievously split. For the first time since Governor Merriam's defeat back in 1938, the old Republican professional touch was missing.

The 1958 general election was a complete Republican debacle. Knowland, who had polled nearly 4,000,000 votes in 1952, lost the governorship battle to Brown by a margin of more than 1,000,000. Democratic Congressman Engle defeated Knight for Senator by better than 700,000. The outgoing governor had the small satisfaction of having run a somewhat closer race than the head of his ticket did. The State Legislature, safely Republican for years in one house or the other, sometimes both, went Democratic. The proportions of the landslide were best illustrated by what happened to the Republican state constitutional officers below the rank of governor and

185

United States Senator. When the campaign opened, all these posts were in GOP hands except for Democrat Brown's attorney-generalship. After the votes were counted, the Democrats had every one of them, save for the job of veteran Republican Secretary of State Frank M. Jordan who somehow managed to weather the storm. So finally the Democrats, for the second time in the century, were in the saddle, after one of the most thoroughgoing reversals of public sentiment which reasonably balanced two-party politics, even in unguessable California, had seen up to that time.

27

"RESPONSIBLE LIBERALISM"

California's unique political mechanism was overhauled, almost as a first order of business, after Governor Edmund G. (Pat) Brown reached the executive mansion. The Democrats, exultantly in control of both the administration and the State Legislature, unceremoniously abolished the primary election cross-filing system which derisive critics east of the Sierra Nevada had been calling a grotesque arrangement and the chief cause of California's political flightiness for nearly fifty years.

Under the "new enlightenment," multiple nominations as the road to political glory were ruled out for the first time since the almost-forgotten chiefdom of Hiram Johnson. Nine governors had lived and ruled under this exceptional plan. Each candidate for partisan office now could seek the primary endorsement of only one party, his own. The revised law made each party primary a closed affair. With the death of cross-filing, the Democrats bade a resounding farewell to the legalized nonpartisanship of Johnson, Warren, Knight and all the governors in between. They proclaimed a political regime of "party responsibility," a California conformity with the rest of the country, at least in restricted nominating procedures. What remained to be seen, of course, was how all this would affect the party-bolting habits of California's turbulent and mercurial population once the nominations had been settled. It was, as the populace soon demonstrated, still a state of political freethinkers.

With the election code rewritten, Governor Brown, a bespectacled, bluff, friendly man, evidently dedicated to political and governmental accomplishments in a hurry, waded into a large and varied assortment of other programs with feverish zeal. His 1959 legislative record, for volume and scope of enactments in a single session, came to be compared favorably, in his own party anyway, with that of Hiram Johnson in 1911. The new Governor was a great admirer of Johnson and Warren, especially of the latter with whom he soon struck up a cordial relationship, despite their difference of party membership, somewhat similar to the personal friendliness which had existed for years between Warren and Harry Truman. Taking his campaign catch-phrase "responsible liberalism" with immense seriousness, Brown tackled the issue of racial discrimination, putting through California's first Fair Employment Practices Commission law and moving to outlaw discriminatory restrictions in restaurants, other public accommodations and publicly-assisted housing establishments. Working with Democratic majorities in his first general legislative session and that of 1961, the new executive wiped out an inherited multimillion-dollar State Treasury deficit, revised the tax system with an increase of rates, balanced the budget, obtained increased pensions and workers' social insurance benefits, established a master plan for higher education, provided for expanded university and state college physical plants, inaugurated a twenty-year $10.5 billion freeway development plan, broadening the earlier Warren work in that respect, and undertook other programs in many fields, ranging from smog control and consumer market-place protection to public school construction planning below the college level to handle an anticipated jump of 200,000 California students every year. Before long, he also had won authorization for state construction and operation of a vast new water conservation and redistribution project.

This enterprise and the political difficulties which delayed its realization for so long a time will be dealt with later on in more detail.

Brown, the politician, had his ups and downs, meanwhile. His honeymoon days with the State Legislature were happy but brief. He had cheers from John F. Kennedy for impressively "preparing to meet tomorrow's challenges" in government. Denunciations as a well-intentioned but inveterate bungler were heaped on him by his political enemies of whom he had quite a number. Even in his own party, Governor Brown succeeded in stirring up a hotbed of opposition with his recurrent insistence on the abolition of capital punishment, a subject on which he had deep convictions. The whole country, in fact, took note of the Governor's death-row reprieve of the convict writer Caryl Chessman, found guilty of a particularly vicious sex crime, and the simultaneous urgent request that the Legislature, during this stay of execution, consider wiping out the death penalty in California altogether. This plea was summarily rejected. It was later conceded in administration circles that the Chessman case had seriously damaged Brown's prestige. Brown belonged unreservedly to the group, quite evidently not a political majority in California at that time, which condemned capital punishment as a barbarous practice and contended it was not a crime deterrent.

The Democratic effort to restore strict partisanship in California, after half a century of carefree political jockeying across party lines, had its backlash, too. The minority Republicans, especially in the Legislature, were compelled to organize tightly and function as a unit, if only for political self-preservation. There was a certain effectiveness in this on legislative issues, such as the growing state budget, which required a two-thirds vote for settlement. The GOP bloc took dead aim at the man in the governor's chair, frequently causing Brown more discomfiture in that regard than any of his predecessors had suffered perhaps in decades, at least since the Olson Democratic administration of the late 1930s and early 1940s. The new-found power of the Democrats, acquired so suddenly after so many lean years, inevitably produced its party cliques and factions, too, in the budding 1960s, not to mention a breed of young, aspiring leaders beginning to maneuver for advancement and clamor for political recognition. All this gave Brown his share of disappointments and often caused his native geniality to wear thin.

On the whole, however, California's thirty-second governor proved to be an earnest, tireless, sometimes mistakenly impulsive kind of man who seemed to be judged with harshness by some and generosity by others, largely depending on the political attitudes of the beholders, frequently on the basis of personal reactions without much apparent concern for the relevancy of his governmental record. He may have been surprised to find himself so controversial. His detractors condemned him as flounderingly unskillful in political maneuver. His friends professed to find him essentially modest, much more prone to questioning self-evaluation than most politicians, as he struggled to provide leadership to a many-phased, subtly evolving state which was moving, in his administration, toward national leadership. He appeared to be trying, these friendly ones concluded, to be "responsible" as well as "liberal." It may have helped a good bit that he was an incurable optimist. As for those in the rest of America who watched, it is probable they thought of Brown, in those days, chiefly as the fellow who had beaten Senate Republican Leader William F. Knowland to a frazzle, as the first California Democratic chief executive in a very long time and as the governor who had put an end to that "silly cross-filing business." Now, at least in the hopeful thinking of Eastern politicians, California could be counted upon to settle down to a sensible orthodoxy, its past eccentricities forgiven, its future behavior nicely manageable. Old California hands knew all too well that complacency in that direction ran the risk of unexpected political booby-traps.

In fact, Brown and the California Democrats stepped on one in 1960. California, still young at heart, may have resented the rumor she was becoming a sweet old lady whose gay flirtatious ways had been abandoned for good. That is as good an explanation as any of why, having smothered the Democrats with wine and roses in

1958, she danced off with another partner entirely the very next political season.

The state's self-confident Democrats were nonplussed, in early 1960, by the array of eager young men around the nation who offered to become President when Eisenhower's second term ended. Governor Brown still had a lingering affection for Adlai Stevenson, but was discouraged, along with a lot of other solicitous politicians, by Adlai's reluctance to say or do anything overtly to help get himself a third Democratic nomination. Stevenson was to say later, at the time of the Democratic national convention, that he would have thought it an impertinence to thrust himself forward as an active seeker of renomination after having been twice beaten for the Presidency. As for the party's other willing candidates, the Democrats of California, early on at least, were unsure of their preference and united chiefly in opposition to Richard M. Nixon, the Californian whom the Republicans were almost certain to nominate.

Up to the time of the crucial 1960 West Virginia primary, the Far Western Democratic liberals were extremely fond of Hubert Humphrey of Minnesota whose drop-of-the-hat oratorical skills entranced them. In more conservative circles, there was a leaning toward Lyndon Johnson and Stuart Symington, though neither had much of a following. At that early stage, strangely, John F. Kennedy seemed to be favorably noted in the state more for his youthful, self-assured drive and the coordinated expertise of his campaigning organization than for other qualities which ultimately attracted millions to his banner. From the start, though, Kennedy's corps of electioneering helpers had a close eye on California, in particular on the vote concentrations of Los Angeles, where Assembly Speaker Jesse M. Unruh, an emerging Democratic power, had enlisted in their crusade. It was the eventual decision of the state's Democratic leaders to send a broadly representative but actually unpledged delegation to the national convention. There was a technical commitment to Governor Brown as a favorite son, the Governor making it plain he would release the delegates when the nomination balloting began. The genuine Presidential aspirants all concluded to take their chances with this local arrangement and skip the California primary. So the Brown slate prevailed handily, but not without more than 600,000 votes going to an eleventh-hour rival ticket headed by George McLain, a Los Angeles pension-plan promoter widely admired by California's "senior citizens."

When Governor Brown's aggregation reached Los Angeles for the national convention, the political fur began to fly almost immediately. Brown finally announced his personal endorsement of Senator Kennedy and attempted, almost at the last minute, to lead his delegates into that camp. He found himself confronted by an annoying revolt of Adlai Stevenson supporters. The delegation was obviously of two minds. To Governor Brown, a former Stevenson man, now working for the Kennedy cause, this development was more than a little embarrassing. His own lieutenant-governor, Glenn M. Anderson, lined up with those prepared to do and die for Adlai. The "We-want-Adlai" chant of demonstrators outside the convention hall, plus Stevenson's somewhat hesitant consent to the presentation of his name, added in no small measure to the California hullabaloo. Stevenson undoubtedly realized he had no real chance. The Kennedy bandwagon, even then, was beginning to roll toward the nomination. Brown was accused of being unable to control his own delegates. Before victory finally came to Kennedy, in fact, the huge California delegation, one of the convention's largest, was obliged to conduct an open caucus roll call in which a hard core of Stevensonites said their piece and even a vote or two went to Johnson and Symington. The Californians could hardly claim much credit for the Massachusetts Senator's triumph, or for the fateful selection of Lyndon Johnson to run for Vice-President. A few of them could boast of their independence, but in the managerial acumen department, so important to political professionals, their score was pretty low.

For the Californians at the subsequent Republican national convention, it was quite another story. They represented—or thought they did—the native state of the next President. Vice-President

Nixon, naturally enough, had been unopposed in the California GOP primary. All Nixon's fellow Californians had to do was lead the convention cheering when the time came to nominate him. Nothing of any great moment marred the serene contentment of the West Coast visitors, or any others, for that matter. There was, to be sure, the so-called "Truce of Fifth Avenue," the compromise between Nixon and Nelson Rockefeller over wording of the Republican platform. And Barry Goldwater was on hand, contending manfully for more conservatism. But neither the Nixon Californians nor the Rockefeller moderates seemed to have any idea at that time that Goldwater and his notions would ever amount to much—perhaps least of all the Californians who would be yelling for the Arizona Senator from the housetops only four years later.

As the state's majority party, comfortably on top both in prestige and voter registrations, the California Democrats entered the Nixon-Kennedy general election contest with considerable aplomb. The head of their state ticket, only two years before, had won by more than one million votes. By any reasonable rule of calculation, they had nothing to worry about. Obviously, there were pockets of Nixon strength south of the Tehachapi, in the vote center of populous Los Angeles County, say, or in nearby Orange County where Republicanism was reputed to be a way of life. But the Democrats had a kind of Prince Charming for a candidate, a smiling, cleancut young fellow who could barnstorm through California to immense and spontaneous acclaim. One quick look at the televised "Great Debate" that fall eliminated all doubt from the thinking of the Democratic hierarchy. And, furthermore, Jesse Unruh and his well-trained aides were supposed to have even the southern California situation well in hand. On election night, the Democratic sense of regional security was reinforced as state after state, including some of the big ones, appeared to be heading safely toward the Kennedy column. On the western edge of the continent, California closed its polls later than most and, simply because of time zones, its vote count ran a little behind the rest of the country. But early precinct reports that night looked all right for Kennedy.

In the last analysis, California proved again, if anybody needed proof, that its heart is restless and a wee bit sentimental. Its much maligned native son, as the vote tally continued, was running a bit closer than the Democrats had reckoned possible. About a week later, when all the outlying precincts in the geographically massive state had reported and the absentee vote had been accounted for, it turned out that more than 6.5 million votes had been cast, that registration tables had been tossed out the window and that the Republicans had carried the state by something like 35,000. Kennedy was the new President, but California's thirty-two electoral votes were solemnly recorded that year for Richard M. Nixon.

28

A MAN-MADE RIVER

Governor Edmund G. Brown often said that the California Water Program, along with the "master plan" for higher education, ranked as one of the chief accomplishments of his gubernatorial incumbency. Some other politician, long before that, had called water "the lifeblood of California." Political speechmakers have been reusing the phrase ever since, almost as automatically as they borrow from the Gettysburg Address. It is a fairly accurate declaration, if a little fancy, in a technically semiarid state such as California, with its unusual length and marked climatic and geographical variations. There is a remarkable difference between some of the northern localities of heavy seasonal rainfall and the low-water-table areas and even desert regions of the south. Winter flood threats and the dangers of summer drought are not peculiar to California, but such problems are aggravated far beyond most other places by size and peculiar local conditions.

The critical nature of this situation was recognized for many decades, almost since American colonization, yet no remedy of a broad and general character was undertaken with statewide approval until the authorization of the Central Valley Project, during the Rolph administration in the 1930s. This contemplated, primarily, the harnessing of the Sacramento River, and later its tributary streams, to prevent floods, control salinity, conserve water for dry-season domestic and irrigation uses, develop hydroelectric power, facilitate navigation and, insofar as possible, reshift surplus water supplies from counties of plenty to districts of severe shortage. It has been described earlier, in a brief way, how the proposed public generation of hydroelectric energy originally aroused stiff opposition to the plan by the privately owned light and power corporations, necessitating a statewide referendum vote for approval of the project legislation; and also how, with state bond sales difficult in depression times, the CVP was taken over and constructed, in the New Deal days and afterward, by the United States Bureau of Reclamation. Thus came the mighty Shasta Dam on the upper Sacramento and eventually the American River's Folsom Dam, along with a series of conduits, canals, pumping plants and other installations for conservation, water transfer, recreation, flood control and related purposes.

It was a remarkable public enterprise, not accomplished without considerable political warfare. Special interests engaged in private production and sale of power resented state or federal intrusion in this field. An argument of the day, among sponsors of the CVP and similar ventures, was that the multipurpose dams and elaborate works which the economy of the West required—not limited to power generation by any means—were of such magnitude that no agency other than governmental was in any position to realize them. They had to be built publicly, it was contended, or never built at all.

It took only a decade or so to demonstrate that even the widespread Central Valley Project was inadequate, or soon would be, to cope with the many-faceted needs of California's industrial and agricultural expansion and its multiplying population. California's "lifeblood" was reaching some of its parts in the merest trickle. To speed and regulate the flow, planning began for a new state government-owned and -operated project of immense potentialities for which the CVP would be, in effect, the prototype. Development of the Trinity River in the extreme north was a new part of the federal program.

Now the state government proposed the Oroville Dam on the Feather River, another stream rising in the Sierra Nevada and flowing into the Sacramento. This Feather River Project involved an intricate plan for water transfer hundreds of miles downstate, eventually carrying northern surpluses beyond the Tehachapi Mountains and into southern California where available Colorado River water was admittedly insufficient to deal with the future demands of ceaseless migration.

Regional bickering commenced almost immediately. Few states are big enough to encounter the drastic differences of interest and opinion which periodically rocked northern and southern California. It was nearly a hundred years since the pre-Civil War scheme to divide California at the Tehachapi into two separate states. The proposal had been renewed from time to time, almost always by angry sectionalists locked in seemingly interminable political dispute. It was practically inevitable that somebody would suggest it again in this new north-south quarrel, with the customary negative result. It was equally likely that family jealousies would erupt into noisy rows with monotonous regularity. In this case, northern California's primary areas of water origin were reasonably willing to share surpluses with less fortunate south-central and southern sections of the state but were insistent on elaborate safeguards for their own protection. They considered this seasonal water abundance their birthright. And what, they asked, was a genuine surplus? There was a stubborn northern reluctance to enter into any water redistribution commitments which might leave the "counties of origin" with allotments too meager for their own development in the years ahead. Southern California, on the other hand, wanted dependable guarantees in this conplex plan that excess northern waters actually would reach the teeming population and undersupplied lands below the Tchachapi. With a majority of the state's voters and taxpayers living in that region, so the argument ran, such contractual assurances were imperative before the South would give its approval to the Feather River Project. The threat of a southern veto hung over the whole endeavor.

This controversy, with innumerable side issues, raged for years in the State Legislature. Regional mistrust and obstinacy resulted in a long chain of parliamentary stalemates. The possibility of compromise appeared remote. No agreement was reached during the considerable span of Earl Warren's state regime or during the shorter administration of Goodwin Knight, though it was not from lack of trying. Formula after formula underwent scrutiny, only to bog down in a morass of intersectional disagreement and political acrimony. A break-through finally came in the early years of "Pat" Brown's governorship. A solution inviting enough to end the deadlock was not easy to devise, since it not only involved reconciling bitter regional and political prejudices in the Legislature but, in terms of financing, also required statewide voter acquiescence. As the upshot of much tortuous maneuvering, California finally authorized the Feather River Project and $1.75 billion in bonds to pay for it, one of the largest issues ever floated by a single state for conservation of natural resources.

The Democratic executive confidently pictured the California Water Plan, obviously more far-reaching than anything of its kind his administration had done up to that time, as "insuring Southern California growth, while protecting Northern California water rights." No sooner had dirt been turned for the huge Oroville Dam, in Butte County where the Feather River roars down through its mountain canyon, than even greater California population and industrial expansion estimates set engineers and planners at the task of mapping still broader developments. It was calculated that in the decades ahead the Eel River and other untapped northern waterways also would have to be harnessed in a continuing effort to keep "lifeblood" coursing through the complicated and maturing California organism. Ultimately, if all went well, these artificial water preservation and redistribution facilities were expected to stretch from the Oregon border country in the north to the international boundary of Mexico. It would be, Governor Brown said proudly, the world's longest "man-made river."

The water problem, however, was only one aspect of an exasperating regionalism which tried the wits of the state's politicians. While California, in the 1960s, led the nation in number of people—with prideful between-census estimates running from around 19,000,000 to upward of 20,000,000—political and governmental management appeared to be growing substantially more difficult than in much smaller geographic entities with denser and more uniform population per given land unit. California provided a remarkable amount of territory for people to rattle around in. Even though urban concentrations were on the increase, the scattering of population over the rural and semirural areas of this immense commonwealth made governmental effectiveness a less than comfortable pursuit and rendered political communication a perplexing, costly and sometimes haphazard business.

The geography of California was made to order for diverse, regional ways of life. A look at its map and its fifty-eight chief political sub-divisions shows an east-west mountainous ridge in the north, dividing its upper tier of counties from the valley floor. The Coast Range on the west separates the Pacific coastal shore from the Sacramento and San Joaquin valleys. These, in turn, are actually one vast prairie-like terrain extending down the middle of the state for more than half its length and bounded on the east by the towering Sierra Nevada. Another cross-state range, the Tehachapi Mountains, boxes in the lower end of the central valley and cuts off southern California from the state's upper two-thirds. This merely accounts for some of the principal natural barriers which stand between strikingly dissimilar regions. The topography is wildly incongruous. It ranges, for example, from the 14,495-foot elevation of Mt. Whitney, highest in the United States until Alaska was admitted to statehood, to the country's lowest spot, Death Valley, only ninety miles away and 282 feet below sea level.

By the 1960s, new Californians, making up a large part of the population and arriving from almost everywhere, not only reflected the oddities of their original environments but differed regionally in their adopted state to a surprising extent. In outlook, mores and even physical appearance, San Francisco and Los Angeles were poles apart, and had been almost from their beginnings. Admirers of style and charm professed love at first sight for "the City by the Golden Gate," yet Los Angeles, fascinated with its own forms of excellence, continued to attract literally millions, as evidenced by the fact that this constantly booming metropolitan area alone was able to claim something like 40 per cent of all California's registered voters.

California's extreme north and extreme south, along with most of the regions in between, entertained contradictory points of view on many things, not excepting politics on frequent occasions. There was, in fact, an active north-south rivalry for governmental power. Despite urbanization, an older, slower manner of existence often prevailed in the mountain counties and other remote areas, coupled with some of the judgments and opinions of an earlier California. The valley farmlands and foothill cattle country had little or nothing in common with, say, the southern oil fields, Carmel's art and tourism concerns or the recreational preoccupations of some of the other coastal towns or high mountain resort villages. Fashionable Beverly Hills and the Negro ghetto of Watts obviously were far apart in affluence and cultural advantages, though both were included in sprawling Los Angeles County. And it is safe to say that, in some upstate valley communities, so-called typical characters from around Hollywood and Vine would have felt completely out of place and easily could have aroused much the same suspicious antipathy as they might on Boston Common. All of which is to suggest that California, a little past mid-century, was the seat of miscellaneous tastes, prejudices and reactions, at marked interregional variance.

All this made for political confusion. What might bedazzle the citizenry of one district frequently was received with resentful displeasure elsewhere. It became commonplace practice for individual candidates to hire public opinion samplers for pseudoscientific researching of local conditions and unorthodox sentiments. Even then, voter behavior in different localities was hard to prophesy. To win a statewide election, the need to capture the fancy of southern California was accepted increasingly as a hard fact of political life. One of the few feasible alternatives was to split the southern vote power, gaining a standoff south of the Tehachapi, and then depend on the north to carry the day. Success in that case, whether for office seekers or ballot measures, usually required a strongly united vote in San Francisco, its adjacent populous counties and the two large interior valleys.

The importance of television grew enormously, though political managers, buying as much time as their budgets would stand, sometimes had reason to wonder whether their candidates were attaining actual idea communication through this medium or merely questionable screen exposure in living rooms irritated by the cancellation of regular entertainment programs. At all events, a much greater premium came to be placed on displaying orators with good looks, personality, soft-sell TV voices and a more infectious smile than Nixon exhibited in 1960. That development alone may have prompted Movieland to begin producing actor-candidates as an industrial by-product.

In addition to intersectional rivalries and idiosyncrasies, racial problems eventually came along, too, to plague the eager, would-be shapers of California's future. Ethnic groups, not such a serious California election factor in earlier years as they were in some of the older Eastern states, became so in later times, particularly with growing Negro elements in the population and an emphasis on civil rights. Japanese-Americans and Chinese citizens, some of the latter with California family backgrounds running back to the Gold Rush days, also assumed a larger share of political significance. In any well-run California campaign, there was always at least one rally in San Francisco's famous Chinatown, locally hailed as the largest outside the Orient. On such gala occasions, electioneering posters were oftentimes printed in two languages. In one of Dick Nixon's streamlined campaign efforts some years ago, this practice was applauded as a stroke of genius until it was discovered that a political ringer had invaded the rally, carrying a large placard which set forth in Chinese a variety of arguments why Nixon ought to be defeated. As for Californians of Latin ancestry, it had been a long time since Leo Carrillo, the stage and movie actor, traveled the state with Earl Warren in the governorship campaign of 1942, delivering ringing speeches in all the hamlets where his forebears had been early settlers long before the American conquest. Warren said gratefully afterward that there appeared to be few places in California where the old Carrillo family or some of its close relatives had not lived at one time or another. As the years advanced, however, the descendants of the one-time Spanish-Mexican rulers of California found themselves far outnumbered by latecomers of Anglo-Saxon or other non-Latin European antecedents, and presently they were treated by most political tacticians, albeit politely, as simply another racial minority.

With all these considerations, many of them peculiar to California electioneering usages, it was a clever politician who could keep all the balls in the air at once. And it was extremely costly. There were records of a single major statewide office seeker spending more than $500,000 simply to be nominated. It was unofficially calculated that overall disbursements on both principal party tickets, appealing to between seven million and eight million enrolled voters, could run in excess of $7,000,000 at a state primary and that $10,000,000 might be a fair prognostication of two-party expenditure sprees in modern-day general-election runoff campaigning. Raising that kind of money was fast becoming one of the nightmares of California politics. It was even more difficult for the public to get a reasonable inkling of where the money came from. California's election fund reporting law was never a paragon of either virtue or candor. Candidates customarily listed overall amounts of contributions, as required by statute, sometimes told how such funds were spent but very seldom revealed in thorough detail precisely who put up the hard cash and how much in each instance. A so-called "Purity of Elections" law, requiring completely open disclosure of all political money collections and the specific sources, without evasion, often was urged in the State Legislature, rather loudly by Governors Olson, Warren and Brown. Over the years somehow, for obscurely explained reasons, these proposals regularly fell by the wayside without enactment.

29

RETURN OF THE NATIVE

Richard M. Nixon came back to his native California and the careful consideration of his political future a few months after his unsuccessful 1960 candidacy for the Presidency. His position in some sense resembled that of another one-time California Republican candidate, John Charles Frémont, after the Presidential campaign of 1856, or perhaps that of Herbert Hoover after 1932. There was this significant difference: Nixon had carried California over John F. Kennedy, whereas Frémont had lost it to Buchanan, and Hoover, after one term in the White House, had been beaten in his adopted state as well as in the nation by Roosevelt. Moreover, in 1961, Nixon was still a very young man, as politicians go—only forty-eight. He would be barely fifty-one at the next Presidential election of 1964 and in his mid-fifties even in 1968.

The course which Nixon followed in California might very well have an important effect on Republican party national decisions and arrangements. Supporters of the former Vice-President, both in his home state and among national Republican leaders to a considerable extent, advanced the thesis early in 1961 that Nixon ought to run for the California governorship the following year. The basis for this was a widely held conclusion that Nixon, though technically the titular national chieftain of the GOP, needed the strength and prestige of the governorship, or some similar elective public position, as a springboard for political recovery. He required a new victory, it was thought, as an eye-catching demonstration of electioneering muscle. A solid base of operations, such as California, was considered essential to his career. Those of that mind evidently felt it would be difficult, if not impossible, for a national politician, even a former Vice-President, to retain the country's favorable attention in the limited roll of practicing attorney and private citizen. The implied suggestion, in short, was that the rejected Presidential nominee go out and get himself a new reputation.

Looking back on 1961, there appears to have been a broad variance between Nixon's intentions, as originally announced at any rate, and the political action which eventually he was impelled to take some months later. Early that spring, he revealed that he had assured the State Legislature's Republican leaders he did not propose to be a candidate for governor. With most of the older Republican state officials eliminated in the Democratic landslide of 1958, the opportunity to help shape party affairs had fallen to a younger group of GOPers in the Legislature, some of whom entertained ambitions for higher honors. Among them was Assembly Republican floor leader Joseph C. Shell, a pleasant forty-three-year-old conservative who had captained the University of Southern California Rose Bowl champions of 1939. Shell was beginning to look wistfully at the governor's chair. Expressing warm praise for all such GOP aspirants, along with confident predictions that some Republican would emerge to beat Democratic Governor Brown, Nixon recommended that those with ambitions get out and campaign and give the public a chance to evaluate them. His own purpose and obligation in 1962, explained Nixon, would be to practice law, speak out on issues, give leadership to the Republican party and devote such time as he could to campaigning for Republican candidates in his native state and nationally. "I have told the legislators," Nixon informed the press, "that I am not a candidate and that I have no intention to be a candidate or institute a draft to be a candidate."

If this was perhaps less than "a Sherman-like statement" of governorship candidacy disavowal, as somebody pointed out, the former Vice-President observed that his intentions were clear, nonetheless, and that he had no expectation of any change of feeling. As to whether he might be a candidate for President in 1964 or 1968, he told questioners, only future events could determine that. It was his belief that trying to calculate the political situation four or eight years in advance usually pointed up a lack of knowledge of history and of the American people. If the times are not right for a man, he indicated, he hasn't a prayer. Immediate California interest centered on the governorship, however, and political reporters importuned Nixon to say whether he might not consider the possibility of running, after all, if other available Republicans appeared unlikely to make the grade. "I am not trying to institute a draft," he repeated. "People are not drafted unless they want to be." Assemblyman Shell promptly predicted Nixon would be subjected to strong pressures to enter the California campaign of 1962. "In my own personal opinion," said Shell, "you can't count him out."

This analysis, as it turned out, was quite accurate. Efforts to persuade Nixon that he, and he alone, would be able to unseat Democratic Governor Brown were soon undertaken with almost hectic fervor and on a statewide basis. Zealous Nixonites, especially in southern California, wasted no time in launching public sentiment soundings which, to nobody's surprise, reinforced the proposition that if the Democrats were to be thrown out of their new California power, Nixon was the man to do the job. A distinct pro-Nixon trend was reported. The glamour of the erstwhile Vice-President's eight-year association with Eisenhower was heavily stressed. So was the circumstance of Nixon's narrow-margin home state victory over Kennedy in 1960, a significant happening considering Democratic voter strength in California and herculean exertions by the Democratic state administration to hold the line. Pollsters surmised, after much

205

opinion-testing, that a pronounced carry-over of Nixon popularity could be anticipated in 1962 and that Brown's prospects of combating it successfully were extremely dim. Only two California governors had been re-elected for second four-year terms. Governor Brown, it was argued, was neither a Hiram Johnson nor an Earl Warren. With the approach of campaigning time, Republican groups broke out in an unusual rash of preprimary resolutions and other declarations of loyalty, imploring Nixon to reconsider his earlier position and consent to lead them to a new party renaissance. Whether the Nixon camp encouraged these manifestations of enthusiasm was beside the point. The overall effect was a diligent, businesslike and flattering draft-Nixon movement which any alert and ambitious politician might have found tempting. Nixon finally consented.

You could probably have consulted half a dozen gypsy fortune-tellers and a roomful of horoscope casters in early 1962 without getting a very accurate forecast on Richard M. Nixon's attempted comeback in the political wars. Certainly the auguries, carefully taken by the busy California entourage of the former Vice-President, were entirely favorable to his election as governor. As the entire country looked on with immense interest, optimistic prophecies also were contributed by many Eastern soothsayers. As a matter of fact, Nixon, whether campaigning on his own or as Dwight Eisenhower's running mate, had never lost a California election. Governor Brown, on the other hand, had endured his share of political unhappiness in earlier years and had undergone several prestige-hurting experiences between state elections. Numerous prognosticators spoke of his 1962 chances in ominous tones. All in all, the crystal-ball gazers, notably those of Republican leanings, appeared to regard the impending contest as a probable mismatch between a scintillating and astute political operator and a governor whose style on the hustings was generally unspectacular and sometimes a bit pedestrian.

The June primary election, on the whole, tended to bolster this estimate in the minds of many, though it produced a few peculiarities which inclined some of the professionals to a modicum of caution.

For one thing, it confronted Nixon with a bothersome Republican challenger, Assembly leader Joe Shell. A husky football star and a Navy flier during World War II, Shell was a plain-spoken conservative. Entertaining strong convictions on this subject, he made no public pretense of semi-liberalism at election time. He energetically tackled Nixon for the Republican nomination, evidently undisturbed by Bill Knowland's ill-fated gubernatorial candidacy on a platform of forthright conservatism in 1958. In the post-Warren years, conservative elements had become a steadily increasing factor in California Republicanism. The Knowland setback may have dismayed them but they were very far from silenced by it. Also, in 1962, the doctrines of the John Birch Society were spreading rapidly, although it was only four years old at that time. Shell emphasized that he was not a member of the Birch organization but said he had encountered some fine citizens who were. Nixon did not much like the term "middle of the road," he said, but traditionally had supported nonextreme candidates. He commended the eight-year posture of the Eisenhower administration. There was room, he suggested, though, for differing points of view within the framework of the Republican party which could not, in its quest for renewed strength, afford the luxury of kicking anybody out.

At the primary, Governor Brown polled 1,739,792 Democratic votes for renomination, while Nixon ran up 1,285,151 on the Republican ticket. Against Nixon, GOPer Shell mustered a surprising 656,-542. And there were other nomination balloting intangibles which made the Brown-Nixon autumn runoff hard to figure. Three minor Democratic candidates, for instance, picked up more than 294,000 voters disinclined to support Brown. Thousands of other Democrats, in this first gubernatorial primary without California's old cross-filing system, chose to write in Republican names on their ballots—35,883 for Nixon and 66,712 for Shell. The Governor collected only 5236 GOP write-ins. Roughly speaking, this added up to more than 1,000,-000 voters who had either bolted party lines or defected from one or the other of the two major party nominees. Trying to guess where all these free-swingers would go in November threw the poll takers, computer jockeys and other skilled hands in the political probability field into a tremendous tizzy.

Two tough professional teams met in the general election campaign. The Republicans gave every sign of confidence that, in Nixon, they had their most accomplished master of political strategy since Earl Warren. The Democrats showed no disposition to roll over and play dead at the former Vice-President's trumpeted approach. Neither underestimating Nixon nor admiring him, they prepared for the interparty clash, if not eagerly, at least with reasonable hopefulness. Richard Nixon had a great deal at stake that year and perhaps something to prove, not only to himself and his California backers but to the nation's Republican kingmakers. He swung into battle with vigor, high spirits, seasoned competence and a formidable grasp of electioneering techniques. Along with Nixon's predictable attacks on the Democratic state administration—which the GOP camp pictured as blundering and inept—it was perhaps natural that the former Vice-President should often address himself to the broad general policies and the national and international concerns with which he had become familiar in his extensive Washington experience. Prior to the Presidential election of 1960, he had been away from California for the better part of fourteen years, serving in Congress, the Senate and the national administration. It was the reputation Nixon had gained in his meteoric climb to high officialdom upon which the Republican strategists undoubtedly depended, in large measure, to carry them back into California power. Celebrity intoxication and a fondness for big-name personalities were traits often attributed to Californians. This was the first time a retired Vice-President, a Californian at that, had offered the state his services as governor.

Handicapped at least in this respect, Governor Brown plunged into the fight with dogged determination and an emphasis on what politicians called the "bread and butter" issues. He and his campaigning aides produced a long recitation of claimed achievements since 1959, stressing such things as the California Water Plan, governmen-

tal reorganizations, workers' insurance, the FEPC, anti-crime legislation, higher old-age pensions, expansion of highways, improvement
of public schools and higher education, tighter regulation of retail
credit practices and even crackdowns on cancer-cure quacks and
mortgage and real-estate irregularities. For these and a hatful of
other recounted governmental doings, the administration pamphlet-
eers hammered home the message that full credit belonged to "Pat
Brown and the Democratic Team." A full-voiced Democratic partisan
pitch—accompanied, of course, by a polite tip of the hat to "all the
people of California"—was, in the very nature of things, essential to
Brown's re-election. The 1962 alignment of California voters, on
paper at least, made it equally imperative for Nixon to poll a full
Republican vote, picking up the Shell nomination supporters, and to
siphon off, at the same time, a substantial segment of the state's
Democratic majority. The large bloc of Democratic affiliates who
had deserted Brown at the primary looked promising to the Nixonites.

Then the Governor's supporters dragged in the Presidential issue.
On the apparent theory that old, tried and true political stratagems
are best, the Democrats replayed their anti-Knowland "steppingstone" record of 1958, substituting the name of their latest adversary. The argument that Nixon wanted the governorship chiefly as a
prelude to another shot at the White House blasted out full volume
from one end of California to the other. In contrast, Brown was depicted as a sincere, liberal and able administrator, his soul untroubled
by dreams of loftier grandeur. The hope seemed to be that in the
general hubbub any angry Republican rejoinders would be largely
unheard or disregarded. The Nixonites struck back sharply and often,
and presently lively barrages of invective rained down on both
camps. As the campaign moved toward its climax, the Democrats
erupted in an indignant round of charges that vicious radicalism
"smear" leaflets were being circulated against Brown. The Nixon organization quickly disavowed any connection with such tactics. Governor Brown's campaign machine, toward the end, appeared to be
picking up steam, while Nixon's, for some reason, seemed to be func-

tioning a little less smoothly than California, over a decade and a half, had come to expect. Referring to Nixon's recently published book, *Six Crises,* recounting the challenging episodes of his political life, Brown sympathizers suggested the former Vice-President very well might be in the quagmire of a seventh critical adventure.

At the November election showdown, California underwent another of its swift and mystifying reversals of sentiment. Having embraced Nixon in 1960, it rejected him out of hand in 1962. Democratic Governor Brown was re-elected with 3,037,109 votes. Nixon got 2,740,351. The country's politicians were astonished and the strongholds of Nixon Republicanism more than a little shaken. Brown had accomplished in California what John Kennedy could not. The 296,758 vote margin by which he had dispatched the former Vice-President was not so sweeping as his majority over the United States Senate Republican leader four years earlier, but it was ample and decisive. Governor Brown was hailed, for the next several years anyhow, as something of a political giant-killer. The election outcome eliminated Nixon as a White House renomination possibility in 1964. It changed him from the acknowledged national leader of the Republicans into a temporarily retired and youngish "elder statesman" of the party, with some years of painstaking labor ahead of him if he were to recapture, at long last, his former supereminence. He set about that task with unflagging zeal almost immediately.*

The complexities of t he progressive-conservative confrontation, which divided the Republicans nationally a few years later, and the Democrats too in some regions, were well exemplified in another phase of the 1962 California election. While the two-term Republican Vice-President and almost President was absorbing a painful drubbing at the hands of the Democrats, Republican United States Senator Thomas H. Kuchel, actually Nixon's successor in the Senate,

* Nixon's survival as a nationally recognized political personality was remarkable in the next half decade. In May, 1967, James Reston wrote in the *New York Times* that Nixon, visiting foreign capitals and getting the headlines without saying anything particularly new about world or domestic affairs, had made "a brilliant comeback" and once more was "in the center of the Republican Presidential arena."

won California re-election by a vote of almost three to two. Not only did Senator Kuchel's vote total exceed that of Democratic Governor Brown but his victory margin was also greater.

Tommy Kuchel, fifty-two years old at the time, was a progressively inclined politician who, in ten years of Washington service, had become Senate Republican whip. He was a native of Orange County, generally regarded in the century's middle decades as one of the most conservative areas in California. Like Democrat Brown, Republican Kuchel was an unabashed admirer of Hiram Johnson and Earl Warren and their gubernatorial records. But, by the time Kuchel reached the Senate at the end of 1952, the Johnson influence as an active factor in Republican thinking had almost disappeared, and Warren's final term as governor was nearly over. Among some of the succeeding right-wing groups of the GOP, Senator Kuchel's professed progressive leanings, even cloaked in the new term "moderate," were evidently looked upon as little short of Republican heresy. The extreme conservatives were provoked further, a bit later on, when Kuchel disclosed open disenchantment with such organizations as the John Birch Society and delivered a public excoriation of "fright peddlers."

Several California Republicans, mostly of ultraconservative stripe, undertook to unseat the Senator at the 1962 state primary. The tirades against him were noisy and often baneful, representing him as something less than a proper Republican. Kuchel weathered the primary, although more than 450,000 GOP votes went against him. Nonetheless, the Senator's primary total was slightly higher than the gubernatorial nomination vote received by Nixon, whose skill at avoiding the pitfalls of progressive-conservative controversy within his party was widely recognized and grudgingly admired. It was, accordingly, something of a feather in Kuchel's cap to win so handsomely in November while Nixon was being snowed under. They did not campaign actively together as a Republican team. The obvious cross-voting of Democrats for the Kuchel general-election candidacy was interesting, especially as the Democratic nominee, State Senator Richard Richards of Los Angeles County, had built up a considerable reputation for liberalism. Kuchel was much better known, after more than a quarter of a century in California public life. The extravagance of right-wing attacks on him, in 1962 anyhow, boomeranged in his favor.

Kuchel had started political life as a kind of boy wonder, rivaling Knowland and Nixon in that respect. He was a state assemblyman at twenty-six, a state senator and chairman of the Republican State Central Committee at thirty. He was on his way to a prolonged political career before most people learned to pronounce his name ("Keekle"). After Navy service in World War II, Kuchel was appointed state controller by Governor Warren, twice retaining that post at the polls. Then, when Kuchel was forty-two, Warren named him to the United States Senate after Nixon moved up to the Vice-Presidency. Some years later, the Senate's Republican "moderate" bloc sponsored the Californian as their party's assistant floor leader. In the California Republican high command, following Warren's departure for the Supreme Court, however, Senator Kuchel was accorded no more than junior rank for some time—up until the elections of 1958 and 1960, in fact, when the "Big Three" of the state's GOP officialdom—Knight, Knowland and Nixon—were eliminated from public office.

Well into the middle 1960s, extremists of the political right continued to view senior Senator Kuchel with marked disfavor. Facing another election test in 1968, Kuchel persisted in his "moderate" views, as of early 1967, and showed no signs of relaxing his opposition to extremism. Already preliminary planning was reported under way in hostile circles to put him on the political skids if possible. Kuchel's friends reminded grimly that the last time this had been attempted, 3,180,483 California voters rallied to his rescue.*

It remained for a 1966 press report to add a belated footnote to

* In 1967, with the next general election year more than six months away, members of the conservative-oriented California Republican Assembly and the United Republicans of California began beating the bushes for a like-minded GOPer to run against Kuchel. There was still indignation in their ranks over moderate Senator Kuchel's failure to endorse Barry Goldwater in 1964 and Ronald Reagan in 1966.

California's 1962 election story. A motion-picture actor named Ronald Reagan had begun to concern himself seriously with politics and had taken an interest in that election. Four years later, by now a candidate for governor, Reagan was quoted as saying at a news conference that he had campaigned for the 1962 re-election of Congressman John H. Rousselot, a Los Angeles County Republican. Rousselot, one of two avowed members of the John Birch Society then in the California congressional delegation, was defeated in 1962 by a Democrat and subsequently served as an official of the Birch organization.

30

YEAR OF CONTRADICTIONS

California bounced around in the 1964 Presidential election year like a lopsided tennis ball, confusing many highly-placed national political spectators and taxing the ability of even experienced local *aficionados* to follow the game with any confidence. Although the Democrats ultimately prevailed in the Presidential balloting, the year, considered as a whole, was a harbinger of reviving conservative sentiment which was to make itself felt in state affairs on an enormous scale in the period just ahead.

In the first place, California assured the Republican Presidential nomination of United States Senator Barry Goldwater of Arizona and then helped banish him to the political sidelines. It devised a crushing Waterloo for New York Governor Nelson Rockefeller whose progressive-cum-moderate attitudes at least approached the traditional position of Earl Warren and other like-minded Californians which had been so readily and repeatedly accepted only a decade or so previously. Nonetheless, Lyndon B. Johnson was accorded the political accolade of a state which, four years earlier, had shied away from the sophisticated charms of John F. Kennedy. At the same election in which they piled up proof of reasonable enthusiasm for LBJ, the Californians became infatuated with a conservative Republican,

George Murphy, the Hollywood motion-picture actor, sending him to the United States Senate, for virtually his first stint of elective public service, by a much larger vote than Goldwater received in the state as head of the GOP ticket. Also, while joining the Johnsonian Great Society, with its commitment to solving or at least attacking the civil rights issue, California voted simultaneously to nullify state legislation which had been enacted to prohibit racial discrimination in housing.

These several verdicts, taken together, emphasized a sharply split majority opinion on various public personalities and affairs. The California conservatives were noisily active at the outset of 1964, the ultraconservatives by far the noisiest of all. They had lost with William F. Knowland in 1958, with Joseph C. Shell in 1962 and the same year with an assortment of right-wingers out to get the scalp of moderate Republican Senator Thomas H. Kuchel. And they had been beaten in the last gubernatorial campaign by Democratic Governor Edmund G. (Pat) Brown. While an exact classification of Richard M. Nixon in the shifting Republican spectrum had always been a bit difficult to arrive at, it was fairly reasonable to suppose that few GOP conservatives had marked their 1962 ballots for Brown. In Arizona Senator Barry Goldwater, the California conservatives of 1964 found a man after their own hearts and began organizing a Presidential primary campaign in his behalf with alacrity and intense devotion.

That year the Republicans had no native California bidder for the White House and no plans for a favorite-son delegation to their national convention. The hefty bloc of California delegates was a tossup among the out-of-state aspirants who cared to contend for it. New York Governor Rockefeller, like Goldwater an outspoken but secondary figure in the Nixon nomination convention of 1960, decided this time to try his luck in California. His slate of proposed delegates at the primary was headed by Senator Kuchel and former Governor Goodwin J. Knight and included an assortment of state legislators and others who customarily sailed under the Republican moderate banner. Among the better-known GOPers on the ticket

215

pledged to Senator Goldwater were Knowland and Shell, conservative Secretary of State Frank M. Jordan and Patrick J. Hillings, a former Los Angeles County congressman and long-time political associate of Nixon.

It proved to be a knock-down-and-drag-out primary contest, not only between Goldwater and Rockefeller but also between the rival advocates of conservative and moderate stances within California Republicanism. The expression "right-wing extremism" already had gained wide currency, and some of the elements to which it was loosely applied were represented as lurking in the wings during much of the electioneering. Meantime, Californians of old-fashioned and perhaps more traditional standpattism also backed Goldwater with the zeal of true believers in the concept that the American people would elect a thoroughgoing exponent of conservatism if the Republican party ever gave them the chance.

The Presidential primary in California is one of the country's last important ones, falling in June, almost on the eve of the national conventions. In 1964, it could scarcely have been more vital. A final triumph for Goldwater would practically wrap up the nomination for him. A victory for Rockefeller well might give the New Yorker's candidacy a needed shot in the arm and undoubtedly would provide important aid and comfort to the faltering block-Goldwater forces. California assured Goldwater's nomination. The primary vote was 1,120,403 for the outspokenly conservative Arizona Senator and 1,052,053 for Governor Rockefeller. The margin was only 68,350, mirroring the troubled division within the state's GOP, but this was lost track of in the psychological boost and substantial increase in delegates which this meant to the Goldwater cause. The national convention in San Francisco, with its Goldwater steam roller both on the nomination question and in the matter of the Republican party's 1964 statement of principles, is too fresh in the public memory to require much recapitulation. Everywhere on that occasion the Goldwater battle flag waved jauntily, while the overall influence of Rockefeller, George Romney, William Scranton and the rest of the party's moderate leadership was methodically reduced to zero, or very close to it.

The California Democrats, all this while, had been beating their drums for President Johnson, whom they had not particularly fancied back in 1960. Two opposed delegation tickets were offered at the 1964 Democratic primary, both officially "expressing no preference," but obviously favoring LBJ. One was headed by Governor Brown and studded with the names of congressmen, leaders in the State Legislature and other prominent party functionaries. The other slate was led by Samuel William Yorty, erstwhile congressman and state assemblyman who had tried for United States Senator and other honors over the years and ultimately had been elected mayor of Los Angeles. Critical stalwarts among the party regulars classed Yorty as something of a Democratic maverick, reminding each other, with much head-shaking, that he had once supported Richard Nixon. The Brown delegation went to the Johnson nominating celebration, having received 1,693,813 primary votes against an unusually large showing of 798,431 for the Yorty contingent.

There were more than 8,000,000 voters registered in California for the 1964 general election, 57.9 per cent of them Democrats, 38.9 per cent of them Republicans. The remaining 3.2 per cent consisted of those declining to designate a party affiliation or connected with one of the state's political splinter groups. With an 88.4 per cent vote cast in November, President Johnson swamped Senator Goldwater, 4,171,877 to 2,879,108. In spite of the Senator's fine showing in June, he captured only 40.8 per cent of the California vote in November. Johnson, with 59.2 per cent, unquestionably polled most of his party's strength and picked up some of the Republican moderates who were unhappy over the Arizona conservative's candidacy. As a matter of fact, Barry led the balloting in only five of California's fifty-eight counties. Los Angeles County alone went to the Democrats by better than 400,000. All this furnished no persuasive hint of the dismal fate which awaited California Democrats only two years later.

There may have been one suggestion of danger for the Democrats,

any of them taken it seriously emough: the 1964 elec-
rge Murphy to the United States Senate. Hollywood had
been playing around the edges of politics for a good many years.
Humphrey Bogart had broken a couple of spears for Adlai Stevenson.
Irene Dunne, Leo Carrillo and others had been active in Earl Warren's campaigns. Indeed, Helen Gahagan Douglas, film actress and
one-time Belasco star on Broadway, represented California in Congress during the New Deal-Fair Deal days. But Murphy made it to the
Senate, an undertaking in which Mrs. Douglas failed. The oddity was
that he won his seat as a conservative Republican in a year which
saw President Johnson and the Democrats spread-eagle the California
Republicans with comparative ease.

Although it was some time since the public had seen George Murphy in major film roles, except on television's late, late shows, he still
had the infectious Irish grin and agreeable personality of his song-
and-dance-stardom days in Movieland's musical extravaganzas. For
some time, he had interested himself actively in Republican committee affairs, gaining considerable prominence and helping to elect
others. In 1964, he decided to elect himself. Murphy's success in
California, where the highly regarded Goldwater suffered a shellack-
ing, elicited the explanation later that the Arizona Senator had Johnson to run against, whereas the former screen star was faced only by
a former Johnson secretary. Pierre Salinger, President Kennedy's
press secretary and later President Johnson's, resigned to return to
California and run for the United States Senate. The senatorial political situation was complicated for months by the fact that incumbent
Democratic Senator Clair Engle had suffered a disabling illness which
eventually resulted in his death. A field of fifteen candidates entered
the senatorial primaries. Among leading contenders on the Democratic side were Salinger, who was to serve briefly in the Senate as
Engle's appointed successor, and State Controller Alan Cranston,
founding president of the California Democratic Council, one of the
largest party-booster organizations of its kind in the country. Before
his connection with the Kennedy political fortunes, Salinger had been

a San Francisco newspaperman and also had engaged for some years in California Democratic organizational and public relations work. Few suspected him of harboring personal ambitions in the elective political field. Fellow newsmen and professional politicians were familiar with his talents, but they, after all, constitute only a tiny percentage of the voting public. It seems altogether probable that more of the general citizenry knew about Salinger in 1966, when his book, *With Kennedy,* made the best-seller list, than in 1964.

The California primary posed a tough test for Salinger and indicated a rocky political road ahead for Murphy. The Democrats nominated Salinger with 1,177,517 votes, while the Republicans were giving the Hollywood actor 1,121,591. Among the other aspirants, Democrat Cranston alone accumulated more than 1,000,000 votes. At first it looked like a Democratic senatorial shoo-in in November, especially with President Johnson heading the party ticket. What the prognosticators apparently overlooked was California's amusement industry enthrallment, the high esteem in which show-business figures were held off-stage as well as on. The Murphy campaign provided a foretaste of that. In 1964, however, the Democrats, though divided in their senatorial preferences after a bloody primary, insisted that Murphy was utterly lacking in experience or aptitude for the responsibilities of the Senate. They dismissed him as just another film-capital song-and-dance man with ridiculous aspirations. Moreover, he was, so they said, pretty far over on the conservative side of Republican politics. As events proved, they ignored all too readily the Murphy smile, stage presence and pleasing mannerisms. A new political day was dawning, for California at least, in which mass-media exposure of agreeable personalities was to count much more heavily at the polling places than old-style vote hustlers were able to imagine.

When the autumn votes had been tallied, Murphy came up with 3,628,555, which was 51.5 per cent of all those cast for Senator and more than 400,000 in excess of the statewide Republican voter enrollment. It was a Hollywood spectacular. The harsh things said about George were left on the cutting-room floor. His vote total not only topped Salinger's but ran well ahead of Goldwater's. Murphy had carried thirty of California's counties. His margin was more than 150,000 in Los Angeles County which had gone Democratic with Johnson at the same election by better than 400,000. He was the new Senator from Beverly Hills.

George Murphy's election walkover, marked by the inability of the California Democrats to hold their ranks intact, was a dress rehearsal of theatrical things to come. Just off stage was another Hollywood actor, Ronald Reagan. Whether dreams of gubernatorial candidacy already absorbed him at that time is hard to guess. But he kept himself busy that fall of 1964 in the vineyards of conservative California Republicanism. He campaigned vigorously for Barry Goldwater.

The California electioneering of 1964 churned up another highly significant development. The state's endorsement of Democratic President Johnson and its contrasting election of conservative Republican Murphy to the Senate were accompanied by a violent, statewide political dispute over housing for Negroes. The previous general session of the State Legislature, after lengthy controversy, had enacted a fair housing measure called the Rumford Act which undertook, broadly speaking, to prohibit racial discriminations in the sale or rental of dwelling property. Previous enactments having dealt with public accommodations, government-financed housing and racial bias in employment, this new legislation sought to regulate transactions involving certain classes of private property. The voters of California, following the most explosive campaign on civil rights which the state had experienced up to that time, not only nullified that enactment but, in effect, restricted the Legislature in the promulgation of any similar measures on the subject without approval of the statewide electorate. A year or so later, the State Supreme Court, in turn, invalidated the 1964 ballot proposition on constitutional grounds. In May of 1967 the United States Supreme Court, to which the fight had been carried, declared the voter-approved amendment unconstitutional.

The Negro civil rights question had been dormant as a source of serious political conflict in California for many years, just as it was for a long time in numerous other Northern and Western states. The Republicans, as "the party of Lincoln," adopted platform planks for social justice as a matter of routine in those years and appealed for Negro support at the polls. The state's Democrats assumed a generally similar position as an accepted part of Roosevelt New Dealism. When Harry Truman insisted on party endorsement of the whole civil rights package in 1948, arousing the ire of angry Southerners, the Democratic national convention fight for his stand was led by a fiery Minnesotan named Hubert Humphrey, loudly seconded by a united California delegation. Among the increasing millions who flocked to California during and after World War II, however, were many members of minority races, including Negroes, whose civil rights soon became a matter of immensely widened political consciousness. Disagreements speedily followed. Although fair employment practices commissions had been set up in other states, notably New York, it was not until 1959, the first year of Democratic Governor Brown's incumbency, that California's Legislature finally voted to outlaw job hiring discriminations based upon religion, race or color.

The difficulties encountered by Negroes in buying or renting residential quarters, except in "colored neighborhoods," led to attempts at remedial legislation later on, and eventually to the Rumford Act. This proposal originated in the population-controlled State Assembly, where it was offered by Assemblyman William Byron Rumford, a Negro pharmacist of Berkeley who held a University of California master's degree in political science. It finally gained passage in the geographically dominated Senate, but only after long delays and much bickering. Modification proposals to exempt individual dwellings in single-family occupancy from the intended new regulations were advanced as part of the effort to prevent a legislative deadlock. Opponents of the Rumford Act renewed battle almost as soon as it cleared the Legislature and was signed by Governor Brown.

The drive to invalidate the housing enactment was spearheaded by real-estate interests, professionally organized on a statewide basis. California election law provided the machinery, by petition, for a general referendum vote on whether any legislative measure should or should not go in the statute books. This permitted public review of legislation in the precise form voted by the lawmakers. In this instance, however, adversaries of the Rumford Act chose to attack it through qualification of an initiative measure, a broader type of direct legislation in which entirely new language was allowable. The plan was not only to strike out the Rumford Act but to lay down mandatory guidelines limiting the power of the Legislature, except with voter authority, to undertake further housing regulations in the anti-discrimination field, at least insofar as private property was concerned. Such an initiative went on the 1964 November ballot.

The basis for opposition to the Rumford Act was a contention that every holder of real property had a fundamental right to manage it and dispose of it as he pleased, without governmental interference. Running along with this was the argument that real-estate values depreciated when Negroes moved into an exclusively white neighborhood. In that respect, the practice of "block-busting" sometimes was cited. This, so it was represented, amounted to the circulation of rumors, true or false, of impending minority encroachment in a given residential area. The reputed purpose was to upset all-white neighborhoods, this presumably leading to hasty disposal of properties at less than ordinary market value. Generally speaking, the Rumford Act was regarded, by those who wanted it repealed, as a measure which would interfere with individual property rights and ruin California real-estate operations. On the other hand, the proponents of the anti-discrimination program, later commonly known as "open housing," stoutly maintained that, in many areas, Negroes and other American racial minorities were the victims of studied intolerance and found it impossible to obtain adequate or desirable residential accommodations. The word "ghetto" assumed new political dialogue significance for California, which heretofore had associated it chiefly with the crowded, dismal living quarters of big-city minorities in much older states. The Rumford Act sponsors insisted that even financially responsible Negroes were being denied the homes their money could buy and found themselves condemned to the role of second-class citizens. A legal remedy, they said, was imperative and a revision of property rental and sales procedures long overdue.

In the ensuing campaign over Proposition 14, as the Rumford Act repeal initiative was called, racial feeling, and in some instances bigotry, reached a level which California seldom if ever had witnessed before. The term "white backlash," for the first time with any real significance, entered the state's political vocabulary. The ballot measure setting aside the Legislature's housing law was approved in November by a landslide. Of all the votes cast, 65.4 per cent favored the anti-Rumford Act proposition, a much higher percentage than California recorded at the same election in support of President Johnson and his Great Society. The sweeping rejection of the position of the Legislature's majority was not expressed by just a few large vote centers but was truly statewide in its scope. The initiative carried in fifty-seven of California's fifty-eight counties.

Coincidentally, the bloody riots of Watts, the Negro "ghetto" concentration in Los Angeles, came in August, 1965. It would be a vast oversimplification to attribute this wild outburst of death and destruction to the housing-issue election of 1964. There were many factors, as an investigative commission later reported, among them lack of job opportunities, transportation problems, educational deficiencies, hate agitation, the misery of poverty and Negro charges of police brutality, which Mayor Yorty and Los Angeles law-enforcement authorities vigorously denied. It is probably reasonable to assume, however, that the political warfare over housing and its decisive outcome did little to ease the overall tensions.

31

LAWMAKING AND "BIG DADDY"

The United States Supreme Court's "one man-one vote" ruling on legislative representation, in June, 1964, affected the California lawmaking setup drastically. The shift of legislative power from rural America to the big cities and suburbia ran counter to the state's long-standing program of legislative organization. Responsive action became mandatory when the Warren court's landmark decision held that "legislators represent people, not trees or acres" and that they had to be "elected by voters, not farms or cities or economic interests." That conclusion necessitated a complete overhauling of the State Senate in California where Chief Justice Warren had served so long as governor.

Once upon a time, the two houses of the California Legislature had been apportioned more or less along population lines. For nearly forty years prior to 1964, however, the Legislature had been divided in its basic allegiances, one branch of it representing population and the other chosen under a complicated geographical formula. This system was considered by its sponsors, back in the mid-1920s, to be much less bizarre than that of some of the other states, where antiquated lawmaking machinery had scarcely been altered at all since the nineteenth century. But it was far from perfect. There was a marked difference between the eighty-member State Assembly which revised its districts in terms of population every ten years after the federal census—though not without a certain amount of gerrymandering—and the forty-man State Senate where a rule of California county or area representation remained largely unchanged for incredibly long stretches of time. The pressures for extensive reorganization of the Legislature became more and more pronounced toward the half-century mark as the lawmaking operations in a state so large and populous approached the status of a full-time business, not to say Big Business in terms of mounting budgets and other manifold responsibilities. It was revamped in the mid-1960s following the federal judicial directive for full representative government without local equivocations.

The California arrangement of split legislative power, as it had long existed in modern politics, was devised and inaugurated toward the end of the 1920s. It was hailed as the "Federal Plan" and patterned roughly after national government provisions which made population the yardstick for membership in the House of Representatives but assured every state, large or small, two seats in the United States Senate. The setup of the upper house of Congress was not disturbed by the 1964 Supreme Court decision. As the somewhat similar plan had worked out in California for a long time, the lower legislative house was in the hands of the big cities and other concentrations of population, while the Senate, based on geography for the most part, was dominated by the state's enormous rural areas, in majority by the so-called "cow counties." Labor, for example, had substantially favorable representation in the Assembly but much less senatorial influence. In 1960, the Senate district contrasts ranged from Los Angeles County, with nearly 7,000,000 residents, to the east-border constituency of Inyo, Mono and Alpine counties, boasting a combination of only about 15,000 inhabitants. Los Angeles County had by far the state's largest single Assembly delegation, yet it was forced to get along with a single senator. No county could have more than one senator.

Such disparities were denounced in some quarters as a distorted parody of representation and warmly defended in others as a highly desirable "balance of power" between the two legislative houses and between urban and agricultural California. The system frequently resulted in bitter and prolonged Senate-Assembly stalemates. A new statewide reapportionment by population, in compliance with the Supreme Court's edict, redrew district lines of the entire Senate, facing numerous "cow county" senators with political elimination. Prior to that revision, it sometimes took an extremely adroit state administration, or nimble special interests, as the case might be, to reconcile inter-house differences engendered by diametrically opposed regional backgrounds and interests. The reorganization, because of population distribution, put Los Angeles County and the rest of southern California in numerical command of both branches of the Legislature. It threw out the old "balance" scheme under which the Senate, where northerners enjoyed control, had long been able to block or veto actions by southern majorities in the Assembly, and vice versa.

In the meantime, the scope of California lawmaking concerns, paced by population gains, had grown immeasurably, in time consumption alone far outstripping the corresponding problems of many other states. What with the diversity of the thousands of proposals offered at each legislative meeting, California's prolonged and often controversial regular sessions, plus budget sessions, special sessions and interim committee activities, were represented as almost paralleling congressional work-loads. A remedial constitutional amendment was drafted, and approved at the polls in 1966, to provide for annual general sessions unrestricted as to duration or subject matter, with Senate-Assembly salary increases geared to year-around legislative service. Legislative pay was hiked from $6000 a year to $16,000. The enactment also incorporated, after years of indecision and false starts, a requirement for regulations outlawing "conflict of interest" practices, including private financial arrangements and interests inconsistent with legislative duties. Proponents called these changes essential to legislative modernization. A minority complained that full-time lawmaking professionals were being substituted for "citizen-legislators."

The same measure rewrote and shortened the California constitution, which patchwork amendments running back to 1879 had made into the third longest constitutional document in the world, described as "cumbersome, inelastic and outmoded" and wordier by far than the fundamental law of many nations. As a first step, with others in contemplation, one-third of the constitution was reduced from 22,000 words to 6000. As for the Legislature, the era of the old-fashioned, "part-time" member, who used to have ample leisure to pursue profitable private business or professional enterprises, was conceded to be over, or just about over, at least in California. The day of the legislative professional, whose entire career might be given over to the complexities of lawmaking and the pleasures of political maneuvering, was well above the horizon. For good or ill, this was a new fact of California public life.

Among the new pros cast up by California's adjustment to mid-century conditions, State Assembly Speaker Jesse M. Unruh of Los Angeles County was in many ways perhaps typical and, at the same time, an extraordinary figure in the exercise of both engaging persuasion and, upon occasion, naked political power. At the height of his incumbency, it used to be said that it was almost impossible to obtain Assembly approval of any consequential measure against which he obdurately set his hand. In 1967, sharing the Legislature's narrow-margin Democratic leadership with Unruh, was Senate President Pro Tempore Hugh M. Burns, an amiable Democratic conservative of Fresno County, a thirty-year veteran of the political wars. First elected to the Assembly in 1936 and to the Senate in 1942, Burns had then been upper house floor manager and rules committee chairman for ten years. His legislative interests had ranged from leadership of the Senate Committee on UnAmerican Activities to authorship of the Burns-Porter Act which created the

California Water Plan. Senator Burns was sixty-five, Speaker Unruh a little over forty-four.

Tagged with the sobriquet "Big Daddy," in affection by his cronies and something less than that by his detractors, husky, strong-willed Unruh became, without much question, the most powerful Assembly Speaker in the state's history up to that time. Born in Kansas and educated at the Wayland Baptist College in Texas and at the University of Southern California, he arrived on the state political scene as, to quote his state-printed biography, "an economist by training" who had become head of an economic research corporation. He reached the Legislature as a Democrat in 1955, three years before his party's gubernatorial victory with Edmund G. (Pat) Brown, and by the fall of 1961 he had the Assembly Speaker's gavel firmly in his grip. A tough-minded Navy Air Corps veteran of World War II, with nearly two years overseas, Unruh projected a new brand of imaginative and pragmatic legislative leadership. In California, the Assembly Speaker not only assigned all bills for preliminary committee scrutiny but also appointed the committees. Unruh called himself a liberal on social issues, offering numerous key measures in that field, and fancied himself a conservative in public finance. He was extravagantly acclaimed by members of his tightly reined Democratic "team" and widely feared in other quarters. Some of the Speaker's flatterers said it was not so much a question of Unruh getting along with the Legislature's army of lobbyists as it was of the lobbyists learning to get along with him. His personal manner was relaxed and jocular, his political posture stubbornly independent. Evidently a firm believer in the overriding importance of money contributions as the sinews of politics, and of the efficacy of "testimonial" dinners for deserving fellow politicians, Unruh was reported to take a lively and influential interest in many campaigns besides his own.

Unruh got into the national political game as an early backer of John F. Kennedy. As time went on, he sometimes supported Democratic Governor Brown and frequently feuded with him. Eventually, he gained a formidable reputation for political strength, especially south of the Tehachapi, and was ranked by his devoted followers as California's second most powerful Democrat at the very least. His friends, in fact, were disposed to step up this estimate after Governor Brown left state office. Whatever the future had in store for him, Unruh certainly held sway for a good many years as the undisputed boss of the State Assembly.

While some observers were inclined to be apprehensive over the intermittent encroachment of legislative bodies around the country on the prerogatives of governmental executive branches, Speaker Unruh professed to see the situation as the other way around, maintaining that for the last two generations the state legislatures of America had been underpaid, denied adequate help and operating facilities and downgraded in authority and prestige. "The executive is becoming more and more powerful," he once said, "and there is only one difference between a dictatorship and a democracy and that is an independent Legislature."*

Whatever the extent of "legislative deterioration," to use Unruh's phrase, may have been in the country generally, the re-emergence of a sturdy cult of the individual, and of a rugged type of partisan legislative leadership in both parties, heavily underscored the growing force of the lawmaking branch in California state government. Even before the legislative reorganizations of 1966, the Californians enjoyed comfortable personal quarters, electric voting apparatus, luxurious committee rooms, television recording facilities, a proliferating bureaucracy of consultants and administrative assistants, an agreeable pension system for retired legislative careerists and other appurtenances of an affluent commonwealth. They had their share of critics, too, who questioned the degree of responsibility exercised

---

* In the spring of 1967, Speaker Unruh, honored for his efforts to improve legislative procedures, became the first state lawmaker to receive the George Washington Award of the American Good Government Society. Legislatures, commented Unruh, too often "vary from obstructionist bodies dedicated to frustrating a Governor's program to rubber stamps validating whatever the Governor presents to carry out federal mandates."

229

by some legislative elements, their tendencies now and then toward complacent "club-like" fraternalism and their occasional displays of political arrogance.

There was no question, in any case, about the magnitude and variety of the work pileup with which lawmakers were confronted each year as the state's inhabitants and their problems continued to multiply. In the 120-member California Legislature, as in the similarly unwieldy lawmaking bodies of other large jurisdictions, the middle and post-middle years of the century produced a widely differing assortment of political characters and personalities. The giddy, irresolute and opportunistic rubbed shoulders inevitably with the dedicated, the strong-willed, the self-reliant and the politically effective. Their parliamentary battles brought forth sound decisions and oratorical brilliance along with numerous eccentric proposals over the years and a staggering array of malapropisms, some of which were real show-stoppers. There was, for instance, one statesman who gave vocal evidence of believing that Barbara Frietchie was a new lobby representative of the cosmetology industry. And long to be remembered is another loquacious floor debater who observed not long ago that the issue under discussion reminded him of "an old Chinese adverb."

32

"DEATH VALLEY DAYS"

The gubernatorial candidacy of Ronald Reagan in 1966 was indubitably another California political first. No other state, so far as anybody could remember, had previously entertained the notion, even briefly, of choosing a motion-picture actor as governor. To a bewitched and curious populace, it seemed that, almost overnight, Reagan had walked away from the studio microphone, where he had been narrator and master of ceremonies for the "Death Valley Days" television show, and casually decided, without need for a political screen test, to become master of California. Actually, the middle-aged film star, at that time fifty-five, had been enamored of politics on an amateur basis for a good many years, with widely ranging sentimental attachments. As gubernatorial aspirant, he apparently had no intention of giving up his amateur standing. He was, judging from preliminary reports, to be a kind of "citizen-candidate," with high-minded disdain for the ways of Governor "Pat" Brown and other such professionals. His brilliant success in this new role left the political world dumfounded.

In terms of the gradual revival of conservatism as a force of consequence in California Republicanism, the timing of Reagan's assault on the Democratic state administration was near-perfect, whereas that of Knowland in 1958 had been unfortunate, that of Nixon in 1962 dubious though understandable. Governor Edmund G. Brown was to say later, after his defeat, that the political tide was running out for him in 1966 as plainly as it had surged in to his advantage during the Knowland and Nixon elections. Although the Democratic executive did not expand on this idea, it was a mathematical fact that many of the young voters of 1966 had been mere school children when he first began waving his banner of "responsible liberalism" around California, and had not yet been born at the time of the New Deal upon which Brown sought to model his public behavior. After all, Governor Brown had been a top figure in California's governing class for sixteen years—eight as head of the State Department of Justice, eight more in the executive mansion. Counting his earlier service as San Francisco district attorney, he had been around on public display for twenty-three years. As he came to the final twelve months of his second administration, Brown had been governor even longer than Hiram Johnson, who held the job a fraction over six years, and was outranked only by Earl Warren who had it for nearly eleven. By this time, almost everybody in California thought they understood Brown perfectly, whether they did or not. Some admired him immensely; others, especially the rejuvenated conservatives of the GOP, plus an unsuspected number in his own party, disliked him thoroughly.

Challenging this political veteran, a third-generation Californian whose grandfather had driven a stagecoach back in the Gold Rush days, Ronald Reagan, six years the Governor's junior, arose to his task with no experience whatever in governmental office-holding but with a background of twenty-nine years of exposure to the public as a Hollywood actor and television personality. Born in Tampico, Illinois, Reagan was educated in that state's Eureka College where he made the football and swimming teams and took a degree (1932) in economics and sociology. During the early 1930s, he was a radio sports announcer in Iowa. Warner Brothers offered him a film contract in 1937 and he moved on to Hollywood, eventually making fifty pictures for Warners, Universal and as a free lance. The actor came out of World War II service as a captain. In 1954, Reagan, then forty-three, signed up as actor, host and emcee with television's "General Electric Theater," a connection which continued for eight years and also involved speaking appearances around the country for G.E. He wound up in 1962 working for Borax as host of that company's "Death Valley Days" TV show. At about the same time, he changed his registration from Democrat to Republican and was warmly welcomed by the GOP's conservative faction.

From the very start, California's campaign of 1966 promised new-fangled twists galore. It was, for example, perhaps the first time the country was privileged to watch a governorship race in which the two most highly-regarded contestants had swung full circle in their political party affections, each representing a party directly opposed to the one in which he previously had served. Governor Brown, having entered political life as a Republican and even as a youthful Republican office seeker, fell in love with the Roosevelt New Deal, switched parties and eventually became, in his own phrase, a "responsible liberal." It was the other way around with Reagan. He cast his first vote in the depression days for Franklin Roosevelt and became "emotionally involved" with the Democratic cause in what he was reported calling, many years later, his "early liberal daze." After nearly three decades, he likewise underwent a change of heart and became a Republican conservative.

In 1966, it had been a long time since Ronald Reagan performed as General George Custer and the like in filmland's winning of the West, though his somewhat dated romantic portrayals still were to be seen in television reruns. His emcee chores in the "Death Valley Days" series were much more recent and continued almost up to the time of his debut as a Republican bidder for the governorship. Behind him were six terms as president of the Hollywood Screen Actors Guild, a job in which George Murphy had been his predecessor. It was half a dozen years since he and Charlton Heston had been negotiators in the guild strike of 1960, which, among other

233

things, gained a percentage cut for actors when new films were used on TV. It was only two years since his involvement in the Johnson-Goldwater Presidential contest as a radiant new voice for Republican conservatism. Hollywood personalities had been avid followers of various political fortunes for decades, and evidently with redoubled interest since the election of George Murphy, one of their own, to the United States Senate. Then, too, such sound-stage paraphernalia and techniques as teleprompting apparatus, professionally produced reading-scripts and sometimes even cue cards were creeping more and more into the field of big-rally political oratory. The day of the long-winded, unorganized campaign harangue, as an efficacious means of mesmerizing voters, was very possibly on the way out. However much an amateur Reagan may have been in the intricacies and hard-eyed realities of governmental management, perhaps even of that vaguely understood phenomenon "practical politics," his performing experience was reckoned to make him a seasoned pro in such newly emphasized electioneering values as stage presence, smiling glamour and engaging all-American boyishness. In short, according to the accurate estimates of his well-wishers, Reagan was starting on his political adventure with the equipment, if all went well, to make the difference between a sure-fire hit and a dismal flop.

Meantime, Democratic Governor Brown was having public image troubles. As current chief executive, he enjoyed no such political worship as former Governors Johnson and Warren were often accorded in generous recollection of their substantial records and long tenure. Allowing for the dissimilar problems with which the three regimes had been confronted, there was really much to be said for the achievements of each of them. Still very actively involved in the hurly-burly of politics as well as state affairs, however, Brown found himself the 1966 victim of a not unusual shortness of public memory. It is somehow easier to look back on a long-departed administration with nostalgia and judge its benefits amiably than it is for the average citizen to measure the attainments and ability of a controversial incumbent. Brown and his lieutenants were proudly aware of a long list of accomplishments over the past seven years and loudly insistent on their recognition. Like the querulous constituent Alben Barkley, the old "Veep," used to tell about, thousands of dissident Californians pelted the Governor and his followers with this irritating question: "What have you done for us lately?"

This experience was not altogether new to Governor Brown. It was perhaps a hallmark of his two terms that Brown's public reputation had bounced up and down fitfully, sometimes hitting a dangerous low between elections, yet stabilizing at a comfortable level for each of his vigorously conducted "I love a fight" campaigns—at least up to that time. Counting on him for retention of Democratic power in the state, his backers prayerfully hoped that this would happen again in 1966. They took heart from the fact that few of his predecessors had demolished such nationally recognized opponents as Knowland and Nixon. Nonetheless, this latest long-term governor was more or less of a riddle to many Californians, judging from their conflicting appraisements of him. He often played the public role of jovial extrovert, while privately he was thoughtful, serious-minded and, for a successful politician, fairly retiring and free of bombast. This was hard for many to see, for he was also bubbling with enthusiasm over hundreds of governmental enterprises and frequently inclined to shoot from the hip with pronouncements of surprising candor. "Sometimes," he said, "I put my foot in my mouth." He likewise voiced some hard truths at times which needed saying. Brown's advocates classed him as an able and sincere administrator, a conscientious and forceful man of imagination, integrity and progressive instincts. His detractors called him a governmental spendthrift in furthering the programs to which he was committed and made him the target of numerous other unpleasant barbs, complaining that as a speechmaker he was perhaps well-meaning but pretty dull, that by and large he lacked finesse and polished urbanity. The contrasting cheers and criticism made Governor Brown a manyfaceted and puzzling figure to many people on whose support his third-term ambitions depended that year. After he lost the election, one widely-read columnist suggested that Brown had too much kindness of heart for his own good as an effective political leader.

Brown's California of 1966 was also a riddle. In his earlier years, the Governor had presided over a vast water plan inauguration, reorganization of the educational system, a broad variety of social and regulatory reforms and a considerable array of other projects. Now the state was busy with industrial expansion in new directions, lunar orbital contraptions, atom smashers, electronics installations and scientific undertakings ranging from desalination of sea water to study of the galaxies. On somewhat less high-flown levels, it was confronted with such additional concerns as sporadic racial difficulties, *de facto* school segregation, labor troubles, public finance problems, protection of natural resources and the complicated plight of modern urban life. One of Brown's cabinet officers ventured the pretentious, freewheeling calculation that California's population, if unchecked, easily could skyrocket from something like 19 million to as much as 1.5 billion by the year 2066. Proper planning, he said, could probably provide for only about 50 million. This peculiar declaration may not have signaled a complete California disenchantment with population grandeur, but it did seem to be a semiofficial admission that thinking, at long last, was proceding in that direction. Looking at the past rather than the future, an association of Mexican-Americans launched an attempt to have the state government conducted on a bilingual basis. This group insisted that the Mexican War peace treaty had guaranteed equality of the English and Spanish languages in California affairs and vociferously demanded, more than a century later, that this promise be carried out.

Some time after asking to be retained as boss man of this wondrous and beguiling place until 1970, Governor Brown observed that his decision to run again had not been an easy one. Had there been any assurance that the Republican candidate would be an experienced man and a political "moderate," the Governor would have been content, he said, to step aside and let some other Democrat carry the banner of his party. Brown explained that when it became reasonably apparent that the Republican nominee would be an "ultraconservative," and one unschooled in government at that, he made up his mind to run a third time, particularly since public opinion polls indicated he had the best chance to win against such a person. Obviously with Reagan in mind, the Governor made a great point of governmental know-how and progressivism as imperative qualities in trying to direct the affairs of so intricate and changing an institution as California. Political fringe reaction to Brown's own slogan of "responsible liberalism" had often been significant over the years. Ultraconservatives spooked at the noun "liberalism"; ultraliberals were suspicious of the modifying adjective. The national command of the Democratic party, in this instance the White House, observed Governor Brown's third-term candidacy decision with careful attention. A 1966 Republican victory in California could be embarrassing, and might even be disastrous, in the event the Democrats encountered an unexpectedly serious national challenge in 1968. Developments speedily established a sound basis for such apprehensions.

No sooner had Reagan begun studying his new part in the spring of 1966 than the California Democrats undertook to recast him in the role of villain. They invited the public to remember him not as the youthful hero of countless Hollywood screen operas but rather as the cochairman of the 1964 Citizens for Goldwater Committee in California. He was, by that token, they argued, a grease-painted false-face for extremists of the political right. The Democrats improvised their own shooting-script in which the good guys were supposed to chase the bad guys clear back to the political badlands, to the desert of Death Valley, so they hoped, in Ronald Reagan's case. The California Republican conservatives, meanwhile, having lost with sober-mannered Knowland, with blunt-spoken Shell and, more recently, with Nixon, often less than uniformly winsome, greeted the appearance of Reagan with every evidence of delight. They remembered, some of them, that one of the most admired pro-

Goldwater speeches of 1964 had been delivered by Reagan. If Brown could carry California where Kennedy had failed, they seemed to reason, then why not this attractive and widely-applauded thespian with all the sturdy supporters the unsuccessful Goldwater had enticed, and maybe a few more? Goldwater himself blessed the Reagan candidacy, predicting its triumphant outcome. He termed Governor Brown a "road company Hamlet" and expressed the opinion that the Democrats, not the Republicans, were guilty of extremist tendencies. "They kid Ronnie a lot about having a good guy image from all of his wonderful movies," the United Press International quoted Goldwater as saying. "All right, it's about time we had a good guy in the Statehouse. You've had Pat What's-his-name long enough." The administration Democrats said this Arizona salute made it clear that Reagan was a thoroughgoing Goldwaterite, backed by the prayers and money—so one campaign handout put it—of "right-wing fanatics throughout the country." Governor Brown added an ironic comment of his own. "The newest bulge in the population crisis of California," he said, "is the sudden influx of conservatives rallying around the Reagan cause."

Jumping the gun a little, since the California primary was yet to be held, at least one impressed political analyst in the East concluded that if Reagan won the governorship, he might be a splendid Republican prospect for President of the United States. A little more than six months later, some of California's rejoicing Republicans were cherishing the same idea.

33

THE "ELEVENTH COMMANDMENT"

Those who anticipated a sparkling and original California political show in 1966, with a real Hollywood celebrity reading one of the principal parts, were rewarded by a first-act innovation called the "Eleventh Commandment." This was an exceptional decree devised by the Republicans to govern the campaign behavior of their candidates and, if possible, prevent quarreling among them. It ushered in a unique political year which merited, and still merits, attentive study, even outside California, as something entirely new in electioneering and kingmaking operations. The whole enterprise was unprecedented in that it encompassed the brilliantly successful build-up of an individual without the slightest participating experience in governmental affairs—in this case, Ronald Reagan, who, regardless of his latent abilities or shortcomings, climbed from political scratch within a year to the governorship of one of the country's leading states. It posed the question whether this extraordinary formula, granted the right leading man, could be employed with comparable results in other regions, or was something peculiar to California.

The "Eleventh Commandment" was issued in the name of Dr. Gaylord B. Parkinson of San Diego, chairman of the Republican

239

State Central Committee, and read as follows: "Thou shalt speak no evil of other Republicans." This ukase, sometimes called "Parkinson's law," was intended for the guidance of GOP participants in the California primary election. It was designed to minimize harsh intraparty bickering and recrimination as Reagan stepped to the footlights to try out for the role of governorship nominee. He was generally expected to get the part, although four other Republicans showed up as rivals, chief among them former San Francisco Mayor George Christopher, a GOP "moderate" who had been beaten for United States Senate nomination by Goodwin Knight back in 1958. Some of that year's party-splitting Republican acrimony may have been remembered in the drafting of Dr. Parkinson's order for harmony. The "Eleventh Commandment" occasioned quite a bit of tart comment, nonetheless, inasmuch as California had rejoined the rest of the United States in the matter of strictly partisan primary procedures in 1959 and its state nomination elections now were supposed to be wide-open, free-swinging intraparty tests. The new rule of polite indulgence among themselves presumably would enable the GOPers, even before the primary, to devote full time to a systematic bludgeoning of State Capitol Democratic incumbents. Within these "guidelines," at any rate, Candidate Reagan tore into the Brown administration from the very start, paying as little attention as he comfortably could to the pretensions of Christopher. He disregarded the other three minor GOP gubernatorial hopefuls almost entirely.

In the Democratic primary, Governor Brown found himself with five opponents and no "Parkinson's law" to protect him from their onslaughts. Los Angeles Mayor Samuel W. Yorty, a perennial bidder for higher political rank, was the Governor's principal nomination challenger. Ignoring Yorty and the others as much as possible, Brown busied himself fending off Republican thrusts. He and his followers seemed chiefly preoccupied with estimating whether Reagan or Christopher presented the greater threat to their survival. The state administration's campaign strategists, at first anyhow, professed to be undisturbed by the reports of public opinion pollsters that Reagan not only was leading on his own ticket but also appeared to be running ahead of the two-term Governor in general popularity. After all, Governor Brown was a man who had been "getting things done"—progressive things at that—and it was inevitable, his supporters said, that he would have made numerous enemies over the years in quarters opposed to those accomplishments. They predicted that such hostility would prove evanescent as the qualities of the candidates became thoroughly understood. There was a complacent disposition in the Brown camp to recall how the straw-vote takers had underrated Harry Truman in 1948. Around the country, political professionals regarded Brown and Reagan with calculating reflection. The situation promised a slap-bang confrontation of reasonably progressive and unmistakably conservative philosophies. It was felt the result might help political weather forecasting considerably.

Governor Brown and his administration missile launchers hastened, even during the primary maneuvering, to introduce the John Birch Society issue into the vote competition. Their contention was that extreme right-wing conservatives, including the Birchers, were beginning to huddle in Reagan's corner and that the actor-politician ought to repudiate such support. They also tried to pin the label of Goldwaterism on Reagan at every opportunity. While the campaigning pursued numerous political byways and side roads, with much extraneous oratory, Brown hammered away most of the time, both before and after the primary, on three principal theses: the declaration that his first two terms had been productive, forward-looking and good for California; the charge that Reagan was "a very dangerous man," a right-wing conservative backed by political extremists who had "an almost pathological fear of government"; the argument that the candidate from Hollywood had no experience in government whatever, even at the lowest local level, and knew little or nothing about California problems. "I'm running against an actor," Brown said on one occasion. "I'm not an actor; I just can't act. And he can't govern."

At least half of this latter statement was patently true. In this uncommon political match, though, there was no profit in deriding an actor, as events proved, especially an actor who had been around for nearly thirty years and whose performances in such roles as George Gipp of Notre Dame were still to be seen on television by those citizens willing to stay up late enough. *Simpatico* was the word for such viewers. Indeed, Governor Brown was up against a baffling exhibition of showmanship which few politicians had encountered up to that time. California, over more than a century of madcap campaigns, had seen a little bit of everything, though probably never such a competent display of magic, so well stage-managed. The star of countless movies delivered his lines with cool effectiveness and considerable charm. Understandably, he muffed his cues now and then. So did old-fashioned politicos, for that matter. Ronald Reagan was an experienced entertainment personality, not to be taken lightly when he faced an audience with a carefully prepared speech to read.

Reagan's broadsides at the incumbent government appeared to favor broad generalities much of the time. There was a lot of crime in California, he said; the state government spent too much money; the California tax burden needed to be reduced; the Big Government in Washington, in exchange for financial handouts to the states, sought to exercise too much control over its political subdivisions and the lives of American citizens; outrageous student demonstrations had taken place at the University of California, with more than a suspicion of radical factors; social welfare was often mishandled; the business climate in California was bad; the management of state affairs in Sacramento was "tired" and inept.

Brown undertook to demolish Reagan's personal appearance tour representations with figures and statistics. On allegations of California economic stagnation, he accused the Republican of distorting the facts. He claimed that corporation earnings, gross individual income and manufacturing payrolls were all on the rise. On the whole, the Governor's stubborn defense and his reliance on particulars in the many fields with which his long career had familiarized him appeared, very early in the contest, to be offset by Reagan's agreeable platform manner, his smiling show of sincerity and his smooth delivery, regardless of the subject matter. Brown found himself tilting at a prefabricated but extremely picturesque windmill.

It became fairly apparent, even before the governorship nominations, that the Democrats were committed to a separation, if possible, of Reagan's reputation in the public mind as a glamorous film player and his record in support of various political causes, the plain intent being to classify him in the latter category as shockingly conservative. For more than fifty years, since Hiram Johnson's first campaign in 1910, this sort of splenetic warfare between progressive and conservative establishments had been a periodic feature of the state's political life, first one faction and then the other pushing into ascendancy. The comparatively unsettled nature of California's millions always made the outcome of such skirmishes hard to prefigure. Now, with the influence of California on the politics of the rest of the country very much greater, the Democratic issue-makers accused Reagan of having, at one time or another, opposed Medicare and the graduated income tax, favored the operation of social security on a voluntary basis and made common cause with political right-wingers on other public questions. Brown belabored Reagan as "Barry Goldwater's stand-in," as a candidate "ignorant of California government," notably when "without his script," and as a man with "dangerous ties to the John Birch Society." He cited Reagan's autobiography, *Where's the Rest of Me?* as an indication of the actor's wavering course from advocacy of liberal Democratic causes in the New Deal days to a later Republican stand so conservative that right-wingers flocked to his banner, bringing their campaign money with them. One Democratic screed charged that these included "some of the most reprehensible groups and individuals in America."

"I'm not an extremist," retorted Reagan. "This is a diversionary tactic to avoid campaigning on the issues." Philip M. Battaglia, state chairman of Reagan's campaign and later his executive secretary after Reagan had won the governorship, asserted hotly that

"McCarthyites on the left" were employing "witch-hunting techniques of guilt by association" to draw public attention away from the Republican charge of "incompetence and lack of leadership" in the Brown administration. "If a man cannot do a job in eight years," added Reagan, "what makes us think he can do it in twelve?" Intent on corralling Republican votes from every quarter and rounding up any and all Democratic strays from the Brown range, Reagan adopted an early position, which he repeated later, that it would be wrong for anybody to set himself up as a judge and jury to decide what constitutes extremism. If Birchers supported him, said the candidate, it was because they bought his philosophy, not because he bought theirs. He saw no reason, however, "to repudiate an organization I don't belong to." On the issue of extremism, Reagan assailed "militant left-wing radicals" and suggested the California Democratic Council was Governor Brown's "good left hand." As for Goldwaterism, Reagan observed blandly that he, and not Barry Goldwater, was running for governor of California. Ridiculed repeatedly by the Democrats as an unschooled hand in government, Reagan noted his long service as head of the Screen Actors Guild and maintained that holding public office is not the only means of gaining important experience. "The founding fathers of this country," he said, "were not professional politicians."

As the campaign dragged on, one political writer, musing over the affair's strange gyrations, offered the guess that the politics of California, 1966 style, had become slightly schizophrenic. He appeared to have a waggish point, at least in connection with the campaign's "image makers" and their efforts to make each candidate fit all the state's variable prejudices as closely as possible. Each camp seemed to shift cautiously toward middle ground, in public utterances anyway. Reagan spoke sparingly of Goldwaterism and far-out conservatism. Governor Brown, who had first been elected under the flag of "responsible liberalism," was now quoted by an Eastern interviewer as regarding himself a "moderate." There was a touch of unintended humor in their choice of public relations agencies. Brown engaged, as an "adjunct" to the Democratic re-election drive, the Los Angeles firm of Baus and Ross, which had handled the 1964 California Presidential primary campaign of Barry Goldwater. Reagan hired another southern California press agent and image-building organization, Spencer-Roberts and Associates, which had represented New York Governor Nelson A. Rockefeller in his bitter fight against Goldwater for the California Republican delegation. Qualified professional campaign tub-thumping outfits were admittedly hard to come by, but the particular selections of Brown and Reagan caused quite a little eyebrow-lifting. The Democrats gleefully announced that Spencer-Roberts, back in its Rockefeller-boosting days of 1964, had described Reagan as just "another Liberty Amendment stalwart." The main points of difference between Brown and Reagan, which actually appeared to be profound, were often lost sight of in a redundance of gibing exchanges along this line.

With desultory sorties into other fields and occasional half-hearted slaps at a few of the other nine would-be governors, the two major candidates finally churned their way through a sea of turgid oratory to the June primary election. Nobody was by any means astounded when the Republicans nominated Reagan and the Democrats renominated Brown. What did surprise a good many was the vote distribution. Reagan polled 1,417,623 Republican votes. The Democrats gave Brown 1,355,262. The Hollywood novice at statewide electioneering, or any other kind, had outpolled the two-term Governor by 62,361. There was more to it than that. Los Angeles Mayor Yorty, Brown's chief Democratic opponent, had mustered 981,088. Former San Francisco Mayor Christopher, on the GOP side, had taken 675,683 votes away from Reagan. The overall tabulations for the eleven gubernatorial nomination seekers showed the five Democrats competing against Brown had amassed more than 1,200,-000 votes, while the four Republicans opposed to Reagan had a combined tally slightly in excess of 760,000. The state administration could take dubious cheer from the fact that, in grand totals, the Democrats had outvoted the Republicans by more than 380,000.

Looked at another way, though, nearly 2,000,000 votes had been cast for the nine Democrats and Republicans who challenged Brown and Reagan, and these would be available for redistribution in November.

Shortly after the primary, Governor Brown talked "frankly and bluntly" about his problems to the board of directors of the California Democratic Council. He pictured Reagan "to the right of Barry Goldwater" and solidly backed by the ultraconservatives. To change the situation between June and November, he warned, would take a long, hot summer of the hardest kind of Democratic campaign work. "I'm a political realist," said Brown. "If the election were held next Tuesday, the right wing of the Republican party would go into office." As matters turned out, he might have mentioned almost any Tuesday.

34

BOOKS, BIRCHERS AND BACKLASH

The summer of 1966 proved to be even longer and hotter than the worried Governor Brown imagined it might. California was on the verge of one of those stunning and complete turnabouts of public sentiment which it had undergone so often in the past, this one, like many of the others, without any major anticipatory realignment of political party registrations. The state was moving inexorably into another of its recurrent struggles between forces which, to borrow Earl Warren's phraseology of fourteen years back, were committed to "social progress" and elements more nearly devoted to the "status quo," in some instances to the uncomplicated values of yesterday. There was, as November election results plainly established, a marked resurgence of conservative thinking, among Democrats as well as Republicans, and a fidgety desire for leadership change. These factors were reflected, not only in the pronouncements of Brown and Reagan, but in the attitudes of their respective party organizations and functionaries on such subjects as housing discrimination, obscenity and left and right political extremism.

Many states have party convention systems of considerable complexity in which a few fractious political cutups can raise election-year havoc with that revered Republican and Democratic loyalist concept called "party unity." Such fragmentation of intraparty harmony would seem to be at least one disaster which Californians easily could avoid, in view of the sharply limited power of the state's postprimary conventions. All nominations are settled at the ballot box, and the subsequent conclaves of both major parties are restricted largely to festive oratory and the drafting of campaign platforms. Yet California party policy-makers, even in these routine operations, often have exhibited a remarkable talent for entangling themselves in discomfiting factional disputes and ideological difficulties.

They did so in 1966. The Democratic and Republican conventions, not to mention some of the rival groups and prominent individuals within each of the state's party structures, soon found themselves at cross-purposes on the merits of the controversial, ultraconservative John Birch Society. There were noisy preliminaries and a number of explosive electioneering sideshows, too. For example, Democratic State Controller Alan Cranston, destined for defeat as it turned out, issued a so-called "white paper," lambasting the Birch Society and attacking "neo-Fascist" hate literature which he claimed could be purchased in "Birch book stores" in several California cities. The Birch Society, "most successful of all in California," he said, planned to spend millions of dollars in 1966 to further its objectives around the country. The Controller also charged that Republican Reagan's campaign fund contributors included "bankrollers of professional right-wing causes." Reagan coolly suggested Cranston's material be turned over for evaluation to some such agency as the State Senate Fact-Finding Committee on UnAmerican Activities. "I'm not a witch-hunter," he told the Democratic official. This somewhat contrived episode provided an early foretaste of the political grimness with which the campaign appeared likely to be waged.

Then, on the eve of the Republican State Convention, made up of GOP officeholders and nominees, Mrs. Lee Sherry, northern California vice-chairman of the party's State Central Committee, made headlines with demands for a platform plank repudiating political extremism to avert the danger of Republican defeat at the polls. "We can no longer straddle this issue," she said in a letter to convention delegates. "We must denounce, in the strongest language possible, the cancer of extremism such as is embodied in the John Birch Society." Her suggestion was that the state's GOP stand with Republican moderate Thomas H. Kuchel, California's senior United States Senator and assistant minority leader, who had condemned the Birchers some time earlier. The Republican state convention, held at Sacramento early in August, adopted a relatively brief platform which assailed Communism, urged an internal security program "ever vigilant against enemies" but did not take a position either for or against the John Birch Society. Republican Nominee Reagan evidently found this declaration acceptable and agreed with the platform as a whole. He had already questioned the wisdom of trying to decide arbitrarily "what constitutes extremism."

Accusing Reagan of "trying to duck this issue," Governor Brown declared: "He wants the support of the Birchers and, most importantly, he wants their money in his campaign." Retiring Democratic State Chairman Robert L. Coate issued a lengthy statement claiming that Reagan's political finance committee included members who were either Birchers or active in other ultra right-wing organizations. The Reagan camp countercharged that the Democratic leadership had resorted to "witch-hunting" to becloud legitimate questions raised about the administration's handling of taxes, state expenditures and the overall management of California affairs. Reagan himself termed the Brown regime "tired and stale." It was guilty of both "erosion of honesty" and "abandonment of principle," he added, and was actuated by "the arrogance that comes from being in power too long." The Democratic state convention subsequently opposed "all forms of political extremism" and rejected "any support" from such sources. "We denounce," said the convention's platform, "those extremists of either the left or the right—from the Communist Party to the John Birch Society—who are attempting to destroy our American way of life."

The extent of Bircher infiltration into official and unofficial political organizations had for some time been a sensitive question in California, especially after a furor in Democratic circles, in the early 1960s, upon discovery that two Republicans in the state's House of Representatives delegation were Birch members. It became the Democratic fashion to suspect Bircher influence in ultraconservative GOP agencies and to search out all available evidence of it. The Republicans, for some years, had been equally outspoken in charges of left-wing proneness on the part of liberal Democrats in some quarters, singling out the California Democratic Council, some of whose members had been critical of government policy in the Vietnam war and had advocated American recognition of Red China. The acrimonious hubbub over Birchism added to the fury of the Brown-Reagan encounter. It goes without saying that, in the general uproar, the Democrats overlooked no opportunity to make California voters aware that their old hero, Chief Justice Warren, had been proposed for "impeachment" by the Bircher slogan writers. Viewed in post-election perspective, it must be concluded that while the Bircher issue may have embarrassed Reagan at times during the turbulent 1966 summer, it did not slow down his drive toward the governorship to any appreciable extent. The right-wing charges continuously leveled at him were not nearly so effective in swinging votes as, say, the left-wing denunciations of Upton Sinclair had been in the angry campaign of 1934. Indeed, after the 1966 votes had been counted, Robert Welch, founder of the John Birch Society, was reported in the press as estimating that, indirectly, his organization had been a factor in the outcome, or at least in helping to pave the way for it, through extensive activity in California for some years. Whether this could be attributed to empty boasting or not, the Welch quotation appeared to be received in fairly general silence among California politicians. No matter who helped to pave the way, the California conservatives, by 1967, were plainly in command.

Brown, Reagan and the other belligerents of 1966 clashed just as blatantly over fair housing legislation for racial minorities. The issue, still a perplexing one although the voters had attempted to settle it in landslide fashion only two years earlier, tempted further political exploitation. As already explained, the State Legislature had outlawed discrimination on racial grounds in the private sale or rental of residential properties, only to have its enactment, the Rumford Act of 1963, overturned by an overwhelming statewide initiative vote in 1964. The Watts riots had centered additional attention on the Negro question in California in 1965. The State Supreme Court, by 1966, had resuscitated the Rumford Act, knocking out the nullifying initiative for constitutional reasons. This protracted course of events, widely followed and arousing strongly-felt public reaction, was still in motion in 1967, with much discussion of further legislation and efforts to obtain a conclusive ruling by the United States Supreme Court.

Democratic Governor Brown had been a supporter of the original Rumford Act and had signed it. Republican Nominee Reagan, while expressing himself as favorably disposed toward civil rights, said he was opposed to invasion of the constitutional right of individuals to dispose of private property as they pleased. He was equally opposed, he stated, to "restrictive covenants" entered into for the purpose of closing certain neighborhoods to minority races. The Democratic campaigners rushed in with the allegation that Reagan himself had signed a couple of such covenants a few years previously. This form of squabbling, on civil rights and numerous other subjects, provided the California political scene with abundant noise, and perhaps a minimum of enlightenment, during most of the 1966 summer and early autumn.

The Republicans, in their platform convention that year, proudly noted once more that they were "the party of Lincoln" and spoke out generally against discriminatory actions of a racial or religious nature. But they also called for "repeal" of the Rumford housing law. Vainly protesting this, a minority in the convention suggested that the advocacy of repeal was, in effect, only a gimmick to seek "white backlash" support at the November general election. One Negro Republican committeeman warned that it amounted to slapping members of his race in the face. The GOP platform plank, in final form, retained the endorsement of "repeal," but also proposed the alternative of Rumford Act "amendment" and substitution of "constructive legislation" which would protect "the free choice and constitutional rights of all citizens."

A few weeks later, while racial unrest and violence were being reported in Chicago, Cleveland and other Northern cities, sometimes on the housing issue, the Democratic state convention also considered the question with what appeared to be cautious improvisation. The Democratic platform resoundingly rejected the idea of Rumford Act repeal, but hastily added that the Democrats stood "ready at all times" to support legislative amendments or improvements which would ensure "equitable application" of the law to everybody. Observing that Californians, by a two-thirds voter majority, had expressed their dislike of at least some aspects of the Rumford law, Governor Brown added a few thoughts of his own, proposing creation of a bipartisan citizens' commission to overhaul it.

Some of the Democratic liberals, evidently against any and all housing law tampering, dissented vehemently, contended Brown had weakened his effectiveness by retreating somewhat from a former posture of liberal vigor and threatened to bolt his ticket. At the same time, an assortment of Republican "moderates" defected from the Reagan camp, called the GOP candidate "totally without qualification" to fill the office of governor and proceeded to form a campaign organization labeled "Californians for Brown." Leaders in both parties seemed keenly aware of a possible "white backlash" vote growing out of the "open housing" altercation. Although the Republicans had advocated "repeal" and the Democrats had not, both platforms contained wary qualifications, and some observers professed to assess the difference between the positions of the two rival groups as chiefly one of semantics. Despite a post-election disposition among politicians to discount the importance of "white backlash" balloting around the country, California was one state where it was widely felt to have played a part. Conceding this by implication, Governor Brown said afterward that he had always tried to be helpful to Californians who needed help, including Negroes. Even Assemblyman Rumford, a legislator since 1949, was beaten in a bid for the State Senate.

252

Brown and Reagan became embroiled in still another confusing statewide issue that fall—this time a privately concocted, offbeat initiative aimed at obscenity. California is shaken, from time to time, by flights of moral apprehension which occasionally alter its way of life and almost always disconcert one group or another of its politicians. These obsessions not infrequently take the form of ballot measures submitted to the public while the voters are looking the other way, so to speak, during a wildly contested Presidential or governorship election. Sex was the subject of such a proposal in 1966, or rather books, magazines and other printed material in which sex was dealt with. Its backers called it a proposal to curb pornography. Its opponents claimed the initiative was so far-reaching in its terms that it might, so one group of church officials contended, prohibit "the works of Shakespeare and even the Holy Bible." The initiative proposed to abolish the "social importance" test which existing law provided as a means of determining whether a novel or other piece of writing, called in question because of its treatment of sex, had an intrinsic literary or scientific value or was deliberately intended to appeal to "prurient interest" alone. The determined outcry for control of obscenity, countered by a warning that the odor of censorship and book burning was in the autumn air, created a modern California furor reminiscent of some of the incidents associated in the past with Boston. Echoes of this new crusade, as a political issue anyhow, probably reverberated over a somewhat larger area, however, due to the rambling size of California and the chosen timing of the crusaders.

Proponents of the initiative, which was entered on the November gubernatorial election ballot as Proposition 16, advertised themselves as the "California League Enlisting Action Now," a somewhat elaborate organizational title evidently dreamed up to produce a kind of campaigning acrostic. The first letters of the five words spelled out "CLEAN," and the ballot measure was extensively publicized as the "CLEAN initiative." A leading sponsor of this movement was a clergyman turned legislator, State Assemblyman E. Richard Barnes, a former Navy chaplain who had retired with the rank of captain, interested himself in Republican politics and first won San Diego election to the Legislature for the session of 1963. His biography in the handbook of the California Legislature listed him as having gained, among other honors, the 1961–1962 San Diego directorship of the Christian Anti-Communism Crusade. The measure went beyond striking out the penal code definition of obscene material as "matter which is utterly without redeeming social importance." Likewise it sought to eliminate a statutory proviso that works cited as catering to prurient interest should be "taken as a whole" in judging their merits or worthlessness, and that one of the factors should be how the material appeared "to the average person applying contemporary standards." In a general tightening up of the law for suppression of pornographic publications, the initiative undertook to limit the power of judges to dismiss obscenity proceedings, to authorize private citizens to sue prosecutors regarded slow in law enforcement, and to make conspiracy to violate an anti-obscenity law a state prison offense.

Both candidates for governor were drawn into the argument, almost inevitably. Reagan rather favored Proposition 16. Governor Brown had legal reservations. A "crack-down on the pornography peddler" was certainly desirable, said Brown, but he "seriously questioned" the constitutionality of "CLEAN." Reagan declared pornography a national scandal. "And California is its fountainhead," he cried. "Crime has skyrocketed." While Brown denied that crime was rampant in California and insisted that juvenile offenses had actually declined in 1965, Assemblyman Barnes raked the gubernatorial campaign battle front with the charge that "some 60 per cent of the nation's lewd paperbacks and magazines are now published in California," many of them falling into the hands of youngsters.

Proposition 16 went down to a resounding defeat, with the California Library Association and the Northern California Council of Churches leading the opposition. They denounced it as "a drastic, badly-written and unconstitutional attempt to impose a system of state censorship of art and literature upon the citizens of California." The scheme was smothered by a November vote of almost three to

254

two. Yet, curiously enough, after all the shouting, the effect on the Republican-Democratic political races was comparatively negligible. Ronald Reagan, who had favored the controversial initiative, was elected governor by a commanding margin. His lieutenant-governorship running mate, Robert H. Finch, who had agreed with Governor Brown that the measure was probably unconstitutional, outpolled Reagan and gained office with the highest vote given any statewide candidate that year.

Assemblyman Barnes, an ardent Reagan supporter, busied himself with yet another unusual project that fall, sponsoring with others a campaign to have California voters reject four justices of the State Supreme Court whose majority decision had invalidated the successful 1964 initiative measure against the Rumford housing law. It was an example of the bitter feeling which the long dispute over "open housing" had engendered. Supreme and appellate justices are not elected on a competitive basis in California as the lower court judges are. The high court jurists are appointed by the governor for fixed terms, subject to approval by the voters. If a judge is disapproved, the governor nominates another, liable to the same ballot-box review. The justices, as their terms expire, continue to face the electorate periodically, but strictly on a yes-or-no question of their retention on the bench. Under this arrangement, effective since 1934, justices of the Supreme Court and the various courts of appeal have rarely been removed by the voters.

"The people can vote their disapproval of these men," Assemblyman Barnes explained, however, "and if there is a majority of 'no' votes cast, the next Governor, who may very well be Ronald Reagan, would have the opportunity to appoint four new Supreme Court justices in California—which is one more reason to vote for Mr. Reagan."

This proposal to throw out a majority of the state's highest tribunal as a form of reprisal was entirely legal, of course. The four jurists, including Chief Justice Roger J. Traynor, were re-elected, but only after an unusually heavy vote, ranging in each case above 1,700,000, had been registered against them.

255

35

"WHERE THE ACTION IS"

The University of California, indeed the whole range of higher education, became implicated in the 1966 Republican-Democratic struggle, before, during and even after the election campaign, probably with more unhinging clamor than the state had heard in any previous gubernatorial contest. This was particularly so at the height of the Brown-Reagan tumult. The managers, plan-makers, regional directors, orators, ghost writers and hired philosophers of both political faiths were up to their necks in a bubbling flood of thoroughly biased rhetoric, while public pulse-takers vied with each other in efforts to forecast the outcome. Most pollsters solemnly reported that only a few percentage points separated Brown and Reagan in their reckonings. The man from Hollywood was still figured ahead, but not so far in front as the actual balloting proved him to be. Nothing was really very certain to those who listened to the political dialogue except that California was, in early autumn, an extremely disjointed and agitated place. The involvement of the state university in all this was perhaps inescapable.

The University of California, by the middle years of the 1960s, had grown to be one of the largest public institutions of its kind in the world, with nine campuses spread around the state and an enrollment of 88,000. It claimed more Guggenheim Fellowship awards than any other university in the country and was rated by the American Council of Education as the best, or one of the best, centers of graduate studies. The size of its faculty at some branches exceeded that of the student body at many smaller colleges. UC had twelve Nobel laureates at that time and led the nation in National Academy of Science members with ninety-seven. Founded in 1868, it was a state institution but separately governed by a Board of Regents, with full powers of organization and administration. The board consisted of sixteen members appointed by the governor for fixed periods and eight ex officio members, largely high-ranking state officials. The Legislature had a degree of fiscal authority in determining university appropriations. The appointive regents were named for long terms to prevent political control of higher education by any given state administration.

The university's first permanent campus in Berkeley found itself, in the mid-1960s, the controversial storm center of a rash of "sit-ins," "teach-ins" and other explosive student and nonstudent demonstrations, running in subject matter from "free speech" to Vietnam war opposition. These disorders led to police intervention, near-riot conditions in one instance resulting in mass arrests. While the chancellor's office later estimated that the so-called "activists" represented only a small percentage of the enrolled total—a few hundred "really far-out students" among some 27,000 at Berkeley—charges about the "New Left," immorality, "student militants" and "outside agitators" reverberated around the state for a long time as a result of the tempestuous doings, and Berkeley was reported to have the reputation among the radically inclined at other American campuses as being the place "where the action is."

By 1966, the Berkeley situation had simmered down to relative quiet as a result of reorganized administrative controls, at least in the judgment of the university authorities, and conditions had been substantially improved by student discipline policies approved in 1965 by the Board of Regents. These, according to UC President

Clark Kerr, were "designed for a free community of learning that seeks to combine freedom with its responsible use." Nonetheless, since education concerns everybody and has always been a handy and tempting target for politicians at election time, the University of California became a Brown-Reagan campaign issue. The State Senate Committee on UnAmerican Activities, in one of its yearly reports, already had reviewed the demonstrations of Berkeley's troubled past and had suspected and decried campus and off-campus radical influences. Reagan, condemning what he called "appeasement of campus malcontents and filthy-speech advocates," wanted the university reinvestigated. Governor Brown, himself an ex officio regent, supported President Kerr and the UC administrative regime, contended Berkeley problems were being worked out satisfactorily, or would be, and argued, in effect, that renewed political attacks, launched for vote-getting purposes, were potentially destructive of a great university. The active participation of a Brown-appointed university regent in the administration's re-election effort drew a statewide outcry by Reagan against what he pictured as political pressure and skulduggery on the part of the Governor. Then another ex officio regent, Dr. Max Rafferty, an outspoken Republican conservative who held the nonpartisan post of State Superintendent of Public Instruction, endorsed Reagan's candidacy. Dr. Rafferty was quoted at one juncture of the political din as saying that "weakness, tolerance and indifference" had made the University of California at Berkeley "look more like a skid row than an institution of higher learning."

This and other developments prompted Democratic Assemblyman Charles B. Garrigus, then chairman of the Assembly Committee on Education, to accuse Reagan and Rafferty of "an alliance of expediency aimed at making a political football out of UC." With Brown characterizing charges against himself and the university as "outrageous," Garrigus, a college teacher, warned in high decibels against "a new set of three Rs for education—Reaction, Raffertyism and Reaganism." Dr. Rafferty indicated he had made his choice of Reagan over Brown pursuant to a questionnaire in which he had asked the candidates whether, if elected, they would "exert leadership" to obtain Board of Regents regulations which would "prevent treasonable and immoral conditions from existing within the university." The San Francisco *Chronicle* called this "a loaded and improper question," meant to imply, its editorial said, that immorality and treason were rampant at UC. Candidate Reagan let it be known that, if chosen governor, he would promote an investigation, headed by former CIA Director John McCone, into university affairs. Governor Brown twitted Reagan with having arrived at this proposal after advancing and abandoning two others—one for the dismissal of UC President Kerr, the other for a Berkeley "witch-hunt" by the State Legislature. Brown suggested his adversary was following the Hollywood production philosophy that "if you muff it the first time around, you can always do a retake." Something certainly ought to be done about an "erosion of standards" in the state administration, Reagan observed, and about a situation in which students at the state university had been guilty of "almost demonstrating for demonstration's sake."

These examples of rough language were fairly typical of the campaign's virulence on most points of difference, whether trivial or not. There was little pretense of political civility. Speech-writers appeared at times to be turning out calculated invective by the yard. Meantime, the embattled gubernatorial nominees, obliged by the size of California to flit from rally to rally by airplane, were frequently hundreds of miles apart—physically as well as ideologically—and often each camp had to depend on political spies and tape recorders to be completely sure what the other camp was saying. Hecklers and pickets for an odd array of causes also played their part. With his university unavoidably caught up in all this, President Kerr attempted to take the long view. The nine campuses of the University of California would have to be increased to fourteen by the year 2000, he predicted, to handle a staggering enrollment total of 274,500. Nobody brings anything really small into California.

"A great university has a duty to the future as great as its duty to the present," Kerr wrote. "Intellectually, it must be both more conservative of established values and more bold in trying innovations than may be fashionable at any given moment. It must maintain scholars in studies which a layman might consider archaic. It must support novel exploration which most people consider speculative. It must take the long view and may often have to defend the unpopular. Neither immediate benefits nor the desire to allay criticism, nor honest exasperation with troublemakers, must tempt the University of California to impair the right of scholars to search and discuss what they find."

There was no abatement of the troubles of the University of California when the electioneering ended in the defeat of Democratic Governor Brown and the elevation of Republican Ronald Reagan to executive power. On the contrary, they multiplied. During the first month of the new state administration, UC President Kerr was fired by the Board of Regents, Governor Reagan voting for the ouster. This coincided with an early demand by the new Reagan regime for a sharp, across-the-board reduction in all state departmental expenditures for 1967–1968 budget-balancing purposes, the program contemplating a severe slash in appropriations not only for the university but likewise for something like twenty regional state colleges scattered around California. President Kerr's reaction was that UC student admissions would have to be restricted if money for support of the huge institution was to be drastically curtailed. The abrupt removal of Kerr aroused widespread condemnation in the press of the country and in educational circles. President Nathan Pusey of Harvard was quoted as terming it "an affront to higher education generally." Deploring the dismissal, the *Christian Science Monitor* called it tragic that the head of a university which had come to be considered the equal of Harvard on the undergraduate level, with one of the world's finest graduate schools, should have been "caught between conservatives on one side and radicals on the other." In an editorial captioned *Twilight of a Great University,* the *New York Times* summarized the California situation in February, 1967, this

260

way: "The interaction of guerrilla warfare by a nihilist minority of students, the beachhead established by non-student disrupters, the Governor's intention to economize at the expense of education and the Kerr dismissal threatens to shatter the high standing of an institution vital to the progress of the nation's largest state."

There were new educational crises to come, and very quickly. Governor Reagan, in another phase of his retrenchment planning, proposed and then temporarily delayed, for 1967 anyhow, the imposition of tuition charges on students at UC and the state colleges. California for years had been one of the few large states which operated its public higher educational establishments tuition-free. Thousands of student "protest marchers" against tuition paraded to the State Capitol in Sacramento, far outnumbering demonstrators for Reagan's point of view. Democratic Assembly Speaker Jesse M. Unruh accused the new GOP government of clumsily trying to punish "student activists." Other critics, evidently remembering Governor Brown's "master plan for higher education" and his generous fiscal policy toward the university and state colleges, expressed fear Governor Reagan's tuition proposal, if approved, would force students of poor families into two-year, home-town junior colleges, with a corresponding rise in the financial burden on local taxpayers. In deferring the tuition issue for the time being, Reagan insisted that his projected state economies apply to UC, contending at one point that a cutback in "intellectual luxuries" for a year or so could be undertaken without any serious harm resulting.*

Governor Reagan emphasized that he had no intention to "downgrade" higher education in California. It was a temporary situation, he said, "like the family that can't have new living-room drapes this

---

* Chief Justice Earl Warren, who had carefully refrained from public discussion of California politics after leaving the governorship in 1953, spoke out with others in 1967 against tuition charges or crippling budget slashes at UC. Estimating California might have a population of forty million in another quarter century, Warren declared that, as a long-term investment, his old alma mater needed to be operated "at its highest potential as it has been for almost a hundred years."

year and has to wait until next year." The Los Angeles *Times,* which had supported Reagan for the governorship, scolded him for what it called his "sarcastic" reference to "subsidizing intellectual curiosity" and suggested he may have misread his mandate from the people and apparently had a "misconception of the purpose of higher education." That was roughly the situation three months after the state government change-over, with the outcome of this and various other controversial matters yet to be determined. However it all might turn out, prestigious UC once more had qualified as the place "where the action is" and California had not experienced such an ear-splitting fracas over higher education since economy-minded Governor Friend W. Richardson tangled with the state colleges back in the 1920s.

36

DEMOCRATIC DEBACLE

As a prelude to Ronald Reagan's difficulties with the University of California and the urgent problems of governmental spending and state taxes, the California election of 1966 closely resembled that of 1958—with the results completely and fantastically reversed. Amid much local and national acclaim and flattering predictions of additional glories to come, Reagan defeated Governor Brown by nearly one million votes, almost as large a majority as Brown had amassed against Republican William Knowland eight years before. Republican Reagan crushed through his opposition with something of the power of Notre Dame's old football hero, George Gipp, whom he had portrayed in that long-ago movie. Democrat Edmund G. Brown's daydreams of a third gubernatorial term ended in baffling disaster, leaving Earl Warren still the only triple-crown winner in California's 116 years of statehood.

The vote was 3,742,913 for Republican Reagan, 2,749,174 for Democrat Brown. It was a sweeping repudiation of the Democratic establishment which had faced the test with a tremendous voter enrollment advantage, a paper superiority of 1,369,607 over Republican registrations. Out of 8,340,868 eligible voters, the Democrats had a potential of 4,720,597 party affiliates against 3,350,990 for the GOP. Yesterday's election statistics are perhaps as dead as yesterday's newspaper, but these deserved a second look. Reagan not only had polled the equivalent of his Republican party's full strength but obviously had picked up several hundred thousand defecting Democrats. Moreover, he had carried in on his fashionably-cut coattails almost the entire ticket of Republican state constitutional office candidates, taking over the executive and principal administrative machinery of the California Capitol lock, stock and barrel. Before the balloting, the Democrats had held every major partisan state office subject to statewide voter decision, except that of seventy-eight-year-old Republican Secretary of State Frank M. Jordan. After the Reagan revolution, Democratic Attorney-General Thomas C. Lynch was the only top state official of the shattered "majority party" who still had his job.

Governor Brown had been fearful of the heavy vote in the state's extreme southern counties. About this he was right, but his optimism about the north was ill-founded. Powerful Los Angeles County went to Reagan by more than 352,000 votes. Orange County, so conservative-minded that it had recently sent a Bircher to the State Senate, gave the Republican gubernatorial nominee an edge which, in round figures, ran around 180,000. San Diego County provided the GOP with a margin of about 110,000. These southern California vote centers accounted for almost two-thirds of Reagan's state majority. Brown was miles off the mark with a forecast he would "come out of the north with a 250,000-vote lead." His native San Francisco favored Brown by some 50,000, and he squeaked through also in Alameda County. The Governor lost, however, in almost all other northern California areas, including the heavily Democratic capital city of Sacramento where he had directed government for eight years. The Democrats had gone to the polls with a registration bulge in all but four of California's fifty-eight counties. As Reagan assumed an early lead in all counties except three, the magnitude of his political conquest became immediately apparent. The result was a complete Democratic debacle.

It was another conspicuous demonstration of the uneasy, changeling nature of California's remarkable population which had been switching political directions spasmodically, like a weather vane in a swirling wind, for more than half a century. It had gone overboard for a political beginner only four years after having rejected native-born and experienced Richard Nixon, twice the Vice-President of the United States and very nearly the President. In 1966, California was part of a general Republican resurgence—but with a difference. Unlike that year's gubernatorial successes of other GOPers—say, for instance, Nelson Rockefeller in New York or George Romney in Michigan—Ronald Reagan's sudden rise from comparative obscurity, at least in any governmental sense, was a smashing victory for the elated forces of refurbished, neo-Goldwater conservatism.

The outcome represented a triumph, too, and an impressive one, for the latest thing in modern public relations methods and image-making expertise. Reagan's quite open and enthusiastic affiliation with the 1964 Goldwater apparatus was deliberately played down, as much as was conveniently possible, in a state where Goldwater had been decisively beaten. The 1966 California conservative vote was rather clearly Reagan's from the outset. What he required was a good lot of Democratic cross-voters and impressionable independents. Accordingly, the conservative phase of the Reagan image was efficiently blurred and the accent shifted, with acute professional skill, to the fifty-five-year-old movie star's charming and oftentimes captivating attributes as a public personality, and to a set of promises and political charges, not excessively specific, which the candidate voiced repeatedly at campaign rallies and over television. Altogether, it was an immensely proficient job, as it had to be, of carefully marketing an unfamiliar political product, with quite a bit of attractive showmanship thrown in for good measure. Against the persuasiveness of these techniques, Brown and his somewhat befuddled Democratic party lieutenants flailed helplessly. They were using relatively old-fashioned selling procedures, as the political market soon demonstrated, in competition with a sparklingly fresh commodity brand which was competently advertised as "new and improved."

It would be difficult to detract in the slightest degree from the scope of Reagan's magnificently managed electioneering achievement, viewed as a practical operation. It seems altogether probable that, starting from taw as a self-styled political amateur, he could not have reached the top in state government with one great bound if any less pragmatic or scintillant *modus operandi* had been used to get him off the ground. From sound stage to governor was a tremendous leap, very possibly the world's political high-jumping record. All in all, Reagan had come a very long way in the twenty-nine years since his first screen test, with a display of alert personal application and self-assurance which quite plainly had bewitched millions. It occurred to a good many, in fact, that, in a new electronics age of computerized decisions and increasingly effective mass-communications facilities, the Reagan campaign of 1966 might very well be taken as a model for instant success in political areas hitherto much less flamboyant than California.

The climactic weeks of the contest, in a manner which almost invariably had characterized major California elections for a good many years, brought the state an influx of outside orators and vote wooers. These were hailed reverently as distinguished visitors or assailed angrily as carpetbaggers, depending upon which ring of the political circus their performances were intended to grace. Not only an appreciation of how the governmental scene might change, if Reagan and his followers took over from Brown and the going establishment, but a shrewd recognition of California's potential role in the Republican-Democratic Presidential decisions of 1968 brought all manner of specialists, political witch doctors and carriers of magic charms scurrying westward over the Sierra Nevada, or at least sending urgent messages. The Kennedys and the visiting Johnson administration speechmakers proved incapable of stemming the Reagan tide, a sobering thought for the Democrats in terms of which way California might be expected to jump two years later.

Among the first of the Democratic lions to come roaring into California in Governor Brown's behalf was Massachusetts Senator Edward Kennedy and an assortment of Johnson cabinet members. It was entirely appropriate for a Massachusetts man to join in the campaign, Kennedy said, since Robert Welch of the same state already had interjected his John Birch Society into California affairs. Other invaders included New York Senator Robert Kennedy. Reagan dismissed the brothers Kennedy as part of "the tourist trade from the East" and complained that some of their fellow spokesmen for the Governor were "trying to tell us how to run California." If Reagan had his way, snapped Brown, he would close California's borders to everybody and everything "except the gold shipments consigned to him by out-of-state extremist organizations." President Johnson was not among the visitors, but Vice-President Hubert Humphrey showed up, testifying that Brown was "one of the finest Governors who ever served in the United States." Out of Independence, Missouri, a communiqué from former President Harry Truman endorsed the Governor, adding that sometimes the people "get confused or diverted by clever propaganda or slick press agents—but not for long." If he were a Californian, announced the peppery old gentleman, he would mark his ballot for Brown.

On the Republican side, Dick Nixon observed that Reagan was something "new" and projected "the mystique of the future," at the same time summarizing Governor Brown's re-election oratory as consisting largely of the "tired old charge" of extremism. Shortly before the election, former President Eisenhower, who customarily wintered in southern California, spoke up for Reagan. So did former Governor Goodwin Knight, for whose neutrality, at least, Governor Brown had been hoping. Unlike California's junior United States Senator, George Murphy, an ardent Reaganite, the state's senior senator, moderate Republican Thomas H. Kuchel, decided not to endorse his party's standard-bearer. Although the 1966 GOP issue selectors had given the impression of being less than anxious to highlight Goldwaterism in their program, Barry Goldwater expressed his political affection for "Ronnie" and his expectations that victory would crown the efforts of his old 1964 campaign helper who had, he explained, "learned to be a statesman." The lions of Hollywood, as well as of Washington and other points east, also became active. Chuck Connors, Pat Boone and, of course, George Murphy, were listed among the filmland and television figures favoring Reagan, while those supporting Brown included Gene Kelly, Frank Sinatra and Dan Blocker, the "Hoss Cartwright" of the "Bonanza" cast. Some of them sang; some of them made speeches. It was a field day for the autograph hunters and celebrity worshipers.

The Brown-Reagan encounter, a strange kind of duel from the beginning, moved toward its bellicose finish as something unique, even by California's political standards. In simple terms, it was the old classic confrontation between a veteran incumbent of basically progressive tendencies and a fresh, new challenger of clearly-delineated conservative inclinations. Simple terms, however, were frequently obscured by dense political fog. Granting a preliminary astonishment at Reagan's ambitious political debut, quite a few natives must have been even more startled by his suave technique, his smiling self-complacency—which the disturbed Democratic leadership preferred to call brashness—and his seemingly enthusiastic reception almost everywhere. Lacking a public record, Reagan did, with consummate skill, what came naturally. All the wiles of stagecraft and charm, learned in long years before movie and TV cameras, were brought convincingly into play. The script was planned with cinematic competence; the staging was effective; the crowds liked it. In short, Reagan, playing his role of candidate for the first time, offered his own brand of professionalism. Confronted with this phenomenon and slashing away at it relentlessly, Brown exuded a kind of grim hopefulness but appeared to suffer discouraging frustrations at times as he endeavored to enlist lively public interest in what he had done as governor over the past eight years and what he considered California's goals ought to be for the future. Having once knocked out such Republican heavyweights as Knowland and Nixon, this time he was up against an unmeasurable consideration—the popularity and glamour of show biz.

Adding to the worries of political managers on both sides, perhaps more particularly on the Democratic side, were recurrent reports of public apathy.

Along with his attacks on extravagant governmental spending and high taxes, Reagan fired broadsides in many other directions, sometimes triggered by little ironic epigrams, such as "Cheating and stealing isn't cheating and stealing if it takes place in the halls of government; then it's just politics." "God," he announced on another occasion, "isn't dead; we just can't talk to Him in a class-room." Brown complained at one juncture that Reagan was relying on the advice of "behavioral psychologists," engaged to "find out what people are afraid of" and devise means to "exploit their anxieties."

Toward the end, the display of mutual aversion approached some kind of a new California record for interparty abuse. Seldom, outside the essentially one-party states of the South, had a major candidate been denounced as a rightist so often and in such language as Brown applied to Reagan. Among other things, the Governor termed his hard-running competitor "the captive of the radical right who will not and cannot repudiate the John Birch Society." With the winning of moderate Republican votes, and indeed a solid body of Democrats, mathematically necessary to the success of his campaign, Reagan decided to discuss the Birch clique and Republicanism. If any group, "whether it be the John Birch Society or any other organization," attempted to take over the Republican party, he finally said, it ought to be "kicked out of the party." He stopped short, the Associated Press noted, of actually repudiating the Birchers, observing that he felt he had no right to issue a blanket indictment. The November vote seemed to establish beyond argument that vast numbers of Californians found themselves in agreement with Reagan's position, or had not been listening very intently.

In the last analysis, 1966 saw a marked swing toward conservatism in California and, on election day, the conservative wing of the GOP, out of power after Merriam's day, won the new lease on political life for which it had been contending tenaciously almost since the departure of Earl Warren for Washington. The size of Ronald Reagan's vote demonstrated he also had attracted many Republican moderates, at the same time cutting deeply into the registered strength of the Democrats. Caught in the middle of a Democratic State Committee organizational quarrel, Brown unquestionably suffered from growing factionalism within his party. Obviously labor votes figured in the outcome, too, despite what Reagan called the efforts of the "self-anointed sultans of labor" to defeat him. Reagan sharply denied that white backlash had swung the election, but Brown insisted it had been an important force in his ouster. In such a political upheaval as California had undergone, though, there are usually many more factors and combinations of factors than even the active participants can enumerate or, for that matter, readily generalize about with any satisfying accuracy.

But politicians continue to try. The "two-party system" had been returned to California, Governor-Elect Reagan announced jubilantly, suggesting almost in the same breath—some thought a bit obscurely—that "partisanship" was ended as of that moment. By and large, Reagan attributed his smashing success to public dissatisfaction with mounting state expenditures and heavy taxes. "The people," he told press association reporters, "wanted to pause to see where we are going, how fast we are going, and how much it is going to cost before we throw everything out the window." There was California discontent, Reagan added, over excessive welfare and other governmental costs and also over what he described as the loss of local government responsibility. In a post-election statement, defeated Governor Brown warned that the conservative trend in California politics had not run its course. So long as the California workingman remained prosperous, he said, there would be more concern about property taxes than about social issues. Brown contended that southern California had been experiencing an influx of Southerners with a conservative bent and that the Democratic party's story was not getting over to them because of the equally conservative inclinations of the southern California press.* It might have consoled the retiring Governor a little to know that even Abraham Lincoln had his southern California troubles, too. Lincoln carried California in 1860 and 1864 but, according to a researcher of old state election records, he lost Los Angeles County both times.

Ardent partisans began boosting Reagan for national honors almost as soon as the 1966 polls closed. Foresighted southern California enthusiasts just happened to have a huge "Reagan for President" banner which was unfurled before the television cameras at a Los Angeles election-night victory rally. Around the country as well, Reagan was acknowledged as one of the personalities who might have to be reckoned with, if only because of California's political importance, at the 1968 Republican national convention. Smiling modestly, the state's latest political superman assured everybody that he had no other intention than to stay on the job as governor for four years. Nobody knew what the situation might be two years hence, however, and "there could be circumstances," Reagan conceded, under which he might be cast in the role of California's favorite-son candidate in 1968, perhaps "to avoid a divisive struggle" at the state's Republican Presidential primary. Meantime, he had other more immediately pressing commitments. For one thing, the freshly crowned Republican state executive had a challenging new script to study, one with a good many more "sides" than any that Hollywood had ever offered him. So he put on his reading glasses, gathered his advisers around him and took up the busy task of giving California what he had promised during the campaign would be a "Creative Society."

* The Democrats faced post-election questions of leadership succession. Seven months after his defeat, former Governor Brown was threatening to withdraw from the California Democratic Council if its ultraliberal factions persisted in plans for a "pro-peace delegation" to oppose President Johnson at the party's 1968 nominating convention.

37

GOVERNOR FROM HOLLYWOOD

Ronald Reagan's "Creative Society" made its bow with celebrational splendor which even surpassed the inauguration fanfare for the late Governor James Rolph, Jr., back in 1930, and certainly would have warmed the heart of ceremony-loving "Sunny Jim." Reagan became California's thirty-third governor amid glittering pageantry, stately political ritual and displays of excited adulation which continued for the better part of four days and sometimes equaled the gala atmosphere of a Hollywood premiere. It was called "Fiesta California." A director of ceremonies with experience at Disneyland, the Pasadena Tournament of Roses parade and half-time activities at University of Southern California football games was called to Sacramento to plan the elaborate series of events in meticulous detail, with careful attention to perfect timing and entertainment-world polish. A fifty-eight-page "Proceedings Manual" was distributed to the participants.

At one minute after midnight on Monday, January 2, 1967, the legal date for Reagan's take-over of government, inaugural formalities began, under close security precautions and before whirring television cameras, in the rotunda of the State Capitol. The new governor took his oath of office on a four-hundred-year-old mission Bible, believed to have been brought to California by Father Junípero

Serra. "I'll try very hard," Reagan promised solemnly. Turning to his old friend, United States Senator George Murphy, he grinned and said, "Well, George, here we are on the late show again." The peculiar timing presumably had been dictated by Reagan's desire to replace Democratic Governor Edmund G. Brown at the earliest possible moment, thus terminating Brown's flood of eleventh-hour patronage appointments. Unhappy Democrats of the outgoing administration suggested irritably that a swearing-in later in the day probably would have run afoul of television's full schedule of holiday bowl football games. It turned out that there was really no need for middle-of-the-night haste, since Reagan already had signed a qualifying oath of office for filing with the secretary of state some days before. "I still don't think it was for real," commented the surprised Governor. "The fellow from the Secretary of State's office should have told me what we were doing. I believed it was a routine loyalty oath."

The enthusiastic festival moved on from Monday through Thursday, with bouncing jollity and many expressions of good will. There were jubilant receptions, blaring bands, a prayer breakfast, a parade through downtown Sacramento, a grand ball where Danny Thomas presented Reagan, and an inauguration symphony concert, with three distinguished conductors sharing the podium, and Jack Benny on hand with his violin. The program ranged from Stravinsky, Bernstein, Gershwin, Richard Strauss and Rossini to Benny playing "Love in Bloom." Topping it all, after a nineteen-gun salute and other germane observances, came Governor Reagan's inaugural address, delivered from a flower-decked platform outside the old Capitol's west portico. Right there festive congeniality made way for political urgency, as the new state management conceived it to be. "We're going to squeeze and cut and trim until we reduce the cost of government," declared Reagan.

Although the "Creative Society," by the very nature of Reagan's swift rise to prominence, was extraordinary, there is always a tendency to compare each new regime, state or national, with those which have gone before. If the introductory pageant in this case had been reminiscent of some of the gay airs of the Rolph days, the prospective overhauling of government and the likely turnover of state job-holders in 1967 caused many veteran politicians to think of Democratic Governor Culbert L. Olson's victory over the Republicans in 1938 and the wholesale revamping of gubernatorial policy which followed it. Like Democrat Olson, Republican Reagan was moving into the executive mansion after its long occupancy by the opposite party. From the standpoint of California fiscal affairs, however, other onlookers were much more forcefully reminded of Republican Governor Friend W. Richardson whose campaign concern with tax relief and whose post-election slogan of "efficiency and economy" had stirred up the early 1920s so mightily. To those of long memory, the Reagan battle cry of "squeeze, cut and trim" had a familiar ring.

It is next to impossible to know how detailed a concept of California's complicated state finances economy-bent Governor Reagan brought to Sacramento with him as a newcomer in government. Annual state disbursements at that time were among the highest in the nation. Their substantial reduction presented exasperating technical problems, since a large segment of the overall budget consisted of subventions in aid of local governments and more than half of the state's colossal program of expenditures represented constitutional and statutory "fixed charges," such as allotments for assistance to education, old-age pensions, bond redemptions and the like. Aside from fantastically large annual appropriations by the Legislature, public works bond issues had been increasingly resorted to, especially during the 1950s and 1960s, to keep pace with the construction needs of higher education and other state institutions. Because of these earlier legislative and voter commitments, only a relatively small proportion of the entire flow of state money was readily within the control of the governor and the lawmakers. A succession of state administrations had been struggling with these perplexities for half a century.

Involved in turn with this dilemma, Governor Reagan roared into office with a preliminary threat to slash all state departmental expenditures 10 per cent across-the-board. The former Brown administration, he charged, had left California finances in critical condition, with a State Treasury general fund deficit of hundreds of millions of dollars in prospect. Supporters of the defeated Democratic government insisted, and the Reaganites denied, that the general fund would be technically in balance at the end of the final Brown budget year. Many conceded, though, that additional state income appeared imperative to finance California's government for the new Reagan budget year of 1967–1968. There had been no major state tax boosts since 1959, the first year of the Brown administration. Governor Brown, inheriting a fund shortage problem, had sponsored a combination of new and increased taxes that year which gave the state something over $200,000,000 in augmented budget-balancing revenue. By various later changes in income-collecting methods and other improvisations, the state had managed to finance government without the actual imposition of further new state taxes during the rest of Brown's eight years in office. With California and its governmental involvements both expanding, however, state expenditures had gone up astronomically during those same years. The last Brown budget had totaled around $4.6 billion. Few could doubt that a day of reckoning for the country's most impressively growing state was far off. As one ready source of extra money, Governor Brown, in his second term, proposed a withholding system, similar to the federal government's, in gathering the state's levy on personal incomes. The Legislature turned him down. Now some of the lawmakers looked dubiously at Governor Reagan's plan for a 10 per cent across-the-board spending reduction, maintaining that the needs of each agency ought to be considered separately and on individual merit. As in the case of the University of California's resistance to Reagan's retrenchment proposals, dealt with earlier, the argument, at the outset of 1967, was that the quality of state government ought to be carefully preserved. The Legislature still had slim-margin Democratic majorities in both houses, enough to spell potential parliamentary trouble for the Republican executive in any strictly partisan dispute.

Choosing his words with something less than customary political prudence, Governor Reagan surprised the Capitol by announcing that, before his arrival, the state had been "looted and drained of its financial resources in a manner unique in our history." Former Governor Brown and his allies erupted in righteous indignation. The state's "fiscal crisis," Brown asserted, existed only in the mind of Reagan whom he described angrily as "the real looter, ready and eager to trade California's potentials for short-range political gains for himself." Reagan explained that he had not intended, by the blunt term "looted," to imply any unlawful actions or wrongdoing by the former Democratic regime, but only to underscore his disapproval of Brown's heavy governmental spending.

By this time, Reagan had sacked most of the key patronage officials of the old Brown administration, replacing many of them with Republicans of business experience rather than political careerists.* Several other headline-catching innovations quickly followed. Governor Reagan urged California's army of more than 100,000 state civil servants to work voluntarily on the Lincoln and Washington birthday holidays, but most of them stayed home. Next came a freeze order on purchase of new state equipment, including desks, chairs and typewriters; state travel expense restrictions; a virtual halt on new hiring. Then a program was unveiled for job eliminations and dismissals of between three thousand and four thousand state workers, a large part of them in the State Department of Mental Hygiene. Picketing workers paraded at the Capitol entrance. Unperturbed by protests, the Governor's office said wage savings could be accomplished without any lessening of necessary service in the mental hos-

---

* Among those no longer in state office under the new regime was Thomas Braden, former newspaper publisher, President of the California Board of Education under Brown, and one-time Central Intelligence Agency official who caused a 1967 stir by reporting (*Saturday Evening Post*) that CIA funds had been funneled through labor organizations after World War II to counteract Communist influences in Europe.

pitals or other state agencies. Concerned over the fire hazards of California's old Victorian executive mansion, dating back to the mid-1870s, Governor Reagan announced plans to move out of it and into a personally leased modern dwelling. Well-wishers promptly launched a movement to finance a new gubernatorial residence by private subscription. Disgruntled critics complained the administration was falsely representing one of the country's richest states as poverty-stricken.

In March the thunderbolt came. On top of a Reagan state budget for 1967–1968 which, subject to revisions by the Legislature, would run close to the $5 billion mark, a new California high, the Governor sent the lawmakers recommendations for a $946,000,000 hike in state taxes, a request seldom equaled around the country. "Governmental frugality marked the beginning of this administration," he declared, "and it will continue to be one of our basic objectives." The Governor's plan called for increases in the big revenue raisers—the sales, income and bank and corporation franchise taxes—and, among other things, heavy boosts in the levies on cigarettes and liquor. This was designed, he said, to meet a state deficit threat, balance the budget and provide $170,000,000 in local property taxpayers' relief the first year, with much more in subsequent years. While a need for additional State Treasury income was not seriously questioned in most quarters, some of the details of Reagan's scheme were predictably controversial. Governor Reagan clearly opposed the old Brown idea for an income tax withholding system. He let it be known, in breezy fashion at a news conference, that he would be apt to approve a withholding tax only if bound hand and foot and burned with a hot iron.

Breeziness and gracious affability often marked Governor Reagan's public behavior as he ploughed into his California problems. He told a group in Washington, D.C., that he felt right at home in the only capital in worse shape than his own. But he was jauntily optimistic, more than ready to match his "Creative Society" against the "Great Society" of President Johnson. "There's a wind of change blowing across this land," he said, and politicians would do well to remember that the people had voted in November, 1966, "against what's going on." Federal tax-sharing with the state governments would be a splendid notion, he suggested, but under no circumstances could federal dictation or interference in state affairs be tolerated. He indicated there was already too much bureaucratic paternalism. "The West was built without an area development plan," he was soon reminding California audiences, "and San Francisco was rebuilt after the great fire and they didn't need urban renewal to do it. . . . We have a great challenge—a great opportunity to show the people of the other forty-nine states what can be done by people deciding their own destiny. I hope to light a prairie fire for the rest of the country."*

Meantime, Ronald Reagan—attractive, self-confident and a shade ambitious—was playing the role of governor to the hilt and, like Jim Rolph before him, evidently enjoying every moment of the spotlight immensely. Relaxed and happy, he celebrated his fifty-sixth birthday, Capitol colleagues presenting him with a birthday cake from which, in festive recognition of administration policy, 10 per cent had been neatly hacked away. A few weeks later, Chief Justice Earl Warren, the only other twentieth-century Republican who had captured the California governorship by knocking the Democrats out of office, observed his seventy-sixth birthday in Washington. The twenty-years difference in the ages of Reagan and Warren spoke, in some sense, of the changes in California between their respective assumptions of power. It appeared to many that Reagan could not conceivably have become a figure of statewide political consequence in the California of Warren's time. Yet the conservative political elements which had spearheaded the Reagan election movement were plainly overjoyed with the new executive and intolerant of any and all criti-

* As time went on, attacks on "the federal government Goliath" appeared to become a stock-in-trade item of Reagan oratory. California, the Governor said as the summer of 1967 approached, "is one state that does not intend to become merely an administrative adjunct of the federal government."

cal appraisals of his doings. Without question, even as a gubernatorial neophyte—perhaps because of that—he was making more news
which attracted national interest than any California governor in a
long time. He was completely at ease and pleasantly agile-tongued
in almost every circumstance. True enough, Governor Reagan's offhand brand of platform quips had reportedly encountered less than
total approbation before the politically apperceptive Gridiron Club
in the national capital. On his home grounds, however, things were
usually different. As a cinema-television personality he had combined
cool self-possession and warm microphone manners to fashion a
new way of political success. "I think Ronnie's doing a great job,"
said his old campaigning comrade, Barry Goldwater, "and the bulk of
the people of California seem to approve."

Governor Reagan reaffirmed his early intention, if circumstances
seemed right, to become a California favorite-son candidate for the
Republican Presidential nomination in 1968—not as a serious White
House bidder, he hastened to add, but just to "keep harmony" and
avoid "any bitter campaign" among GOPers at the Presidential primary. Not only among the ousted Democrats but, to some extent, in
Republican ranks, too, there seemed to be cautious and somewhat
awkward factional efforts to adjust to the new fact of Reagan's 1966
triumph and make ready for whatever repercussions might follow.
Any number of Democrats yearned for advancement, with Brown
out of the way. Possibly borrowing a page out of Reagan's success
book, the irrepressible Democratic mayor of Los Angeles rushed on
TV with a weekly, commercially-sponsored "Sam Yorty Show." Conservative Republican Max Rafferty, head of the state school system
and also ambitious, expressed the judgment that GOP moderate
United States Senator Thomas Kuchel, up for re-election in 1968,
was about as popular among Republicans "as a skunk at a picnic."
Superintendent Rafferty was gently reprimanded for breaking the
"Eleventh Commandment" against Republicans making ill-mannered
remarks about each other. Dr. Gaylord Parkinson, who devised this
local rule for party behavior, announced Presidential build-up activi-

ties in behalf of perpetually busy Richard Nixon. Governor Reagan said gravely that one of the benefits of his favorite-son undertaking would be to prevent "Eleventh Commandment" violations. Regarding the California governor's plans much more seriously, the *Ripon Forum,* a national publication of Republican moderates, inveighed excitedly against "creeping Reaganism." Whatever else might have been said of Reagan at this early date—and praise and condemnation were poured out in abundance—he had risen from very nearly a political cipher to the governorship in twelve months and was tentatively committed to a venture which might make him at least a technical aspirant to the White House in a little more than another twelve.

This account covers only the highlights of the Hollywood governor's first hundred days in office. By then there had been compromise negotiations on his proposed appropriation slashes for the University of California and the state colleges, and the fate of his intended 10 per cent cutback in overall state spending, even modified, was in doubt. Against any interparty mischief-making by a Democratic majority in the State Legislature, Reagan possessed the weapon of gubernatorial veto. The effectiveness of post-session "pocket vetoes" had been vitiated, though, at the same election which made Reagan governor, and the Legislature had been authorized to reassemble, if it wished, and act again on any eleventh-hour measures killed by the Governor.

As the first year of the Reagan administration ended, with the 1968 primaries, party conventions and Presidential election just ahead, the California governor turned his attention more and more to the heady field of national politics and the elaborate maneuvering of Republican White House hopefuls. On the California home front, he continued to be controversial: his attitudes toward various welfare and humanitarian functions were severely criticized as a reversal of the policies pursued by his predecessors for nearly three decades; the new administration's proposed slashes in state medical aid for the needy faced litigation; the Governor's personal staff underwent considerable reshuffling; hostile press editorial comment in the fall of 1967 marveled at the executive's shrewdly fashioned political image, noting that Reagan still was being effectively "packaged" as a great "economizer," despite the fact his first budget and his program of tax increases had established a state governmental record for extraordinary size. Nonetheless, the State Legislature, grinding through one of its longest sessions, had failed to overturn his basic decisions in any important degree, and his partisan foes, by and large, had been unable to dent his charismatic reputation as a good and graceful knight out of Camelot, armed with the sword of conservatism and intent on slaying the dragons of public extravagance.

Committed to a "non-candidate" candidacy as a Presidential favorite son in California, the beguiling gubernatorial tyro invaded the East, the South, the Midwest and most other parts of the country as a welcome orator at GOP "party unity" and political fund-raising functions. He became a hawk on Vietnam, a critic of President Johnson on both the conduct of the Asian war and the domestic war on poverty, a figure of dazzling charm in the right-wing ranks of Republicanism. In the Reagan camp, demure disclaimers to the contrary notwithstanding, there were ill-concealed hopes that what had happened in California might, with astute management, very well happen ultimately in a much broader arena. The thought was contagious. Even Shirley Temple, the Hollywood child star of yesterday, and incidentally a co-performer with Reagan and Senator Murphy in long-ago cinema entertainments, ventured out of housewifely retirement in California to run for Congress. The campaign of the former movie moppet (now Mrs. Shirley Temple Black) enlisted worldwide notice, one London newspaper headlining her defeat as "The Sinking of the Good Ship Lollipop." National press coverage of Reagan as an arresting phenomenon was in itself phenomenal. But the Governor was not a party, he insisted, to any campaign-year arrangements or private electioneering agreements with Richard Nixon or anybody else. "I don't make deals," he announced curtly. Although some observers grumbled that the freshman Governor was trying to move ahead too early and much too fast for his own eventual good, Reagan, always the seasoned trouper, took to his new role as national administration gadfly with gusto and evident enjoyment. Long exposure on millions of television and motion-picture screens indubitably had invested the adopted Californian with a certain polish and undimmed glamour which, fully as much as his speeches and tart impromptu sallies, presently gained him a modest but fairly consistent rating in the early Presidential popularity polls. General Eisenhower expressed public admiration for him. *Time* magazine ran his picture on its cover as one of the outstanding Republican national ticket possibilities. Suddenly he was in the big time, or at least on its fringes.

However preposterous the Democrats and many moderate Republicans considered Governor Reagan's pretensions to be, in fact, he had become the first Californian, perhaps the first politician anywhere in the country, to be touted with apparent seriousness for national leadership consideration in his very first year of public officeholding. This was, in some sense, a sobering testimonial to the newfound political magic of Movieland, California's latest contribution to the science of public affairs.

Epilogue

DESTINATION UNKNOWN

California had been saddled with the shopworn image of glorified paradise unaccountably invaded by eccentricity for most of the twentieth century, but not very often perhaps had its way of life been examined more eagerly or superficially than in the closing days of 1966 and the early months of 1967. In living color, for instance, an attractive young matron, presumably intended to represent a "typical Republican" in her garden, was exhibited to the nation on television as one qualified exponent and analyst of the state's carefree mannerisms. The substance of her opinion appeared to be that Californians were happily blessed with sunshine, beauty, material plenty and joyous outdoor living and were preoccupied largely with security, affluence, gracious modern homes, elaborate swimming pools (of which the state had a record number), abundant leisure fun and all the other pleasures of assured status. On the other hand, a well-dressed gentleman, billed as a "radical Democrat," was reported as accounting for West Coast election surprises with the contention that the state's newly arriving millions—an increase of something like five million since Governor Brown took office in 1959—had included a large sampling of the maladjusted from other regions, perpetually out of sorts with the established pattern of things and periodically

283

impelled toward political leaps in the dark. However the rest of the land may have reacted to such points of view, California was much more complex, of course, than either of these impromptu testimonials indicated.

Indeed, the state and its residents, whether well or poorly adjusted, prosperous or otherwise, seemed considerably less atwitter over the Ronald Reagan phenomenon than many other parts of the country. His background as an actor, though adding a bit to his sparkle, was hardly flabbergasting to a population within comfortable driving distance of Hollywood. With almost casual acceptance of the governmental change-over, as the new year propelled Reagan from political show to political showdown, Californians generously wished the new governor the best of all possible administrations. Nobody actually quoted the sixteenth President but, even among dejected campaign losers, there was obvious agreement with Lincoln's dictum that, so long as the people remained virtuous and vigilant, no administration could "very seriously injure the government in the short space of four years." The majority of the natives were neither restless nor particularly concerned with the *pourquoi* of Reagan's spectacular victory. If he made good, they were prepared to cheer wildly and urge him on to possibly higher pinnacles. If his performance was less than brilliant, they could always dump him after one term, as they had every other California governor with three exceptions. It may be, too, that the great body of Californians had learned to live agreeably with their recurrent political convulsions, erratic innovations and cyclical transformations, without quite understanding them or experiencing any strongly-felt need for self-analysis.

Ronald Reagan undertook his gubernatorial incumbency amid a rare combination of problems, advantages and possibly unforeseen preoccupations, a juxtaposition of magnificent agricultural and industrial productivity, of remarkable technological and educational developments. Added to this was an enormous urban and suburban concentration, with all its benefits and woes, attendant glitter, racial unrest, pseudo sophistication, squalor and pageantry. Like his immediate predecessors, Governor Reagan was up against one of the country's most complicated operations.

As in many other regions, California's technological inventiveness and material prosperity had moved ahead through the century with much less clanking than its political machinery. There was a mounting tendency to regard the specialized field of political and governmental affairs a trifle apathetically, as something slightly esoteric, touching the average citizen's daily life only peripherally. It was for many an entertaining circus to become stirred up about seasonally around election time and then left pretty much to the professional politicians and bureaucrats. Nonetheless, this land of contrasts by the Pacific, with its eager optimism and predilection for hazy cure-alls, its impulsive switches back and forth between progressive and conservative management, had muddled through more than half a century of significant advancement, in some respects to national leadership. If only because of an uneasy concern for the judgments of history, most of its governors had somehow managed to handle themselves a bit more ably in the executive chair than often seemed probable while they were campaigning for it.

The California political shake-up of 1966–1967 had an immense regional significance. Aside from the power transfer from the Democrats to the Republicans, it also represented a potential southern California take-over. The new governor and lieutenant-governor came from south of the Tehachapi. So did both of California's United States Senators. And the southern end of the state, with its brimming rservoir of votes and the court-directed reapportionment of the State Senate, had enough muscle to dominate the Legislature. It is doubtful if southern California's newly enhanced prospects of influence and political ascendancy had been equaled since the faraway days of the Spanish and old Governor Portolá who stuck reasonably close to the south and south-central coast. From the viewpoint of regional approval and understanding, whatever the strength of his partisan base turned out to be, Governor Reagan of Pacific Palisades and Lake Malibu scarcely could have taken up his novel adventure in government under more favorable auspices.

At the same time, with louder or at least more persistent uproar than elsewhere, new socioeconomic manifestations and behavior patterns, especially evident among younger Californians, demanded attention. The period produced an almost unprecedented array of contrived demonstrations, nonconformist fanfare and "protest marches" for a staggering collection of causes. To a greater extent than perhaps some of them realized, leaders of the Establishment—political and governmental as well as social and educational—faced a need in the late 1960s to take increasing cognizance of broadly varying and oddly assorted minorities, frequently bewildering and sometimes alarming to the older generations. The manifestoes of the New Left may have been noisier than the stylized pronouncements of the New Right but scarcely more resentful of governmental bigness or the ways of conventional politics. Adherents of the Students for a Democratic Society and like-minded organizations often were as incomprehensible to many onlookers of settled status as were the dedicated sympathizers of, say, the John Birch Society or other right-wing aggregations. There was inevitable dispute over what the influence of Marxist radicalism and neo-Fascist attitudes might be in the general hubbub. Aside from that, some professed to see, on and off college campuses, an earnest sincerity, however misguided, in the discontent of many youngsters with the management of public affairs, a mistrust seemingly extending to the precepts of old-fashioned liberalism and conservatism alike. On top of that, the racial minorities —Mexican-Americans as well as Negroes—persisted in demands for betterment of their lot. In some of the larger cities, bohemian elements such as the beatniks and later the hippies got most of the headlines, especially for their use of psychedelic drugs. All in all, the doings of California's young activists, following a kind of offbeat conventionalism of their own, veered from the faintly ridiculous to the menacing edge of terrorism. One day in May, 1967, for instance, a dozen or so young Negroes, self-styled members of the "Black Panther" party, invaded a session of the State Assembly. In protest against proposed anti-firearms legislation, they carried loaded pistols, rifles and shotguns until disarmed by the police.* To older partici- pants in political life, the diversified preoccupations of newly emerg- ing extremists, whether left or right, often appeared to be negative, a disenchantment with the *status quo,* accompanied with only a rela- tively vague notion of what ought to be substituted. New undercur- rents of thought and conduct obviously existed, though, regardless of what their ultimate directions and significance might turn out to be.

The miscellaneous nature of the California population in which these yeasty ingredients bubbled to the surface was re-emphasized in the spring of 1967 by a survey reporting that 74 per cent of the state's inhabitants had been lured there from other states and na- tions, reducing the native-born residents to a mere 26 per cent of the whole. The California Poll of the Field Research Corporation was widely quoted as finding that 36 per cent of the "Californians," as of then, had come from the Midwest, 15 per cent from the East, 9 per cent from the South, 13 per cent from the Southwest, 12 per cent from other states of the Far West and 15 per cent from foreign countries. At about that time, Lieutenant-Governor Robert H. Finch revived the observation that "what California is today, the rest will be tomorrow." He called the state a "microcosm" of the future.

Meanwhile, California, indifferent to the passage of years, was still the winsome and irresolute beauty of yesterday, with the same smile of an angel and the same wayward heart of a coquette. No swain, however handsome or polished of manner, could really be sure of her undivided tenderness for any appreciable space of time.

* After the "Black Panther" incident, Governor Reagan, at a news conference guarded by armed State Police, advocated outlawing the carrying of loaded fire- arms in public but opposed a proposal that vigilante-type armed posses be formed to assist lawmen in stabilizing communities. A few days later, according to the United Press International, "Nazi Party" members, uniformed and wear- ing swastikas, staged a weapons drill in front of the "Black Panther" headquar- ters in Oakland.

Fundamentally, as many an erstwhile favorite had learned to his sorrow, her butterfly ways had not altered very much since she fluttered from Stephens to Richardson far back in the 1920s, from Merriam to Olson in the 1930s, to Warren in the 1940s and to Brown in the late 1950s, only to change her pretty little mind and ditch him for romantic Ronald in the mid-1960s. She was, and promised to be for a very long time to come, a precious and seductive darling, loved to distraction by almost everybody. In an odd sort of way, she was likewise an extremely moody and deceptive girl, high-strung and easily swayed, captivating but often unreliable. Her frothy, headlong love affairs, rapturous enough while they lasted, still gave her a dubious name around the country.

But she had many good points, too; more, perhaps, than most. For one thing, adoration and riches had never completely spoiled her. She could be every bit as gracious and well-mannered as the next girl when she wanted to be, which was actually most of the time. The hot blood of Spain and Mexico and the modifying strains of the Anglo-Saxon generations, what with Northern vigor, adopted Eastern style, an occasional Southern drawl and sometimes even the accents of Texas, made quite a combination. It was fairly irresistible. And California, dressed up for visitors, was unquestionably something to whistle at. When you saw her in the blue of Tahoe, in the green lace of the redwoods or in the shining off-white of the Pacific beaches—preferably at a little distance to hide the billboards and a possible background of beer cans and other litter discarded by her nineteen million admirers—she was an enchanting vision, still comparatively ageless and as lovely as ever.

But somehow, with the best intentions in the world, the big, wayward girl, forever mettlesome and impetuous, did manage to land herself in a surprising amount of trouble. Those who held her in enduring affection, and worried about her a good bit, could perhaps do no better than say to her, as her Spanish forebears were in the habit of saying long ago: *Vaya con Dios.*

Index

289

Index

293